VITAL RECORDS

OF

BELLINGHAM,

MASSACHUSETTS

Notice

In many older books, foxing (or discoloration) occurs and, in some instances, print lightens with wear and age. Reprinted books, such as this, often duplicate these flaws, notwithstanding efforts to reduce or eliminate them. The pages of this reprint have been digitally enhanced and, where possible, the flaws eliminated in order to provide clarity of content and a pleasant reading experience.

Vital Records of Bellingham, Massachusetts, to the Year 1850

Originally published
Boston, Massachusetts
1904

Reprinted by:

Janaway Publishing, Inc.
732 Kelsey Ct.
Santa Maria, CA 93454
(805) 925-1038
www.JanawayGenealogy.com

2003, 2011

ISBN: 978-1-59641-107-4

Made in the United States of America

VITAL RECORDS

OF

BELLINGHAM,

MASSACHUSETTS,

TO THE YEAR 1850.

PUBLISHED BY THE
NEW-ENGLAND HISTORIC GENEALOGICAL SOCIETY,
AT THE CHARGE OF
THE EDDY TOWN-RECORD FUND.

BOSTON, MASS.,
1904.

THIS publication is issued under the authority of a vote passed by the NEW-ENGLAND HISTORIC GENEALOGICAL SOCIETY, 6 November, 1901, as follows:

Voted: That the sum of $20,000, from the bequest of the late Robert Henry Eddy, be set aside as a special fund to be called the Eddy Town-Record Fund, for the sole purpose of publishing the Vital Records of the towns of Massachusetts, and that the Council be authorized and instructed to make such arrangements as may be necessary for such publication. And the treasurer is hereby instructed to honor such drafts as shall be authorized by the Council for this purpose.

Committee on Publications.

C. B. TILLINGHAST, FRANCIS EVERETT BLAKE,
CHARLES KNOWLES BOLTON, DON GLEASON HILL,
EDMUND DANA BARBOUR.

Editor.
HENRY ERNEST WOODS.

Stanhope Press
F. H. GILSON COMPANY
BOSTON U.S.A.

THE TOWN OF BELLINGHAM, Norfolk County (formerly in Suffolk County, until 1793), was established November 27, 1719, from parts of Dedham, Mendon, and Wrentham.

February 23, 1832, bounds between Bellingham and Franklin were established.

Population by Census: 1765 (Prov.), 468; 1776 (Prov.), 627; 1790 (U.S.), 735; 1800 (U.S.), 704; 1810 (U.S.), 766; 1820 (U.S.), 1034; 1830 (U.S.), 1102; 1840 (U.S.), 1055; 1850 (U.S.), 1281; 1855 (State), 1413; 1860 (U.S.), 1313; 1865 (State), 1240; 1870 (U.S.), 1282; 1875 (State), 1247; 1880 (U.S.), 1223; 1885 (State), 1198; 1890 (U.S.), 1334; 1895 (State), 1481; 1900 (U.S.), 1682.

EXPLANATIONS.

1. WHEN places other than Bellingham and Massachusetts are named in the original records, they are given in the printed copy.

2. In all records the original spelling is followed.

3. The various spellings of a name should be examined, as items about the same family or individual might be found under different spellings.

4. Marriages and intentions of marriages are printed under the names of both parties, but the full information concerning each party is given only in the entry under his or her name. When both the marriage and intention of marriage are recorded, only the marriage record is printed; and where a marriage appears without the intention recorded, it is designated with an asterisk.

5. Additional information which does not appear in the original text of an item, i.e., any explanation, query, inference, or difference shown in other entries of the record, is bracketed. Parentheses are used only when they occur in the original text, or to separate clauses found there — such as the birth-place of parents, in late marriage records.

ABBREVIATIONS.

a. — age
abt. — about
b. — born
ch. — child
chn. — children
Co. — county
c.r. — church record, Baptist
d. — daughter; died; day
Dea. — deacon
dup. — duplicate entry
g.r.1. — gravestone record, North Bellingham Cemetery
g.r.2. — gravestone record, Bellingham Center Cemetery
g.r.3. — gravestone record, South Bellingham Cemetery
g.r.4. — gravestone record, Rakeville Cemetery
g.r.5. — gravestone record, Scammell Cemetery
h. — husband
hrs. — hours
inf. — infant
int. — publishment of intention of marriage
Jr. — junior
m. — married; month
p.r.1. — private record, from Wight Diary, 1755-1849, kept by Samuel Wight and his daughters, now in the possession of the Town Clerk
p.r.2. — private record, from Crooks family Bible
prob. — probably
rec. — recorded

ABBREVIATIONS.

s. — son
Sr. — senior
w. — wife ; week
wid. — widow
widr. — widower
y. — year
1st. — first
2d. — second
3d. — third

BELLINGHAM BIRTHS.

BELLINGHAM BIRTHS.

To the year 1850.

ADAMS, Abby Amelia, d. Ruel and Julia Ann, Apr. 7, 1835. [Abbie A., w. Edwin Darling, G.R.2.]
Abby C., d. Daniel P. and Abby T., Sept. 14, 1837.
Abigail, d. David and Sally, May 21, 1836.
Abigil, d. Amos and Abigil, Mar. 20, 1782.
Abigirl, d. Obediah and Sarah, Oct. 22, 1746.
Albert Galatine, s. John Q. and Celista, July 12, 1839.
Albert M. [h. Hellen], ———, 1829. G.R.1.
Alce, d. Caleb and Miltiah, May 14, 1806.
Alfred, s. Peter and Anna U., June 9, 1816.
Amos, s. Obadiah and Sarah, Oct. 6, 1758.
Amos, s. Amos and Abigil, Jan. 25, 1787.
Amos Jr., s. Amos and Abigail, June 8, 1818.
Ann Elizebeth, d. Daniel P. and Abby T., Apr. 17, 1847.
Anna, d. Caleb and Lydia, w. Edwin Darling, June 3, 1834. G.R.2.
Asa, s. Silas and Mary, Dec. 3, 1768.
Asenath Partridge, d. David and Sally A., July 5, 1841.
Austin, s. William and Emeline, July 27, 1849.
Benjamin Spear, s. Peter and Anna U., Dec. 15, 1818.
Caleb, s. Caleb and Milletiah, Nov. 9, 1801.
Catharine B., June 8, 1817. G.R.2.
Charles Monroe, s. John Q. and Celista, Mar. 24, 1837.
Christopher Naham, s. Lewis Chamberlain and Susan Ann, Oct. 7, 1843.
Daniel, s. Samuel and Chloe, Oct. 16, 1777.
David, s. Amos and Abigail, Oct. 18, 1801.
David Franklin, s. David and Sally A., Oct. 10, 1844.
Edward Everett, s. John Q. and Celista, Mar. 26, 1835.
Edwin Stanley, s. Ruel and Julia Ann, Aug. —, 1841.
Elason, s. Amos and Abigail, Feb. 17, 1793.
Elisabeth Partridge, d. Joseph 2d and Asenath, July 15, 1821.
Elisha, s. Obediah and Sarah, Oct. 23, 1745.
Emeline M., d. Amos and Abigail, Oct. 19, 1830.

ADAMS, Emily, d. Joseph 2d and Asenath, Dec. 5, 1826.
Emily T. [———], w. Joseph, Nov. 6, 1807. G.R.1.
Gilbert A., s. Joseph and Jemima, Dec. 17, 1828.
Harriet E., d. Daniel P. and Abby T., Mar. 25, 1841.
Hellen [———], w. Albert M., ———, 1830. G.R.1.
Joel, s. Silis and Mary, Feb. 10, 1774.
Joseph, Jan. 23, 1796. G.R.1.
Joseph, s. Amos and Abigail, Jan. 23, 1797.
Joseph Edmund, s. Joseph 2d and Asenath, Nov. 28, 1824.
Julia A., d. Ruel and Julia M., July 11, 1845.
Julian, d. Peter and Anna U., Dec. 12, 1814.
Levi, s. Sillis and Mary, Mar. 26, 1772.
Lewis, s. Silas and Mary, Oct. 3, 1777.
Lewis Leander, s. William and Emeline, Mar. 13, 1848.
Lydia, d. David and Sally, Sept. 25, 1833.
Margaret, d. Silas and Mary, Apr. 29, 1770.
Mariah A., d. Joseph and Jemima, Dec. 4, 1819.
Mary [———], w. Samuel, Apr. 5, 1839. G.R.1.
Milly, d. Caleb and Miletiah, Feb. 9, 1804.
Naby, d. Caleb and Milletiah, Nov. 17, 1799.
Nahum, s. Amos and Abigail, Oct. 23, 1791.
Nance, d. Amos and Abigil, Nov. 4, 1784.
Nancy, d. David and Sally, Mar. 9, 1828.
Nathan, Feb. 22, 1797. G.R.1.
Obediah, s. Samuel and Chole, Mar. 3, 1780.
Olive, d. Obediah and Sarah, Jan. 1, 1753.
Olive, d. Silis and Mary, Feb. 19, 1776.
Olive, d. David and Sally, Sept. 25, 1830.
Rebeckah, d. Samuel Jr. and Mercy, Sept. 12, 1813.
Reuel, s. Samuel Jr. and Mercy, Dec. 7, 1810.
Roxanna [———], w. Nathan, Apr. 22, 1794. G.R.1.
Royial Quincy, s. Edmund J. and Amanda L., Apr. 9, 1849.
[Royal Q., s. Edmand J. and Amanda, G.R.1.]
Salle, d. Amos and Abigil, Dec. 23, 1789.
Sally, d. David and Sally, Feb. 23, 1838.
Samuel, s. Samuel and Chloe, Dec. 27, 1781.
Samuel Adison, s. Ruel and Julia Ann, May 29, 1837.
Samuel S., ———, 1837. G.R.1.
Samuell (Admams), s. Obediah and Sarah, Nov. 7, 1755.
Sarah Sumner, d. Joseph 2d and Asenath, Dec. 14, 1829.
Seneca, s. Amos and Abigail, Oct. 18, 1815.
Silas, s. Obediah and Sarah, Apr. 17, 1748.
Tryphena, d. Amos and Abigail, Mar. 4, 1813.
Wilber F., s. Daniel P. and Abby T., July 3, 1844.

ALBEE (see Allbee), Allven, s. Nathon and Elisabeth, Mar. 31, 1781.
Beulah, d. Nathan and Elisabeth, May 7, 1776.
Elisabeth, d. Thomas and Jemima, June 28, 1755.
Hipsibah, d. Nathon and Elisabeth, Jan. 25, 1784.
Hipzibah, d. Peter and Rhoda, Dec. 28, 1772.
Huldah, d. Thomas and Jemima, Feb. 26, 1753.
Jonathan, s. Thomas and Jemima, Oct. 30, 1751.
Phile, d. Nathon and Elisabeth, Nov. 8, 1778.
Polly, d. Alpheus and Susanah, July 21, 1796.
Ziba, s. Peter and Rhoda, Oct. 10, 1776.

ALDEN (see Aldin), Derius, s. Elisha and Irene, Jan. 26, 1778.
Elijah, s. Noah Jr. and Joanna, Apr. 4, 1776.
Jemima, d. Noah Jr. and Joanna, Nov. 10, 1777.
Joanna, d. Noah Jr. and Joanna, Nov. 30, 1783.
Laura, d. Elijah and Polly, Dec. 31, 1799.
Lydia, d. Noah Jr. and Joanna, Jan. 7, 1782.
Noah, s. Noah Jr. and Joanna, May 1, 1785.
Noah Jr., s. Elijah and Polly, Feb. 3, 1802.
Samuel, s. Elisha and Irene, Feb. 21, 1776.
Zelpha, d. Noah Jr. and Joanna, Jan. 4, 1780.

ALDIN (see Alden), Fear, d. Elisha and Irene, Apr. 7, 1774.
Irene, d. Elisha and Irene, Feb. 24, 1772.
Nathan, s. Elisha and Irene, Sept. 5, 1768.
Simeon, s. Elisha and Irene, June 27, 1770.

ALDRICH, Abigale, d. Laban and Ama, Apr. 19, 1782.
Alpha, d. Laban and Ama, Oct. 22, 1778.
Alvah, Nov. 16, 1802. G.R.3.
Amy [———], w. Alvah, June 15, 1826. G.R.3.
Anna, d. Laban and Ama, Jan. 9, 1787.
Asenath, d. Laban and Ama, Aug. 14, 1789.
Ida A. [———], w. James O., Oct. 18, 1848. G.R.4.
Nicholas, s. Abner and Elisabeth, July 3, 1768.

ALLBEE (see Albee), Lucretia, d. Peter and Rodah, Mar. 5, 1770.

ALLEN, Asa, s. Samuel and Polly, Oct. 23, 1820.
Bethesda, d. Samuel and Polly, Mar. 18, 1819.
Charlotte [———], w. ———, Apr. 22, 1836. G.R.1.
Ethan, s. Nethaniel and Lucy, Sept. 2, 1808.
Lucinda, d. Samuel and Polly, Oct. 17, 1817.

BELLINGHAM BIRTHS.

ALLEN, Mary Adams, d. Nathaniel and Lucy, Nov. 13, 1810.
Milton, s. Samuel and Polly, Sept. 16, 1821.
Nancy, d. Samuel and Polly, May 5, 1823.
Reuel, [twin] s. Samuel and Polly, Nov. 27, 1824.
Rufus, [twin] s. Samuel and Polly, Nov. 27, 1824.

ALVERSON, Simeon, s. Simon and Eunice, Mar. 5, 1776.

AMES, Adeline Maria, d. William and Sophia, July 17, 1831.
Charles Henry, s. William and Sophia, Sept. 3, 1839.
Edwin Mason, s. William and Sophia, Oct. 2, 1849.
Emily [———], w. George, Feb. 19, 1838. G.R.1.
George William, s. William and Sophia, Apr. 14, 1834.
Jane Amanda, d. William and Sophia, Aug. 9, 1836.
Maryann, d. Ezekiel H. and Mary, Dec. 31, 1815.
Polly Laurania, d. William and Sophia, Jan. 9, 1842.
Sophia Elizebeth, d. William and Sophia, Jan. 10, 1848.

ARMINGTON, Lydia, d. George W. and Eliza, ——— 16, 1838.

ARNOLD, Albert, s. Daniel Jr. and Jane M., Feb. 24, 1839.
Almon Whitman, s. Noah J. and Mary W., Oct. 26, 1848.
Amanda Levina, d. Noah J. and Mary W., Apr. 25, 1840.
Amos, Aug. 13, 1807. G.R.4.
Andrew, s. Daniel and Jane M., July 13, 1843.
Catherine P., d. Dea. William, w. Rev. Joseph T. Massey, Apr. 24, 1816, in Charlestown. G.R.2.
Daniel, s. Daniel and Jerusha, Oct. 25, 1802.
David, s. Bowley and Unice, Nov. 1, 1752.
Hannah, d. Seth and Martha, Dec. 7, 1768.
Hannah 2d, d. Seth and Martha, July 21, 1778.
Henrey, s. Seth and Martha, Dec. 12, 1772.
Henry Clay, s. Noah J. and Mary W., Aug. 8, 1845.
Lewis, s. Daniel Jr. and Jane M., Mar. 13, 1841.
Lucy [———], w. Amos, Oct. 5, 1808. G.R.4.
Lydia, d. Seth and Martha, Sept. 27, 1774.
Maranda, d. Daniel Jr. and Jane M., Apr. 19, 1836.
Mary, d. Daniel and Jerusha, Aug. 24, 1799.
Mary Adeliad, d. Noah J. and Mary W., June 19, 1842.
Orinda, d. Daniel and Jerusha, Feb. 7, 1805.
Pamelia, d. Daniel and Jerusha, Sept. 14, 1807.
Rebecca, d. Bowley and Eunice, Sept. 12, 1765.
Richard, s. Seth and Martha, Nov. 15, 1770.
Seth, s. Seth and Martha, Nov. 10, 1776.
Willam, s. Boley and Unice, May 7, 1762.

AUSTIN, Charles, s. Moody and Ann, Aug. 4, 1823.
George, s. Moody and Ann, Nov. 16, 1821.

BAILEY (see Baley, Baly, Bayley).

BAKER, Eben, ———, 1814. G.R.2.

BALCOME, Elmer Hubert, s. James H. and Louisa D., Mar. 13, 1842.
James Arthur, s. James H. and Louis D., May 23, 1847.

BALEY (see Baly, Bayley), Anne, d. James and Susanna, Dec. 21, 1769.
Elijah, s. James and Susanna, Feb. 13, 1768.
Sarah, d. James and Susanna, Apr. 19, 1766.

BALLOU, Almira, w. Oren Sayles, Jan. 22, 1805. G.R.4.
Lorinda Arnold, d. Arnold and Lorinda, May 28, 1817.

BALY (see Baley, Bayley), Abigal, d. Phillip and Abigal, Feb. 26, 1791.
Elisabeth, d. James and Susanna, Oct. 2, 1773.
Experance, d. James and Susanna, Nov. 3, 1771.
Hannah, d. James and Susanna, Apr. 16, 1776.

BARBER, Adams J. Jr., s. Adams J. and Orinda, Nov. 16, 1826.
Adams Jones, s. Calvin and Chloe, Oct. 26, 1801.
Adin, s. Adams J. and Orinda, Sept. 1, 1834.
Calvin, s. Calvin and Chloe, Aug. 7, 1808.
Daniel A., s. Adams J. and Orinda, Jan. 8, 1825.
Elial, s. Calvin and Chlloe, Jan. 20, 1803.
Emeline O., d. Adams J. and Orinda, July 15, 1837.
Horace E., s. Adams J. and Orinda, Nov. 8, 1828.
William Marsh, s. Calvin and Chloe, Feb. 28, 1805.

BASS, Benjamin, s. Benjamin and Mary, Aug. 7, 1775, in Midway.
Hannah, d. Benjamin and Mary, Mar. 20, 1773, in Boston.
Mary, d. Benjamin and Mary, Aug. 11, 1777.

BATES (see Batte), Abigail, d. Laban and Olive, May 26, 1789.
Abigail, d. Eli and Abigail, Apr. 7, 1808.
Abigil, d. Ezekiel and Abigial, Sept. 3, 1787.
Alanson, s. Ezekiel Jr. and Sabra, Oct. 18, 1818.
Albert, s. Peter and Sibyl, Sept. 15, 1811.
Albert G., s. Elijah and Sarah, June 29, 1811.
Andrew A., s. Elijah and Sarah, Jan. 28, 1810.

BELLINGHAM BIRTHS.

BATES, Ann Elizebeth, d. Francis D. and Julia A., Feb. 13, 1844.
Asa, s. Ezekiel and Abigal, Oct. 8, 1775.
Asa Fairbanks, s. Lyman and Jerusha, Apr. 1, 1806.
Caroline Elisebeth, d. Peletiah S. and Caroline B., July 5, 1842.
Caroline R. [———], w. Peletiah S., ———, 1813. G.R.2.
Carrie A. [———], w. Elias T., ———, 1838. G.R.2.
Catherine Frances, d. Peter and Sibyl, Dec. 6, 1824.
Charlotte Maria, d. Albert G. and Maria M., Mar. 2, 1838.
Cynthia Abigail, d. Otis and Electa, Apr. 30, 1807.
Daniel Hill, s. Peter and Sibyl, Oct. 27, 1815.
Davis Herbert, s. John Jr. and Sarah, Aug. 1, 1843.
Dexter Daniels, s. Peletiah S. and Caroline B., May 4, 1836.
Electa, d. Otis and Electa, Dec. 21, 1813.
Eli, s. Laben and Olive, Sept. 19, 1769.
Eli, s. Eli and Abigail, Apr. 5, 1799.
Eli, s. Peter and Sibyl, Mar. 9, 1822.
Eli Willard, s. Eli and Abigail, Sept. 30, 1800.
Eliacam Adams, s. Ezekiel Jr. and Sabra, June 30, 1817.
Elijah, s. Ezekiel and Abigail, Aug. 20, 1780.
Elijah, s. Elijah and Sarah, Mar. 24, 1815.
Elisabeth, d. Ezekiel and Abigail, July 28, 1767.
Ezekiel, s. Ezekiel and Abigal, Jan. 21, 1771.
Ezekiel, s. Ezekiel and Abigal, Nov. 4, 1777.
Francis, s. Ezekiel Jr. and Cyrena, Jan. 30, 1805.
Francis Augustus, s. Francis D. and Julia A., Mar. 11, 1841.
Francis D., s. Elijah and Sarah, June 22, 1813.
George, s. Eli and Abigail, June 27, 1793.
Hannah E., d. Albert G. and Maria, Apr. 15, 1845.
Horace Rockwood, s. Peletiah S. and Caroline B., Aug. 16, 1834.
Isaac, s. Joseph and Sarah, Feb. 28, 1763.
James Henry, s. James Madison and Ann Eliza, Aug. 14, 1843.
Jervis, s. Peter and Sibyl, Oct. 8, 1809.
Joanna, d. John and Margaret, Nov. 22, 1799.
John, s. Ezekiel and Abigal, May 20, 1773.
John, s. John and Margaret, Jan. 2, 1802.
John Erving, ———, 1847. G.R.2.
Julius, [twin] s. Peter and Sibyl, Feb. 27, 1827.
Junius, [twin] s. Peter and Sibyl, Feb. 27, 1827.
Laban, s. Isaac and Mary, Oct. 30, 1749. G.R.3.
Laban, s. Laban and Olive, Nov. 5, 1784.
Laban, s. Eli and Abigail, Apr. 1, 1810.
Levi Dunbar, s. Elijah and Sarah, Aug. 28, 1825.
Levina, d. John and Margaret, May 26, 1812.
Liberty, s. Laben and Olive, July 16, 1775.

BATES, Lorinda, d. John and Margaret, Apr. 3, 1798.
Louisa Ann, d. John and Margaret, May 9, 1815.
Lucius R., s. Otis and Electa, July 19, 1827.
Lucretia, d. Ezekiel and Abigail, Jan. 16, 1769.
Lucretia, [twin] d. Ezekiel and Abigal, Dec. 15, 1782.
Lydia, d. Eli and Abigail, Aug. 17, 1802, in Pelham.
Lyman, [twin] s. Ezekiel and Abigal, Dec. 15, 1782.
Madison, s. John and Margaret, Apr. 3, 1808.
Margaret, d. Eli and Abigail, Dec. 3, 1795.
Margaret, d. John and Margaret, Jan. 20, 1806.
Maria B., ——, 1818. G.R.2.
Martha, d. Joseph and Sarah, Dec. 20, 1764.
Mary, d. Joseph and Sarah, Feb. 10, 1767.
Mary, d. Ezekiel and Cyrena, Mar. 28, 1807.
Mary Abigail, d. Mellens B. and Mary A., Mar. 19, 1842.
Mellen, s. Otis and Electa, Oct. 21, 1811.
Metcalf Adams, s. Peletiah S. and Caroline B., July 14, 1839.
Micah, s. Joseph and Sarah, May 13, 1769.
Nahum, s. Laban and Olive, Apr. 8, 1773.
Olive [——], w. Laban, Apr. 12, 1750. G.R.3.
Olive, d. Laban and Olive, June 23, 1779.
Olive, d. Capt. Eli and Abigail, Sept. 17, 1797.
Otis, s. Ezekiel and Abigil, Apr. 4, 1785.
Otis Jr., s. Otis and Electa, Apr. 22, 1809.
Peletiah Smith, s. John and Margaret, May 11, 1810. [[h. Caroline R.] G.R.2.]
Peter, s. Laben and Olive, June 23, 1771.
Peter, s. Laban and Olive, Mar. 29, 1782.
Peter Jr., s. Peter and Sibyl, Dec. 20, 1817.
Polly, d. Laban and Olive, Nov. 8, 1791.
Rhoda, d. Ezekiel and Levina, May 1, 1800.
Rhoda, d. Otis and Electa, June 20, 1818.
Sarah, d. Laban (Bat[e]s) and Olive, May 1, 1777.
Sarah A. [——], w. Sullivan, Dec. 25, 1816. G.R.2.
Sarah A., d. Andrew A. and Abigail L., Mar. 28, 1839.
Sarah Elizabath, d. Elijah and Sarah, Aug. 30, 1817.
Sarah Josephin[e], d. John Jr. and Sarah, Sept. 25, 1836.
Sarah P. F., ——, 1812. G.R.2.
Sena, d. Ezekiel and Abigil, Jan. 13, 1790.
Senah Adeline, d. Otis and Electa, Apr. 6, 1816.
Seneca, s. Otis and Electa, Apr. 12, 1824.
Sibyl, d. Peter and Sibyl, May 16, 1813.
Smith, s. Laban and Olive, Nov. 28, 1786.
Smith, s. Laban and Olive, Oct. 25, 1794.

BELLINGHAM BIRTHS.

BATES, Smith, s. Laban Jr. and Chloe, Jan. 30, 1805, in Pelham.
Smith George, s. Peter and Sibyl, Dec. 7, 1819.
Stephen Albert, s. Albert G. and Maria M., Sept. 18, 1841.
Stephen Gano, s. Otis and Electa, Mar. 9, 1822.
Sullivan, s. John and Margaret, Mar. 14, 1804.
Susan Jane, d. Andrew A. and Abigail L., Aug. 10, 1835.
Watee H., d. Peter and Sibyl, Oct. 13, 1807.
Whiteman, s. Nahum and Parley, Jan. 21, 1800.
William, s. Ezekiel Jr. and Sabra, Jan. 26, 1820.

BATTE (see Bates), Amasa, s. Silvanes and Deborah, Mar. 1, 1773.
Amos, s. Silvanes and Deborah, Jan. 24, 1776, in Chesterfield, N.H.
Robart, s. Silvanes and Deborah, Sept. 7, 1771, in Gloscester, R.I.

BAYLEY (see Baley, Baly), Esther, d. James and Susanna, Oct. 25, 1764.
Phillips, s. James and Susanna, Jan. 26, 1763.

BEASLEY (see Bezely).

BELCHER, Martha A. [———], w. A. Hezeltine, Feb. 8, 1824.
G.R.2.
Samuel, s. David and Rachel, June 14, 1779.
Sarah, d. David and Rachel, Nov. 4, 1781.

BEMBO, Cloe [negro], d. Jack and Cloe, Mar. 1, 1782.
Cyrus [negro], s. Jack and Cloe, Apr. 23, 1785.
Pegey [negro], d. Jack and Cloe, Nov. 17, 1777.

BENEDICT, Olive A. [———], w. Dea. Benedict, May 22, 1817. G.R.1.

BENT, Amos Roswell, s. Roswell and Tryphena, Aug. 31, 1843.
Charles Elbridge, s. Micah and Betsey, Oct. 10, 1830.
Edward Micah, s. Roswell and Tryphena, July 1, 1846.
Eugene Alonzo, s. Micah and Betsey, June 8, 1833.
Frederick Augustus, s. Micah and Betsey, July 24, 1836.
Waldo Adams, s. Roswell and Tryphena, Jan. 18, 1849.

BEZELY, Diana Smith, d. Sofarla Smith, Dec. 2, 1814.

BILLINGS, Samuel, s. William and Esther, Dec. 8, 1789.

BLACKMAN, Phillip, s. Eleazer and Mary, July 13, 1768.

BLAKE, Aaron H., s. Solomon and Mary Ann, Oct. 2, 1836.
Abraham, s. Abraham and Silence, Mar. 11, 1767.

BLAKE, Ebenezer, s. Asa and Hannah, May 8, 1772.
Elionia, d. Abraham and Silence, Sept. 6, 1770.
Elisabeth, d. Asa and Mary, Mar. 4, 1764.
George W. [h. Levina], ———, 1813. G.R.2.
Henry Harison, s. George W. and Lavina, Oct. 19, 1840.
Joanah Bates, d. George W. and Lavina, Sept. 21, 1836.
Levina [———], w. George W., ———, 1812. G.R.2.
Mary, d. Asa and Hannah, June 8, 1770.
Olive, d. Asa and Mary, Jan. 18, 1766.
Silas, [twin] s. Abraham and Silence, Mar. 10, 1765.
Silence, [twin] d. Abraham and Silence, Mar. 10, 1765.
Timothy, s. Abraham and Silence, Aug. 13, 1763.
———, s. George W. and Lavina, Mar. 4, 1844.

BLOOD, Ann, d. Richard and Joanah, Feb. 9, 1725.
David, s. Joseph and Abagail, Sept. 26, 1743.
Ichobod, s. Joseph and Abigail, Mar. 17, 1747–8.
Isaiah, s. Richard and Joannah, Jan. 19, 1720–1.
Jahanh [Joannah], d. Richard and Joanah, Jan. 3, 1723.
Joana, d. Richard and Joanah, Oct. 16, 1729.
Joanna, d. Joseph and Abigial, May 9, 1746.
Joseph, s. Joseph and Abigail, Oct. 18, 1738.
Leusee, d. Joseph and Abagail, Apr. 10, 1741.

BOLSTER, Daniel [h. Susan E.], ———, 1821. G.R.2.
Susan E. [———], w. Daniel, ———, 1823. G.R.2.

BOSWORTH (see Bozworth), Eliza Abigail, d. Stacy and Abigail, Oct. 21, 1820.
Fisher Ames, s. Stacy and Abigail, Jan. 3, 1817.
George Whitefield, s. Stacy and Abigial, Sept. 30, 1818.
Pollina Scott, d. Stacy and Abigail, Oct. 24, 1822.
Timothy, s. Stacy and Abigail, Aug. 30, 1826.

BOWERS, Abby Adaline, d. William C. and Adaline E., Oct. 31, 1847.
Hannah [———], w. William, Aug. 13, 1779. G.R.2.
Nathan J., s. William C. and Adaline E., July 11, 1849.

BOZWORTH (see Bosworth), Ichabod, s. Jonathan and Susanna, Mar. 21, 1745.
Jonathan, s. Jonathan and Susanna, Sept. 1, 1748.
Joseph, s. Ichabud and Chloe, May 21, 1771.
Mary, d. Jonathan and Susanna, Nov. 2, 1746.

BRIGGS, Richard A., June 15, 1830. G.R.2.

BELLINGHAM BIRTHS.

BRODBENT, Elias, s. Samuel and Sarah, July 11, 1819.
James, s. Samuel and Sarah, Feb. 24, 1822.

BROWN, Betsy Chapin, d. Ebor R. and Betsy, Jan. 15, 1824.
Cynthia Cook, d. Eber R. and Betsey, Oct. 15, 1828.
Eber Rize, s. Eber R. and Betsy, Aug. 12, 1826.
Philo Washington, s. Ebor R. and Betsy, May 3, 1820.
Rhoda Thomson, d. Ebor R. and Betsy, Oct. 17, 1821.

BRYANT, Philip Henry, s. Philip C. and Amanda H., June 25, 1843.

BULLARD, Austin, s. Elisha and Rachel, Dec. 5, 1800. "September 14th AD 1821 at the request and by the Directions of Elisha Bullard I add to the Name of Austin Bullard Above recorded Samuel Austin Bullard he being yet under age."
Balis, s. Daniel and Molley, May 9, 1779.
Bathshaba, d. Elisha and Rachel, Sept. 25, 1778.
Cephas, s. Elisha and Rachel, June 8, 1790.
Cinthia Mariah, d. Ellis and Cinthia, May 28, 1847.
Clarysa, d. Elisha and Rachel, Feb. 16, 1784.
Deborah, d. Daniel [and] Molley, Apr. 1, 1777.
Elijah, s. Elisha and Rachel, Jan. 11, 1786.
Elisha, s. Elisha and Rachel, Mar. 6, 1793.
Ellis Richards, s. Wheelock and Sary, Aug. 12, 1811.
Fisher, s. Elisha and Rachel, Mar. 24, 1782.
Laura Ann, d. Ellis and Cynthia A., July 9 [9, written in pencil], 1844.
Leonard Pierce, s. Wheelock and Sary, Jan. 19, 1819.
Luther, s. Elisha and Rachel, Apr. 23, 1780.
Mari, d. Dr. Daniel and Ruth Wiswell, w. Eli Pond, Aug. 23, 1804. G.R.2.
Maria Louisa, d. Z. and Mary, Aug. 10, 1829. G.R.1.
Mary, d. Jonathan and Sarah, May 26, 1741.
Mary [——], w. Zebina, Aug. 9, 1794. G.R.1.
Olive Polena, d. Ellis and Cyntha, Aug. 31, 1840.
Poley, d. Daniel and Mary, Dec. 16, 1786.
Pyam, s. Elisha and Rachel, May 22, 1788.
Rachel, d. Elisha and Rachel, Mar. 22, 1795.
Sabra, d. Elisha and Rachel, Jan. 2, 1798.
Samuel Austin (see Austin Bullard).
Wheelock, s. Daniel and Mary, Oct. 8, 1783.
Zebina [h. Mary], Apr. 4, 1792. G.R.1.
——, ch. Daniel and Deborah, Nov. 7, 1775.

BURCH, Abigall, d. Thomas and Sarah, Dec. 5, 1728.
Hannah, d. Thomas and Sarah, Sept. 21, 1723.
Jerimiah, s. Thomas and Sarah, Feb. 10, 1718–19.
Mary, d. Thomas and Sarah, Feb. 21, 1720.
Sarah, d. Thomas and Sarah, Oct. 24, 1721.

BURDICK, Ellen Frances, d. Isaac and Sylvia, Nov. 17, 1844.

BURLINGAME, Adin B., July 31, 1840. G.R.1.

BURNHAM, Andrew, Sept. 27, 1796. G.R.2.

BURR, Abby Maria, d. Laban and Maria, Oct. 31, 1832.
Addison, s. Laban and Maria, Oct. 19, 1830.
Albert, s. Laban and Maria, Jan. 14, 1824.
Angeline, d. Elisha and Electa, Jan. 3, 1820.
Asa, s. Elisha and Lucretia, Apr. 8, 1777.
Calvin Chickering, s. Seneca and Lucy, June 30, 1840.
Charles [crossed out], ch. Laban and Maria, Mar. 18, 1845.
Charles Edgar, s. Laban and Maria, Oct. 11, 1842.
Charlotte Eliza, d. Seneca and Eliza B., May —, 1832.
Cynthia, d. Asa 2d and Polly, Sept. 1, 1805.
David, s. Elisha and Lucretia, May 28, 1769.
Edmund, s. Laban and Maria, Mar. 11, 1827.
Electa, d. Elisha and Electa, Feb. 24, 1806.
Eli, s. Elisha and Electa, Jan. 13, 1811.
Elisha, s. Elisha and Lucretia, Apr. 14, 1780.
Elisha, s. Elisha and Electa, Dec. 13, 1812.
Emerline, d. Elisha and Electa, Sept. 1, 1817.
Ezekiel, s. Elisha and Lucretia, Mar. 7, 1783.
Hannah A. [———], w. Addison S., Apr. 12, 1830. G.R.2.
Hannah Ellis, d. Asa and Polly, Apr. 19, 1814.
Harriet, d. Elisha and Electa, Nov. 19, 1822.
John M., s. Elisha and Electa, June 28, 1826.
Joseph Massey, s. Laban and Maria, July 25, 1837.
Julia Ann, d. Laban and Maria, Aug. 11, 1825.
Laban, s. Elisha and Lucretia, Aug. 24, 1790.
Lucretia, d. Elisha and Lucretia, Oct. 12, 1787.
Mary Eliza, d. Albert G. and Rebecca, Nov. 29, 1849.
Mary Jane, d. Asa and Polly, July 20, 1833.
Meranda Maria, d. Asa and Polly, May 15, 1812.
Nabby Smith, d. Asa and Polly, Jan. 13, 1817.
Nathan, s. Asa and Polly, May 9, 1802.
Olive, d. Elisha and Lucretia, July 3, 1774.
Olive, d. Elisha and Electa, Nov. 3, 1808.

BURR, Olive W. [————], w. Seneca, ———, 1833. G.R.2.
Paulina, d. Asa and Polly, May 9, 1810.
Polly, d. Asa 2d and Polly, Dec. 30, 1803.
Polly M. R. [————], w. Asa, Mar. 13, 1791. G.R.2.
Polly Sabrina, d. Asa and Polly, Nov. 16, 1820.
Rebecca, d. Elisha and Lucretia, Nov. 4, 1766.
Sabra Ann, d. Asa and Polly, Nov. 6, 1822.
Sarah, d. Asa and Rhoda, June 14, 1764.
Sarah, d. Elish[a] and Lucretia, Dec. 7, 1771.
Seneca, s. Elisha and Electa, Dec. 21, 1803.
Seneca Jr., s. Seneca and Eliza B., Oct. 16, 1830. [[h. Olive W.] G.R.2.]
Sophia, d. Asa and Polly, Apr. 4, 1808.
William Oscar, s. Laban and Maria, Jan. 16, 1829.

BURRILL, Mary, w. Parker Wheeler, Apr. 23, 1842. G.R.1.

BUTTERWORTH, Elizabeth Holbrook, d. Otis and Anny, Dec. 10, 1798.
Esther, d. Nathaniel and Elisabeth, Aug. 1, 1762.
Ezuba, d. Nathaniel and Elisabeth, Aug. 15, 1770.
Maria, d. Otis and Anny, Jan. 31, 1802.
Nathaniel, s. Otis and Anny, May 15, 1800.
Niles, s. Nathaniel and Elisabeth, Jan. 20, 1773.
Ottes, s. Nathaniel and Elisabeth, Oct. 7, 1768.
Sarah, d. Nathaniel and Elisabeth, Dec. 9, 1764.

CAPRON, Benjamin, s. Banfield and Hannah, June 20, 1724.
Hannah, d. Charles and Mary, Oct. 16, 1743.
Leah, d. Banfield and Hannah, Mar. 10, 1722.
Nancy, youngest d. Philip and Priscilla, w. Elisha Scott, Oct. 20, 1783, in Cumberland, R.I. G.R.3.
Phebe, d. Charles and Mary, May 17, 1747.
Phillip (Copron), s. Banfield and Hannah, Feb. 1, 1719–20.
Phylip, s. Charles and Mary, Apr. 28, 1745.

CARPENTER, Amos, s. Reuben and Sarah, Aug. 31, 1779.
Daniel, s. Daniel and Chloe, Sept. 7, 1771.
Hephzibah, d. Daniel and Chloe, July 27, 1773.
James, s. Daniel and Chloe, Nov. 24, 1777.
Lydia, d. Reuben (Corpenter) and Sarah, Mar. 6, 1782.
Reuben, s. Reuben and Sarah, Jan. 7, 1776.
Reuben, s. Reuben and Sarah, Oct. 29, 1777.
Samuel, s. Daniel and Chloe, July 19, 1775.

CASK, Ealce, d. John and Ealce, Feb. 7, 1743-4.
Mary, d. John and Ealce, Aug. 14, 1742.

CASS, Emily Marion, d. Jarvis and Rachel, Jan. 19, 1849.
Rachel C., Apr. 26, 1822. G.R.4.

CHACE (see Chase), Isabel, d. William and Isabel, May 12, 1758.
Joseph, s. William and Isabel, Aug. 16, 1764.
Tryphose, d. Allen and Lidia, May 10, 1798.

CHAMBERLAIN, Eunice, d. Sam[ue]ll and Margret, Mar. 6, 1763.

CHAPIN, Charles, s. Elias and Rhoda, Mar. 6, 1816.
Cyrus, s. Elias and Rhoda, Mar. 16, 1822.
Hollis, s. Elias and Rhoda, Dec. 12, 1819.
Mariah, d. Elias and Rhoda, Feb. 2, 1818.

CHASE (see Chace), Ebenezer Perry, s. Allen and Lidia, Aug. 17, 1796.
Horace Grandville, s. Elisha and Adaline A., July 11, 1848.
———, d. Hiram and Matilda, Oct. 15, 1849.

CHICKERIN, Abigail [———], w. John, Sept. 12, 1774. G.R.2.
John [h. Abigail], Mar. 25, 1771. G.R.2.

CHILLSON (see Chilson), Jedidiah, s. Joseph and Lydia, Apr. 18, 1758.
John, s. Joseph and Lydia, Feb. 3, 1754.
Joseph, s. Joseph and Lydia, July 17, 1751.
Joseph, s. Joseph and Hannah, Jan. 18, 1791.
Joshua, s. Joseph and Lydia, July 8, 1756.
Martha, d. Joseph and Marcy, Apr. 13, 1746.
Mary, d. Joseph and Lydia, June 23, 1761.

CHILSON (see Chillson), Aliddia, d. Joshua and Margaret, Oct. 26, 1785.
Anna, d. John and Abiagil, Oct. 28, 1783.
Asa, s. Joshua and Margaret, Feb. 25, 1793.
Caleb Adams, s. Ichabod and Deborah, Jan. 11, 1813.
Diadama C., d. Orrin and Diadama, Oct. 28, 1832.
Draper, s. Ichabod and Deborah, Mar. 29, 1811.
Esther Thayer, d. Paul and Mary, Mar. 29, 1829.
Hannah, d. Josiph and Hannah, Aug. 25, 1788.
Ichabod, s. John and Abigil, Aug. 29, 1785.
James O., s. Orin and Diadama, Mar. 28, 1837.

CHILSON, Jedediah, s. Joshua and Margaret, Oct. 12, 1791.
Joanna, d. Joshua and Margaret, Nov. 26, 1802.
John, s. John and Abigil, Jan. 11, 1788.
John, s. John and Abigil, Oct. 25, 1790.
John Draper, s. John and Almira, Oct. 29, 1824.
Jonathan, s. Ichabod and Deborah, Jan. 30, 1810.
Joshua, s. Joshua and Margaret, Nov. 18, 1788.
Laura Jane, d. Paul and Mary, Apr. 6, 1843.
Lebbeus, s. Orin and Diadama, Mar. 1, 1835.
Lucius Adison, s. John and Almira, May 31, 1830.
Margaret, d. Joshua and Margaret, Apr. 23, 1809.
Martha W., d. Orren and Diadama, Mar. 20, 1826.
Martin, s. John and Abigail, Apr. 25, 1796.
Mary Mariah, d. Paul and Mary, July 7, 1839.
Nabbe, d. John and Abigil, June 27, 1793.
Nathan, s. Joshua and Margaret, Oct. 9, 1795.
Nathen, s. Joshua and Margret, May 16, 1784.
Orin, s. John and Abigail, July 26, 1799.
Orrin, s. Orrin and Diadama, Oct. 6, 1830.
Paul, s. Joshua and Margaret, Mar. 18, 1801. [Mar. 13, G.R.2.]
Paul Davis, s. Paul and Mary, May 25, 1833.
Phebe Ellen, d. Nathan and Susan R., Sept. 5, 1847.
Polly, d. Joshua and Margaret, June 8, 1787.
Polly, d. Joshua and Margaret, May 3, 1790.
Reuben, s. Orren and Diadama, Oct. 13, 1828.
Suky, d. Joshua and Margaret, Oct. 10, 1799.
Sulivan, s. Ichabod and Deborah, Nov. 2, 1808.
Whipple Olney, s. John and Almira, June 4, 1827.
Willard, s. Joshua and Margaret, Dec. 8, 1797.

CLAFLIN, George Hoppins, s. Luther and Nancy, May 13, 1816.

CLARK (see Clerk), Alice Augusta, d. Joel J. and Almira Elizebeth, Feb. 26, 1844.
Alvin Henry, s. Mason and Polly, Oct. 30, 1835.
Amos M., Apr. 12, 1820. G.R.2.
Charlotte Amanda, d. Alfred and Abigail M., Apr. 10, 1842.
Elizabeth J., Mar. 15, 1824. G.R.4.
Laura Catherine, d. Joel J. and Almira, June 8, 1845.
Mary M., Aug. 18, 1829. G.R.4.
Orlando David, s. Mason and Polly, Mar. 20, 1840.
Peggy, d. John and Olive, Mar. 11, 1802.
Rachel, d. Anson and Rachel, Apr. 26, 1822.

CLERK (see Clark), Marcy, d. John and Sarah, Aug. 26, 1756.

BELLINGHAM BIRTHS.

CLERK, Nathan, s. John and Sarah, Aug. 24, 1758.
Samuel, s. John and Sarah, Dec. 30, 1760.

COBB, Clarissa, d. Samuel and Rhoda, July 3, 1778.
Ortensa, d. Luther and Rachel, Jan. 27, 1797.

COMBS (see Coombs), Abijah, s. John Jr. and Mary, Apr. 17, 1781.
Amos, s. Jesse and Sarah, Oct. 20, 1808.
David, s. Jesse and Sarah, Nov. 14, 1811.
Elizabeth, d. John and Mary, Apr. 13, 1775.
Jesse, s. John and Mary, Mar. 4, 1773.
Jesse, s. Jesse and Sarah, Mar. 13, 1806.
John, s. John and Mary, Mar. 27, 1758.
Jonathan, s. John and Mary, Oct. 2, 1762.
Louis Bacon, d. Odid and Polly, Mar. 26, 1803.
Meletiah, d. John Jr. and Mary, July 13, 1783.
Noah, s. Jesse and Sarah, Mar. 7, 1804.
Odid, s. John and Mary, Dec. 21, 1777.
Odid, s. Jesse and Sarah, Apr. 22, 1814.
Sally, d. John and Mary, Oct. 2, 1760.
Stephen Adams, s. Jesse and Sarah, May 15, 1798.
Valentine Rathbun, s. Jesse and Sarah, July 25, 1800.

COOK (see Cooke), Aaron (see Aron Clark).
Abigail, [twin] d. Caleb and Provided, June 19, 1754.
Abigail, d. Daniel and Elisabeth, Mar. 20, 1767.
Abigail, d. Stephen and Joanna, Apr. 7, 1785.
Abigal, d. Nicholus and Elezebath, Nov. 1, 1731.
Abijah, s. David Jr. and Susannah, Sept. 24, 1784.
Abner, s. David Jr. and Susannah, June 20, 1778.
Abner Legg, s. Seth and Susan, Feb. 21, 1832.
Alma, d. Fenner and Miranda, July 1, 1829.
Alpha, d. Reuben 2d and Martha, July 28, 1813.
Anson, Apr. 10, 1792. G.R.4.
Arnold Dean, s. Aquilla and Olive, Jan. 9, 1825.
Aron Clark, s. Anson and Rachel, June 27, 1819. [Aaron, G.R.4.]
Caleb, s. David and Susanna, Aug. 16, 1793.
Calib, s. George and Phebe, June 23, 1773.
Calista, d. Abijah and Roxanna, Jan. 7, 1821.
Calvin, s. Nicholas and Phillis, Mar. 4, 1771.
Candes, d. Stephen and Joanna, Aug. 18, 1771.
Charles, s. Abijah and Roxanna, Jan. 7, 1815.
Charles F., s. Seth and Susan, Aug. 17, 1839.
Charles Francis, s. Emery and Maria, Mar. 24, 1849.

COOK, Crusa, d. Stephen and Joanna, Mar. 14, 1775.
Daniel, s. Nicolas and Elizebeth, Sept. 12, 1722.
Daniel, s. Daniel and Elisabeth, Apr. 11, 1756.
Daniel, s. Daniel and Charlotte, Nov. 18, 1791.
David, s. Daniel and Elisabeth, Nov. 8, 1751.
David, s. Lealend and Sofarla, Oct. 1, 1816.
Diadama, d. Reuben 2d and Martha, May 5, 1808.
Eddy C., ——, 1817. G.R.4.
Edgar L., s. Lewis F. and Phila H., Dec. 9, 1849. G.R.4.
Eleania, d. Abner and Wata, June 7, 1806.
Elias, s. Daniel and Elisabeth, Dec. 30, 1770.
Elias Jr., s. Elias and Mary, Dec. 18, 1804.
Elisabeth, d. Daniel and Elisabeth, July 16, 1758.
Elisha, s. Stephen and Joanna, Mar. 19, 1773.
Elizabeth, d. Caleb and Provided, Aug. 31, 1772.
Elizabeth Jillson, d. Anson and Rachel, Mar. 15, 1824.
Elizebath, d. Nicholas and Elizebath, July 15, 1729.
Ella A., w. George A. Crooks, ——, 1830. G.R.4.
Ellen Eliza, d. Amory B. and Mary, Aug. 16, 1840.
Ellis, s. Abner and Wata, Aug. 4, 1810.
Ellis Wheaton, s. Seth and Susan, Aug. 1, 1820.
Elona Maria, d. Seth and Susan, Jan. 30, 1825.
Elsey Rockwood, d. Seth and Susan, July 4, 1828.
Emma S., d. W[illia]m W. and Eliza E., Apr. 17, 1845.
Emory, s. Abner and Wata, Aug. 3, 1803.
Emory Bangs, s. Emory and Maria, May 6, 1830.
Esther, d. Ezekiel and Jerusha, Nov. 22, 1784.
Esther P. [——], w. Pliny, ——, 1796. G.R.2.
Eunice, d. Ezekiel and Jerusha, Jan. 26, 1779.
Ezekiel, s. Nicholas and Elisabeth, June 19, 1744.
Ezekiel, s. Ezekiel and Jerusha, Aug. 18, 1771.
Freelove, d. Caleb and Provided, Dec. 21, 1757.
George, [twin] s. Caleb and Provided, June 19, 1754.
George Adelbert, s. William W. and Eliza E., Sept. 30, 1843.
George Bates, s. Aquilla and Olive, July 20, 1822.
George E., s. N. A., ——, 1847. G.R.4.
George U., July 30, 1842. G.R.4.
George W., s. Fenner and Miranda, Feb. 11, 1831.
Gilbert Emanuel, s. Seth and Susan, Dec. 30, 1833, in Mendon.
Hannah, d. Ichabud and Elisabeth, Jan. 21, 1773.
Harriet Jane, d. Charles and Zylpha, Apr. 22, 1849.
Henrietta Paine, ——, 1808. G.R.2.
Hiram Everett, s. Emory and Maria, Nov. 26, 1838.
James, s. William and Priscilla, June 7, 1760.

BELLINGHAM BIRTHS. 25

Cook, James, s. Fenner and Miranda, Apr. 28, 1839.
James M., Apr. 15, 1823. G.R.4.
Jamima, d. Nicolas and Elizaba[th], Nov. 16, 1716.
Jemima, d. Daniel and Elisabeth, Jan. 29, 1747-8.
Jemima, d. Caleb and Provided, Oct. 10, 1765.
Jeremiah, s. Nicholas and Phillis, Aug. 4, 1766.
Jerusha, d. Ezekiel and Jerusha, Nov. 10, 1777.
Joanna, d. Nicolues and Elisebath, Nov. 14, 1740.
Joanna, d. Daniel and Elisabeth, Feb. 3, 1754.
Joanna, d. Stephen and Joanna, June 6, 1793.
John, s. Daniel and Elisabeth, Aug. 5, 1749.
John, s. Elias and Mary, Feb. 8, 1795.
John L., s. Lealend and Sofarla, Sept. 18, 1820.
John Mayo, s. John 2d and Nancy, June 14, 1831.
Joseph, s. Daniel and Elisabeth, Apr. 14, 1769.
Julia, d. Fenner and Miranda, Feb. 24, 1827.
Julia Maria, d. John 2d and Nancy, Nov. 28, 1818.
Katheron, d. William and Priscilla, Mar. 6, 1763.
Kezia, d. Noah and Kezia, May 14, 1733.
Lalon [Lealand], s. David and Susannah, Apr. 3, 1789.
Levina, d. Daniel and Elisabeth, Dec. 21, 1760.
Lewis F., Sept. 1, 1824. G.R.4.
Louisa, d. Fenner and Miranda, Mar. 10, 1821.
Lucius Austin, s. John 2d and Nancy, July 20, 1833.
Lucretia, d. William and Priscilla, Apr. 17, 1767.
Lucy, d. Daniel Jr. and Charlotte, Feb. 7, 1784.
Lutinia, d. Nicholas and Phillis, Mar. 8, 1764.
Lydia, d. Nicholas and Phillis, Oct. 13, 1768.
Marcus Moreton, s. Seth and Susan, Sept. 6, 1837, in Mendon.
Marietta, d. Fenner and Miranda, Jan. 19, 1824.
Martha Daniels, d. John 2d and Nancy, Oct. 1, 1825.
Mary, [twin] d. Elias and Mary, Dec. 26, 1808.
Mary Emeline, d. Amory B. and Mary, Feb. 18, 1844.
Mary Mayo, d. John 2d and Nancy, May 25, 1823.
Maryan, d. Reuben 2d and Martha, Jan. 22, 1810.
Mayo, s. Elias and Mary, May 15, 1798.
Monroe, s. Fenner and Miranda, Aug. 5, 1835.
Nabby, [twin] d. Elias and Mary, Dec. 26, 1808.
Naham Herbert, s. Nathan A., Jan. 12, 1849.
Nahum, s. Ezekiel and Jerusha, Sept. 21, 1782.
Nahum Adams, ——, 1835. G.R.2.
Nancy, d. Fenner and Miranda, Oct. 21, 1822.
Nancy Wight, d. John 2d and Nancy, Mar. 20, 1821.
Nathan A. [h. Sena A.], ——, 1828. G.R.4.

BELLINGHAM BIRTHS.

Cook, Nathanael, s. Nicolas and Elizbath, Sept. 15, 1718.
Nicholas, s. Nicholas and Ele[za]bath, Feb. 7, 1735-6.
Nicholas, s. Stephen and Joanna, Feb. 27, 1777.
Olive, d. Caleb and Provided, Mar. 30, 1756.
Olive Eliza, d. Seth and Susan, Aug. 3, 1830.
Olney, s. Fenner and Miranda, July 15, 1837.
Otis, s. Stephen and Joanna, Oct. 26, 1769.
Paciance, d. Caleb and Provided, Oct. 30, 1760.
Peter, s. Nicholas and Elizebeth, Aug. 26, 1720.
Peter, s. Stephen and Joanna, Mar. 12, 1779.
Phebee, d. Daniel and Elisabeth, Apr. 10, 1763.
Phila H. [———], w. Lewis F., Apr. 15, 1826. G.R.4.
Philenda, d. Noah and Patience, Dec. 11, 1791.
Pliny [h. Esther P.], ———, 1800. G.R.2.
Priscilla, d. William and Priscilla, Apr. 26, 1765.
Rachel, Aug. 3, 1791. G.R.4.
Reuben Olney, s. Reuben 2d and Martha, June 18, 1822.
Rhode, d. Stephen and Joanna, Feb. 12, 1790.
Ruben, s. David Jr. and Susannah, Dec. 7, 1780.
Sally, d. Daniel and Charlotte, Sept. 15, 1785.
Sally, d. Daniel and Charlotte, Aug. 28, 1789.
Samuel, s. William and Priscilla, Nov. 12, 1755.
Samuel, s. Stephen and Joanna, Apr. 17, 1789.
Sena A. [———], w. Nathan A., ———, 1828. G.R.4.
Seth, s. Seth and Experience, Mar. 27, 1720.
Seth, s. Daniel and Elisabeth, Jan. 27, 1765.
Seth, s. David Jr. [and] Susannah, Mar. 19, 1783.
Seth, s. Abner and Wata, Feb. 5, 1800.
Seth Aldrich, s. Seth and Susan, Sept. 20, 1826.
Silvanus, s. William and Priscilla, Sept. 5, 1758.
Simeon, s. Caleb and Provided, Dec. 8, 1770.
Stephen Warren, s. Stephen and Joanna, July 2, 1795.
Stillman R., Dec. 1, 1834. G.R.4.
Stillmon, s. Daniel and Charlotte, May 15, 1793.
Susan Ann, d. William W. and Eliza E., Mar. 17, 1847.
Susan Emily, d. Seth and Susan, July 14, 1823.
Susanna, d. Nicholas and Elizabath, Mar. 6, 1738.
Susanna, d. William and Priscilla, Nov. 30, 1756.
Susanna, d. Reuben and Esther, July 13, 1802.
Sylvia Freeman, w. Levi A., Sept. 20, 1836. G.R.1.
Urania, d. Ezekiel and Jerusha, Sept. 18, 1775.
Uriah, s. Nicholas and Phillis, June 27, 1760.
Vernon, s. Daniel and Charlotte, Dec. 13, 1801.
Warren Foster, s. Amory B. and Mary, Sept. 10, 1838.

BELLINGHAM BIRTHS.

Cook, Wata, d. Abner and Wata, Jan. 29, 1815.
Wata Ann, d. Seth and Susan, Nov. 12, 1835, in Mendon.
William, s. Nicolas and Elizebeth, Dec. 12, 1724.
William, s. William and Priscilla, Mar. 11, 1770.
William, s. Nicholas Jr. and Phillis, Apr. 10, 1773.
William, s. Stephen and Joanna, Nov. 6, 1782.
William Wilcox, s. Seth and Susan, Oct. 4, 1821.
Ziba, s. Ezekiel and Jerusha, May 6, 1764.
Zuriel, s. Caleb and Provided, Oct. 22, 1763.

COOKE (see Cook), Calib, s. Nickolas Jr. and Elezebath (Cook), Sept. 25, 1727.
Jarvis, June 7, 1805. G.R.I.

COOMBS (see Combs), Charlotte Matilda, d. Stephen A. and Charlotte B., Apr. 22, 1836.
Clarissa [――――], w. Valentine R., Nov. 16, 1802. G.R.I.
David, s. Stephen A. and Charlotte B., Feb. 10, 1839.
Eicanors, ch. Valentine R. and Clarissa, Aug. 11, 1835. G.R.I.
George V., ch. Valentine R. and Clarissa, Aug. 10, 1830. G.R.I.
John N., ch. Valentine R. and Clarissa, Apr. 5, 1828. G.R.I.
John Vars, s. Stephen A. and Charlotte B., May 11, 1843.
Levina, d. John and Mary, Aug. 3, 1786.
Marion [――――], w. Valentine, Jan. 1, 1807. G.R.I.
Marriam Woolsom, d. Stephen A. and Charlotte B., Mar. 29, 1833.
Mary Olivia, d. Stephen A. and Charlotte B., July 25, 1845.
Melitiah, d. John and Mary, July 15, 1784.
Nancy (see Nancy Hayward).
Stephen Francis, s. Stephen A. and Charlotte B., May 20, 1829.
William Earl, s. Stephen A. and Charlotte B., Nov. 15, 1830.

CORBET (see Corbett, Corbitt), Bethiah, d. John and Hopstill, Mar. 21, 1740-1.
Briget, d. Daniell and Sarah, Feb. 25, 1726.
Daniel, s. Daniel and Sarah, July 8, 1720.
Eunice (see Unices).
Marcy, d. Daniel and Sarah, Sept. 2, 1718.
Mehetabell, d. John and Hopstill, Oct. 24, 1747.
Pricilla, d. John and Hopstill, Apr. 17, 1745.
Sarah, d. Daniell (Corbit) and Sarah, May 4, 1722.
Unices, d. Daniele and Sarah, May 4, 1728.

CORBETT (see Corbet, Corbitt), Abigel, d. John and Hopstill, Jan. 19, 1730.

CORBETT, Allice, d. Daniel and Sarah, Feb. 23, 1733.
Elijah, s. John and Hobstill, Apr. 9, 1736 [*sic*, see Rachel].
John, s. John and Hopstill, Oct. 25, 1729.
Josiah, s. John and Mehetabell, June 13, 1725.
Josiah, s. John and Hopstill, Apr. 29, 1734.
Loes, d. Daniel and Sarah, Dec. 24, 1730.
Mahetabel, d. John and Mahetabel, July 13, 1722.
Melitiah, d. John and Hopstill, Nov. 5, 1732.
Nathaniel, s. Danaiel and Mary, May 20, 1742.
Priscilah, d. Danill and Sarah, May 9, 1732.
Priscilla, d. John and Hopstill, Oct. 7, 1728.
Rachel, d. John and Hopestill, Nov. 14, 1736 [*sic*, see Elijah].
Seth, s. John and Hopstill, Mar. 25, 1743.

CORBITT (see Corbet, Corbett), Nathanael, s. Daniel and Sarah, Mar. 21, 1724.

CRAIG, Catharine Amelia, d. Edward C. and Cynthia A., May 15, 1837.
Catharine Amelia, d. Edward C. and Cynthia A., Sept. 5, 1843.
Charles Bates, s. Edward C. and Cynthia A., May 3, 1835.
George Edward, s. Edward C. and Cynthia A., Aug. 30, 1833.
Henry Elijah, s. Edward C. and Cynthia A., Aug. 5, 1841.
James Otis, s. Edward C. and Cynthia, Mar. 27, 1839.

CROOKS, Amos Darling, s. Jeremiah and Anna, May 24, 1816.
Beriah, d. John and Beriah, Feb. —, 1781.
Charles Francis, s. Joel and Esther, June 14, 1841.
Deborah, ch. Jeremiah and Phebe, May 16, 1801, in Me. P.R.2.
Delia Eliza, d. Joel and Esther, Sept. 10, 1832.
Ella A. (Cook), w. George A., ——, 1830. G.R.4.
George Augustus, s. Joel and Esther, June 23, 1830.
Jeremiah, Dec. 16, 1766. P.R.2.
Jeremiah, ch. Jeremiah and Phebe, June 10, 1791. P.R.2.
Jeremiah Mayo, s. Jeremiah and Anna, Mar. 24, 1823.
Joel, Maj., Feb. 21, 1803. G.R.2. [ch. Jeremiah and Phebe, in Me., P.R.2.]
Joel Aldrich, s. Joel and Esther, Feb. 8, 1828.
Marcus Duffee, s. Jeremiah and Anna, Oct. 18, 1830.
Mary, d. Jeremiah and Anna, Oct. 14, 1818.
Phebe, ch. Jeremiah and Phebe, Jan. 30, 1796. P.R.2.
Polly, ch. Jeremiah and Phebe, Nov. 18, 1788. P.R.2.
Sally, ch. Jeremiah and Phebe, Oct. 25, 1798. P.R.2.
Sally Ann, d. Jeremiah and Anna, Jan. 21, 1827.

CROSBY (see Crossby), Sarah Lavina, d. Pardon and Alsada, July 21, 1841.

CROSSBY (see Crosby), Alsada Malissa, d. Pardon and Alsada, June 17, 1843.

CUMMINGS, Augusta Melvina, d. Lucius G. and Lorinda, May 8, 1842.
———, ch. Lewis G., ——— [rec. between July 18 and Aug. 8, 1845].

CURTICE (see Curtis), Addenon Nelson, s. Wright and Aurilla, Nov. 25, 1811.

CURTIS (see Curtice), Artiman Hill, s. Wright and Aurilla, Sept. 23, 1815.
James Munroe, s. Wright and Aurilla, Feb. 20, 1818.
Marcus Arnold, s. Wright and Aurilla, Aug. 14, 1813.
Phila Ballou, d. Wright and Aurilla, Feb. 23, 1819.

CUSHING, Hannah, d. Solomon and Mary, Oct. 24, 1774.
Isaac, s. Solomon and Mary, Mar. 30, 1779.
Rhody, d. Solomon and Mary, Mar. 23, 1781.
Selah, d. Solomon and Mary, May 6, 1785.
Solomon, s. Solomon and Mary, Dec. 29, 1776.

CUSHMAN, Albert Tenney, s. Charles F. and Olive M., Feb. 1, 1848.
Amaziah, s. Amaziah and Marthe, Apr. 14, 1789.
Asa, s. Amaziah and Marthe, Nov. 3, 1779.
Charles Fisher, s. Sabin and Mary, Oct. 3, 1825.
Cyrena, d. Amaziah and Marthe, Mar. 1, 1785.
Cyrene, d. Amaziah and Lydia, Apr. 5, 1817.
Luis, s. Amaziah and Marthe, June 8, 1787.
Martin, s. Amaziah and Marthe, Feb. 11, 1782.
Martin Gray, s. Martin and Hannah, Nov. 16, 1825.
Mary [———], w. Sabin, Aug. 9, 1800. G.R.2.
Matthew Smith, s. Amaziah and Marthe, Nov. 15, 1777.
Sabin, Aug. 5, 1796. G.R.2.
Sarah, d. Amaziah and Marthe, June 28, 1775.

CUTTLER, William, s. Jonathan (Cutler) [and] Abigail, Mar. 24, ———.

DAMAN, Benoni, s. Ebenezer and Es[t]her, May 16, 1756.
Ebenezer, s. Ebenezer and Esther, June 4, 1757.
Jonathan, s. Joseph and Hopstill, Apr. 11, 1751.

DAMAN, Mary, d. Ebenezer and Esther, Feb. 4, 1760.
Rebakah, d. Joseph and Hopstill, Aug. 17, 1752.
DANELS (see Daniels), Esther, d. Ephram and Elezebath, Dec. 15, 1733.
DANIELS (see Danels), Abigail, d. David and Magdelon, Aug. 28, 1726.
Elisabeth, d. Samuel and Elisabeth, May 26, 1761.
DARLIN (see Darling), Jobe, s. Cornelus Jr. and Hanah, Jan. 2, 1727-8.
Ruth, d. Sam[ue]ll and Mary, July 3, 1728.
DARLING (see Darlin), Abbie A., w. Edwin, d. Ruel Adams and Julia, Apr. 7, 1835. G.R.2.
Abigal, d. Samuel and Maray, Feb. 16, 1731.
Abisha, s. Joshua and Martha, Apr. 2, 1767.
Ahimaaz, s. Joshua and Martha, Mar. 19, 1765.
Ahimaz, s. Ahimaz and Margeretta, June 11, 1829.
Albert Welcome, s. Welcome B. and Alpha, July 18, 1848.
Alfred O., Nov. 23, 1824. G.R.4.
Amasa, s. Joshua and Martha, Apr. 30, 1769.
Anna, d. John and Anna, Oct. 30, 1770.
Anna, w. Edwin, d. Caleb Adams and Lydia, June 3, 1834. G.R.2.
Asa, s. Sam[ue]l Jr. and Sarah, July 18, 1783.
Benjamin, s. Samuel Jr. and Esther, July 4, 1761.
Caraloine, d. Samuel Jr. and Sarah, Sept. 17, 1801.
Charles, s. Samuel Jr. and Margaet, Jan. 21, 1817.
Charlotte, d. Enoch and Lois, Sept. 14, 1768.
Collins, s. Samuel Jr. and Sarah, Oct. 14, 1785.
Corneleas, s. Corniles and Hannah, Mar. 15, 1732.
Deborah, d. Cornelius and Mehitabel, Dec. 22, 1775.
Dennis (see Dennis Thompson).
E. A. [———], w. Almon, Jan. 27, 1821. G.R.4.
Edwin, s. Jefferson and Joanna, July 3, 1826. [Edwin R., G.R.2.]
Edwin, s. Samuel Jr. and Margaret, June 14, 1834.
Elijah, s. Enoch and Louis, Sept. 14, 1756.
Elizebeth, d. Samuel and Mary, Aug. 31, 1725.
Emma Marion, d. Collins C. and Marion P. of Boston, May 26, 1846.
Esther, d. Samuel and Esther, Sept. 1, 1765.
Esther, d. Sam[ue]ll and Sarah, Aug. 8, 1791.
Eunice, d. Enoch and Lois [dup. Louis], Aug. 11, 1758.
Fisher, s. Simon and Peggy, Mar. 11, 1796.

BELLINGHAM BIRTHS. 31

DARLING, George, s. Samuel Jr. and Margaet, Aug. 15, 1815.
George Cook, s. George and Susan B., Nov. 17, 1846. G.R.2.
Gilbert, s. Samuel Jr. and Margaet, Jan. 21, 1819.
Gilbert G., s. Fisher and Rebecca, Oct. 3, 1823.
Hannah, d. John and Anna, Apr. 9, 1773.
Hannah A. [———], w. Alfred O., Nov. 25, 1834. G.R.4.
Hester, d. Ebenezer and Abiel, May 28, 1724.
Hulda, d. Cornelias and Hannah, Oct. 29, 1725.
Huldah, d. Job and Margery, June 16, 1765.
Huldah, d. Job and Margery, Sept. 11, 1766.
Jean, d. Cornelias and Sarah, Dec. 17, 1721.
Jefferson Burr, s. Samuel and Sarah, May 2, 1803. [May 21, G.R.2.]
Jemima, d. Timothy and Kezia, Aug. 24, 1765.
Jershua, s. Samuel and Mary, Nov. 2, 1737.
Jerusha, d. Samuel Jr. and Esther, July 27, 1756.
Joab, s. Timothy and Kezia, Oct. 23, 1763.
Joanna, d. Samuel and Esther, Oct. 10, 1757.
Joanna S. [———], w. Jefferson B., Aug. 29, 1803. G.R.2.
John, s. Ebenezer and Abigall, Nov. 7, 1729.
John, s. Samuel and Mary, Apr. 29, 1733.
John, s. John and Anna, Nov. 1, 1761.
Joseph, s. Ebenezer and Abiel, July 29, 1722.
Kezia, d. Timothy and Kezia, Jan. 21, 1759.
Keziah, d. Simon and Peggy, Dec. 19, 1801.
Lanson, s. Samuel Jr. and Sarah, Sept. 10, 1795.
Lucius, s. Samuel Jr. and Margaret, Oct. 3, 1827.
Lucy, d. Samuel Jr. and Esther, Aug. 15, 1772.
Lydia, d. Enoch and Lois, Jan. 11, 1752.
Lyman Cook, s. Welcome B. and Alpha, Apr. 7, 1838.
Martha Ann, d. Welcome B. and Alpha, May 9, 1833.
Mary, d. Cornelios and Hannah, July 25, 1724.
Mary, d. John and Anna, July 21, 1757.
Mary Ann, d. Jefferson and Joanna, Apr. 8, 1824.
Matildia A., d. Fisher and Rebecca, Apr. 3, 1820.
Mayo Cook, s. Jefferson and Joanna, Jan. 12, 1830.
Mercy, d. Timothy and Kezia, Aug. 22, 1762.
Michel, s. Joshua and Martha, Feb. 20, 1773.
Michell, s. Samuell and Mary, Mar. 6, 1723.
Nancy, d. Samuel Jr. and Sarah, Dec. 23, 1797.
Nathan, s. Samuel and Esther, May 10, 1770.
Nathaniel, s. John and Anna, Jan. 11, 1764.
Olive, d. Samuel and Ester, June 30, 1779.

BELLINGHAM BIRTHS.

DARLING, Orson, s. Fisher and Rebecca, Oct. 31, 1821.
Paty, d. Joshua and Martha, Nov. 29, 1770.
Peggy, d. Simon and Peggy, June 29, 1804.
Penelape, d. John and Anna, Nov. 20, 1759.
Penellepe, d. Samuel and Penellepe, Aug. 25, 1742.
Phebe, d. Corniles and Hannah, Nov. 14, 1735. [d. Cornelius and Hannah, Nov. 15, P.R.2.]
Phebe, d. Cornelius and Mehitabel, Mar. 18, 1767.
Philee, d. Joshua and Martha, Mar. 27, 1763.
Prudence, d. John and Anne, May 26, 1756.
Rachel, d. Samuel and Mary, June 11, 1735.
Rachel, d. Enoch and Louis, Dec. 9, 1753.
Reuel, s. Samuel Jr. and Margaret, May 3, 1830.
Rhoda, d. Samuel and Esther, Sept. 24, 1776.
Rhoda, d. Samuel Jr. and Sarah, Sept. 4, 1787.
Rhoda, d. Samuel Jr. and Sarah, May 28, 1789.
Ruben, s. Samuel Jr. and Esther, Apr. 12, 1763.
Ruth, d. Simon and Peggy, Mar. 23, 1794.
Sabra, d. Sam[ue]l and Esther, Apr. 25, 1774.
Samuel, s. Samuel and Mary, Jan. 9, 1719–20.
Samuel, s. Samuel Jr. and Esther, Aug. 8, 1759.
Samuel, s. Samuel Jr. and Sarah, Aug. 15, 1793.
Samuel, s. Samuel Jr. and Margaret, ———— [rec. between ch. b. Jan. 21, 1819, and ch. b. Oct. 3, 1827].
Sarah, d. John and Anna, June 12, 1766.
Sarah Augusta, d. Jefferson and Joanna, Aug. 9, 1836. [Aug. 6, G.R.2.]
Sarah Burr, d. Sam[ue]l Jr. and Sarah, Oct. 13, 1800.
Seth, s. John and Anna, Apr. 28, 1777.
Simon, s. Timothy and Kezia, Dec. 6, 1769.
Simon, s. Simon and Peggy, June 15, 1806.
Stephen, s. John and Anna, July 10, 1768.
Timothy, s. Ebenezer and Abiel, Jan. 30, 1726.
Timothy, s. Timothy and Kezia, Apr. 19, 1767.
Uriah, s. John and Anna, Sept. 15, 1781.
William, s. Joshua and Martha, Sept. 30, 1778.
William Addison, s. Ahimaz and Margaretta, Mar. 23, 1838.
William Wallace, s. Jefferson and Joanna, Mar. 2, 1829.
Ziba, s. Samuel and Esther, Sept. 19, 1767.

DAWLEY, Adoneram Judson, s. Perry and Elvira, June 1, 1830, in Ex[e]ter, R.I.
Elizabeth Jane, d. Perry H. and Elvira, Feb. 2, 1836.
Elvira S., d. Perry and Elvira, Apr. 12, 1828, in Exeter, R.I.

BELLINGHAM BIRTHS. 33

DAWLEY, George Foristall, s. Perry and Elvira, June 6, 1834.
Perry, s. Perry and Elvira, May 4, 1832, in Ex[e]ter, R.I.

DEWING, Angeline A. [———], w. Charles, ———, 1831. G.R.1.
Charles [h. Angeline A.], ———, 1821. G.R.1.
Elijah [h. Mary], Oct. 13, 1790. G.R.1.
Mary [———], w. Elijah, July 3, 1796. G.R.1.

DRAKE, Ichabod Jones, s. John and Betsey, June 25, 1843.

DRAPER, Abigail, d. Jonathan Jr. and Abigail, Dec. 23, 1756.
Ichobad, s. Jonathan Jr. and Abigail, Jan. 16, 1760.
Jonathan, s. Jonathan and Mary, May 10, 1730.
Jonathan, s. Jonathan and Abigail, Oct. 14, 1762.
Jotham, s. Jonathan and Abigail, Oct. 6, 1769.
Malley, d. Jonathan and Abigail, Nov. 25, 1766.
Mary, d. Jonathan and Mary, May 11, 1735.
Rachel, d. Jonathan and Mary, Mar. 14, 1738–9.
Rachel, d. Jonathan and Abigail, Mar. 8, 1764.

DUDLEY, George, s. Sumner and Elizabeth G., Mar. 18, 1844.
[George A., soldier, G.R.1.]

DUKEWILLIAM, Margret, d. Marvellous and Margret, July 6, 1758.

EAMES (see Ames).

EATON, Pamelia A. [———], w. John H., ———, 1830. G.R.2.
——— [———], mother of John H., ———, 1808. G.R.2.

EDDY, Augustus W., Mar. 7, 1830. G.R.3.
Berack, Nov. 19, 1842. G.R.3.
Elvira (Hawkins), w. John R., May 11, 1811. G.R.3.
John R. [h. Elvira Hawkins], May 5, 1808. G.R.3.
Rebecca B., Nov. 13, 1836. G.R.3.

ELLIS, Abijah, s. John and Mary, Feb. 22, 1765.
Amos, s. Amos and Hannah, May 4, 1769, in Midway.
Betsey, d. Amos and Hannah, Mar. 1, 1784.
Hannah, d. Amos and Hannah, Dec. 8, 1778.
Hannah, d. Amos and Hannah, Jan. 17, 1786.
Jonathon [dup. Jonathan Elis], s. Amos and Hannah, June 28, 1774.
Joseph, s. Amos and Hannah, July 31, 1772, in Medway.
Nathan, s. John and Mary, Nov. 4, 1762.
Nathan, s. Amos and Hannah, Mar. 7, 1777.

ELLIS, Polly, d. Amos and Hannah, Sept. 22, 1780.
Presson, s. Timothy and Deborah, Oct. 28, 1803.
Preston Partridge, s. Preston and Cymentha, Dec. 15, 1831.
Rosanna, d. Amos and Hannah, June 21, 1782.
Sabra, d. Amos and Hannah, Dec. 19, 1770, in Medwey.
Vespasian, s. Amos and Hannah, Aug. 26, 1767, in Wrentham.

ESTEN (see Estes), Lucia E. [———], w. Samuel, Mar. 25, 1825. G.R.4.

ESTES (see Esten), Clarinda, d. Samuel and Lovina, Feb. 18, 1811. G.R.4.

FAIRBANKS, Calvin, s. Elijah and Nancy, Oct. 25, 1825.
Edwin, s. Elijah and Nancy, July 12, 1816.
Elijah, s. Joseph and Mary, May 29, 1788.
Emery, s. Joseph and Mary, Jan. 23, 1792.
George, s. Elijah and Nancy, Dec. 29, 1819.
Jemima Adams, d. Elijah and Nancy, Apr. 9, 1829.
Joseph, s. Elijah and Nancy, Nov. 25, 1823.
Leonard Francis, s. James and Maria, Jan. 19, 1844.
Lucy, d. Joseph and Mary, Feb. 19, 1795.
Nancy Metcalf, d. Elijah and Nancy, Jan. 8, 1835.
Rufus, s. Elijah and Nancy, Oct. 8, 1813.
William, s. Elijah and Nancy, June 10, 1818.

FALES, John Marshall, s. James D. and Mary, Jan. 27, 1835.

FARRINGTON, Charles Hesekiah, s. Aaron Jr. and Rebecah, Apr. 3, 1825.
Eliza Adaline, d. Aaron Jr. and Rebecah, Aug. 13, 1819.
Naomi (Forinton), d. Elijah and Jemima, July 31, 1757.
Nelson Winn, s. Aaron Jr. and Rebecah, Apr. 22, 1823.
Orren Gardner, s. Aaron Jr. and Rebecah, May 31, 1821.
Permelia Ann, d. Aaron Jr. and Rebecah, Oct. 22, 1830.
Susan Maria, d. Aaron Jr. and Rebecah, May 28, 1827.

FISH, Ann [———], w. George, ——, 1819. G.R.1.
George [h. Ann], ——, 1817. G.R.1.

FISHER, Ella Francena, d. Lewis L. and Sarah, Aug. 2, 1848.
Horace, s. Abial Jr. and Betsey, Nov. 16, 1817.
Sarah, d. Abial Jr. and Betsey, Feb. 13, 1828.

FISK, Elizabeth J., w. George Thayer, Jan. 25, 1842. G.R.2.
Hamblet Barber, s. James T. and Rebeckah, Mar. 27, 1838.

BELLINGHAM BIRTHS. 35

FISK, Marion Eliza, d. James T. and Rebeckah, Nov. 15, 1835.
Willard Ira, July 13, 1824. G.R.2.

FLING, Elisabeth, d. Morris and Elisabeth, June 20, 1758.

FORCE, Amelea, d. Ameriah and Keziah, June 1, 1795.
Lawson Partridge, s. Ameriah and Keziah, Aug. 9, 1796.

FORESTALL (see Foristall, Forristall), Caroline N., Jan. 17, 1845. G.R.1.
Edmund H., Sept. 4, 1843. G.R.1.
Polly [――――], w. Olney, Sept. 29, 1791. G.R.1.

FORISTALL (see Forestall, Forristall), Amasa Jr., s. Amasa and Sarah, Apr. 11, 1807.
Benjamin, s. Amasa and Sarah, Feb. 26, 1803.
Bethiah, d. Ezra and Bethiah, Mar. 3, 1772.
Caroline Amanda, d. Olny and Polly, Aug. 30, 1815.
Charles, s. Amasa and Sarah, Oct. 12, 1809.
Eleazer Howard, s. Amasa and Sarah, Aug. 14, 1805.
Electa, d. Ezra and Bethiah, Feb. 19, 1782.
Elijah Haven, s. Amasa and Sarah, May 5, 1813.
Elmeria, d. Amesa and Sarah, July 10, 1796.
Elmira, d. Amasa and Sarah, Aug. 4, 1799.
Junia, d. Amesa and Sarah, Nov. 9, 1797.
Luther, s. Ezra and Bethiah, Aug. 16, 1778.
Mary, d. Ezra and Bethiah, Mar. 1, 1774.
Mary Ann [――――], w. Benjamin, July 3, 1800. G.R.1.
Olney Daniell, s. Amesa and Sally, May 5, 1823.
Oney, s. Ezra and Bethiah, June 7, 1784. [Olney Forestall, June 17, G.R.1.]
Poley, d. Ezra and Bethiah, Aug. 10, 1776.
Sally, d. Ezra and Bethiah, Apr. 12, 1787.
Sarah, d. Ezra and Bethiah, Mar. 15, 1780.

FORRISTALL (see Forestall, Foristall), Amasa, s. Ezra and Bethiah, Nov. 18, 1769.
Elisabeth, d. Ezra and Bethiah, July 13, 1765.
Lucy, d. Ezra and Bethiah, July 4, 1767.

FOSTER, Francis, ――, 1808. G.R.1.
Martha, ――, 1809. G.R.1.

FRANKLIN, Mary Jane [――――], w. George, Apr. 28, 1846. G.R.1.

FREEMAN, Clark (Phreeman), s. Samuel and Elisabeth, Aug. 6, 1772.
Dexter, s. Nathan and Anna, Aug. 10, 1774.
Edward Harris, s. James M. and Nancy L., Aug. 27, 1843.
Esther, d. Benjamin and Mary, Sept. 5, 1761.
Ezra, s. Benjamin and Mary, Nov. 11, 1759.
Mary Adalade, d. James M. and Mary, Oct. 8, 1849.
Sylvia w. Levi A. Cook, Sept. 20, 1836. G.R.1.

FULLER, Asa, s. Asa and Meletiah, Dec. 26, 1781.

GATCHELL, George Hawley, s. Increase and Almira, Dec. 18, 1848.

GERSTLE, Magdalena, d. John J. and Magdalena, Mar. 27, 1847.

GETCHELL (see Gatchell).

GILMORE (see Guilmor).

GLOVER, Laura, d. Joel and Maria, May 8, 1840.
Morton, s. Joel and Maria, June 28, 1841.

GODMAN, Comfort, d. John and Anna, Mar. 26, 1773.
Eleazer, s. John (Godmon) and Anna, May 25, 1782.
Moses, s. John and Anna, Nov. 24, 1775.
Sarah, d. John and Anna, Oct. 4, 1777.
William Hayward, s. John and Anne, Oct. 12, 1770.

GOOGINS, Betsey Matilda, d. William H. and Matilda, Aug. 8, 1837.
Keziah Elizabeth, d. William H. and Matilda, Apr. 20, 1835.
William Henry, s. William Henry and Matilda, Mar. 10, 1839.

GOULD, Charlottee, d. Isaiah and Lucretia, Mar. 6, 1805.
Isanna, d. Isaiah and Lucretia, Sept. 29, 1810.
Izanna, ——, 1808. G.R.1.
Jemima, d. Isaiah and Lucretia, Aug. 5, 1808.
Lucretia, d. Isaiah and Lucretia, Sept. 12, 1806.

GOULDSBURY, Abigail, d. John and Abigail, Mar. 27, 1761.
Christopher, s. John and Abigail, Aug. 27, 1762.
Eunice, d. John and Abigail, Aug. 19, 1758.
James, s. John and Abigail, Dec. 24, 1756.
John, s. John and Abigail, July 21, 1766.
Mary, d. John and Abigail, June 3, 1754.

GRAY, Frances Elizabeth Smith, d. Smith Gray and Permela Thompson, May 4, 1833.

GRANT, A. C., ——, 1813. G.R.1.
Adaline C., d. Ezekiel C. and Adaline S., July 1, 1829.
Harriot A., d. Ezekiel C. and Adaline S., Nov. 29, 1831.
Lucy C. [——], w. William, Dec. 12, 1812, in Dover. G.R.2.
Martha E., d. Ezekiel C. and Adaline S., July 9, 1830.
Mary Jane, d. Ezekiel C. and Adaline S., May 3, 1833.
Roselda, d. Hervy and Lydia, Sept. 22, 1840.
William, Apr. 3, 1817. G.R.2.

GUILMOR, Lewis, s. Appollos and Julia, Jan. 17, 1792.

HALL, Abigall, d. Zuriell and Su[s]anah, July 8, 1712.
Anna, d. John and Joanna, May 8, 1777.
Asa, s. Seth and Elisabeth, May 29, 1766.
Benjamin, s. Seth and Elisabeth, July 9, 1770. [[h. Sarah] July 11, G.R.3.]
Chloe, d. John and Joanna, Apr. 1, 1772.
Deborah, d. Seth and Abigail, Aug. 17, 174 [sic].
Deborah, d. Marvelos and Esth[er], May 11, 1775.
Elezebath, d. Zuriell and Susanah, June 8, 1698.
Elisabeth, d. Seth and Elisabeth, Nov. 26, 1772.
George, s. Seth and Elisabeth, May 3, 1762.
Joanna, d. John and Joanna, Feb. 26, 1770.
John, s. Seth and Abigail, June 18, 1747.
Lemuel, s. Seth and Elisabeth, Apr. 24, 1768.
Martha, Sept. 15, 1804. G.R.3.
Marvellous, s. Seth and Abigail, Nov. 26, 1752.
Mary, d. Zuriell and Susanah, July 24, 1700.
Mary, d. John and Joanna, Dec. 17, 1781.
Mary, d. John and Bridget, June 10, 1787.
Patiancess, d. Zuriell and Susanah, Nov. 4, 1704.
Ruth, d. Zuriell and Susanah, July 21, 1720.
Sarah [——], w. Benjamin, ——, 1775. G.R.3.
Selissa [——], w. Asa Esq., Sept. 21, 1789. G.R.3.
Seth, s. Zuriell and Susanah, Apr. 2, 1707.
Seth, s. Seth and Abigail, May 15, 1739.
Seth, s. John and Joanna, Apr. 11, 1774.
Seth Capen, Mar. 28, 1800. G.R.3.
Susanah, d. Zuriell and Susanah, Aug. 2, 1702.
Urania, d. Zuriell and Susanah, Jan. 11, 1709.
William, s. Seth and Elisabeth, May 23, 1764.

HALL, Zurial, s. Seth and Abigail, Mar. 23, 1738.
Zurial, s. Seth and Abagaial, July 17, 1741.
HANCOCK, Louisa Alice [———], w. Charles P., July 11, 1838. G.R.2.
HARTSHORN (see Heartshorn).
HARWOOD, Charles H., ch. Elbridge G. and Caroline S., Mar. 13, 1832. G.R.1.
George Abner, s. Levi and Ann P., June 15, 1838. G.R.1.
Harriet M., ch. Elbridge G. and Caroline S., Mar. 12, 1844. G.R.1.
HAWKINS, Elvira, w. John R. Eddy, May 11, 1811. G.R.3.
HAYDEN, Franklin Leroy, s. Lot and Lucinda, Mar. 19, 1843.
Walter Handel, s. Lot and Lucinda, Nov. 10, 1841.
HAYFORD, Chancy C., s. Lewis S. and Abigail A., Dec. 3, 1848.
HAYWARD, Abigial, d. Ezekiel and w., Nov. 6, 1771.
Anne, d. Eliezer and Mary, Apr. 25, 1753.
Asa, s. Ebenezer and Hanah, Sept. 19, 1739.
Asa, s. Elisha and Elisabeth, Jan. 21, 1767.
Bethiah, d. Eleazer [dup. Elezer] and Mary, Jan. 28 [dup. Jan. 29], 1744–5.
Caleb, s. Samuel and Hannah, July 25, 1720.
Doritha, d. Ebenezer Jr. and Hannah, Mar. 7, 1767.
Ebenezear, s. Ebenezer and Hannah, May 24, 1736.
Ebenezer, s. Elisha and Elizabeth, May 19, 1786.
Eliezer, s. Eliezer and Mary, Sept. 29, 1750.
Elijah, s. Ebenezer and Hannah, May 30, 1754.
Elisabath, d. Ebnezer and Hannah, Feb. 3, 1740.
Elisabeth, d. Oliver and Sarah, Dec. 3, 1747.
Elisabeth, d. Elisha and Elisabeth, Feb. 25, 1777.
Elishire, s. Ebnezer and Hannah, May 15, 1743.
Elizebath, d. Samuel and Elezebath, Jan. 1, 1736.
Ezeakel, s. Samuel and Elezebath, Aug. 22, 1741.
Hannah, d. Samuel and Hannah, June 20, 1718.
Hannah, d. Ebenezer and Hannah, Sept. 12, 1746.
Henery, s. Ebenezer and Hanah, Aug. 3, 1749.
Jacob, s. Willam and Sarah, Apr. 27, 1728.
Jason, s. Ezekiel and Hannah, Apr. 15, 1768.
Jemima, d. Eleazer and Mary, Aug. 13, 1747.
Julia, d. Samuel and Bothiah, Dec. 12, 1764.

HAYWARD, Lucy, d. Elisha and Elisabeth, Feb. 19, 1772.
Macy [Mercy], d. Elisha and Elisabeth, June 25, 1783.
Maray, d. Elezar and Mary, Aug. 9, 1740.
Melatiah, d. Sam[ue]ll and Elisabeth, Sept. 22, 1745.
Metilda, d. Samuel and Bothiah, Apr. 24, 1769.
Nabee, d. Samuel and Elisabeth, Apr. 10, 1749.
Nancy "Alias Coombs," d. Lucy Hayward, May 6, 1789.
Nathan, s. Samuel and Elisabeth, June 4, 1744.
Nathan, s. Ebenezer and Hanah, May 31, 1757.
Nathan, s. Elisha and Elisabeth, Mar. 28, 1781.
Parker, s. Elisha and Elisabeth, Dec. 18, 1778.
Pearlle, d. Ebenezer Jr. and Hannah, Apr. 27, 1764.
Phebee, d. Samuel and Elizabeth, Sept. 4, 1747.
Priscilla, d. Samuel and Bothiah, Sept. 20, 1766.
Rachel, d. Ebenezer and Hanna, July 21, 1751.
Rodah, d. Ezekiel and Hannah, Oct. 11, 1769.
Rosanna, d. Elisha and Elisabeth, Feb. 28, 1788.
Ruben, s. Samuel and Elezebath, May 22, 1740.
Ruth, d. Elisha and Elisabeth, Mar. 7, 1774.
Samuel, s. Samuel and Elezebath, Mar. 22, 1735.
Samuel, s. Elisha and Elisabeth, Jan. 18, 1770.
Sarah, d. Elezar and Mary, Mar. 25, 1743.
Seth, s. Ebenezer and Hanna, Oct. 9, 1752.
William, s. William and Johannah, Jan. 15, 1736–7.
William, s. Eliezer and Mary, Aug. 10, 1738.

HEARTSHORN, David, s. Eben[ezer] and Lydia, Oct. 24, 1772.

HILL, Abijah, s. Aaron and Sally, Mar. 14, 1794.
Albert Henry, s. Henry and Hannah, Dec. 16, 1831.
Amos, s. David and Mercy, July 6, 1789.
Aron, s. Aaron and Sally, Mar. 19, 1798 [*sic*, see Sally].
Artemon, s. David and Mercy, Jan. 23, 1792.
Charles Austin, s. David and Mary, July 10, 1815.
Claricy, d. Aaron and Sally, Oct. 28, 1783.
David, s. David and Mercy, Sept. 23, 1787.
David, s. Sylvester and Olive, Apr. 17, 1812, in Ashford, Conn.
Huldah, d. Aaron and Sally, Dec. 28, 1785.
Jane [———], w. Geo[rge] W., ———, 1843. G.R.5.
Jonathan, s. Aron and Sally, Aug. 17, 1789.
Laura A. [———], w. Asa, Mar. 10, 1809. G.R.1.
Lewis, s. Sylvester and Olive, July 3, 1818.
Mary Ann R., d. Sylvester and Olive, July 19, 1820.

40   BELLINGHAM BIRTHS.

HILL, Moses, s. Aaron and Sally, July 8, 1782.
Paulina, d. David and Mercy, Mar. 4, 1803.
Paulina, d. Sylvester and Olive, Nov. 8, 1815.
Phebe, d. David and Mercy, Aug. 14, 1799.
Polly, s. Aron and Sally, Mar. 23, 1792.
Sally, d. Aron and Sally, Sept. 24, 1797 [sic, see Aron].
Sarah, d. Moses and Mary, Oct. 22, 1775.
Silvester, s. David and Mercy, Apr. 12, 1786.
Solon, s. David and Mercy, Feb. 4, 1794.
Solon, s. David and Mary, June 12, 1805.

HINKLEY, Oscar Smith, s. Hazen and Bulah, Apr. 18, 1839.

HIXON (see Hixson), Abraham, Mar. 3, 1802. G.R.I.
Amos L., s. Ellery and Cynthia, June 5, 1835.
Amos R., s. Ellery and Cynthia, Aug. —, 1833.
Charles R., s. Ellery and Cynthia, June 5, 1839.
Elery, ch. Luther T. and Sarah V., June 1, 1796. G.R.I.
George A., s. Ellery and Cynthia, Mar. 5, 1831.
Jemima, ——, 1806. G.R.I.
Levi, s. Ellery and Cynthia, July 15, 1843.
Lydia A. [————], w. Luther T., Dec. 19, 1843. G.R.I.
Silas, May 12, 1806. G.R.I.

HIXSON (see Hixon), Hannah, d. Elkanah and Hannah, May 9, 1767.

HOLBROKE (see Holbrook, Hoolbrook), Jesse, s. Joseph (Holbrok) and Mary, July 21, 1729.

HOLBROOK (see Holbroke, Hoolbrook), Aaron, s. John and Hannah, Aug. 31, 1730.
Aaron, s. Amzi and Sarah, July 25, 1793.
Abbagail, d. Asa and Mercy, Aug. 13, 1824.
Abi, d. Aaron and Hannah, Dec. 16, 1764.
Abigell, d. Peter and Hannah, May 7, 1722.
Abigial, d. Eliphelet and Abigial, June 9, 1776, "Six weeks after the Death of her father."
Abigil, d. Amariah and Moley, May 12, 1780.
Abigil, d. Amariah and Moley, June 2, 1789.
Adaline, d. Lyman and Hypsalanty [dup. Hypsa L.], Oct. 29, 1820.
Almira, d. Amos and Lucretia, Apr. 28, 1822.
Amanda, d. Sabin and Mary, June 2, 1819.
Amariah, s. Jesse and Abigail, June 6, 1756.

BELLINGHAM BIRTHS.

HOLBROOK, Amariah, s. Amariah and Moley, Jan. 23, 1785.
Amasa, s. Stephen and Rachel, Dec. 31, 1769.
Amos, s. Luke and Marcy, Jan. 23, 1754.
Amos, s. Amariah and Moley, Apr. 27, 1783.
Amos Harrison, s. Amos and Lucretia, Nov. 23, 1818.
Amos Wales, s. Whitman and Nancy W., Apr. 4, 1836.
Amzi, s. Aaron and Hannah, Mar. 4, 1763.
Anna, d. Asael and Anna, May 24, 1747.
Anna, d. Henry and Elisabeth, Mar. 29, 1786.
Anna, d. Asa and Meletiah, Nov. 23, 1790.
Asa, s. Asael and Anna, Mar. 26, 1757.
Asa, s. Amariah and Moley, May 18, 1792.
Asa Newell, s. Cephas and Polly, July 19, 1820.
Benajah, s. Aaron and Hannah, Apr. 15, 1771.
Benajah, s. Aaron and Hannah, Nov. 19, 1772.
Bethiah, d. Joseph and Grace, Apr. 13, 1741.
Betsy, d. Amzi and Sarah, Aug. 31, 1795.
Caleb, s. Eliphelet Jr. and Abigail, Nov. 1, 1760.
Calib, s. Eliphelet and Joannah, Jan. 14, 1731.
Catherine Hill, d. Simeon and Catharine, Nov. 30, 1813.
Cephas, s. Asa and Meletiah, Nov. 16, 1787.
Chrstopher Gore, s. Simeon and Catharine, Mar. 6, 1809.
Clare, d. Seth and Dinah, Jan. 22, 1779.
Clarecy Lethbridge, d. Eliphalet and Julia, Apr. 20, 1816.
Clark Bates, s. Peter and Mary, Apr. 11, 1794.
David, s. Joseph and Mary, Mar. 15, 1721.
Deborah, d. Asa and Meletiah, Sept. 30, 1783.
Denis, s. Nathan and Sarah, July 10, 1799.
De Witt Clinton, s. Pliny and Martha, Oct. 16, 1828.
Diana, d. Nathan and Sarah, Jan. 31, 1808.
Dinah, d. Luke and Marcy, May 1, 1757.
Edena, d. Joseph and Meletiah, Dec. 25, 1786.
Edward, s. Eliab Jr. and Julia, June 7, 1849.
Eliab, s. Eliphelet Jr. and Abigail, Feb. 20, 1772.
Eliab, s. Henry and Elisabeth, May 6, 1784.
Eliab, s. Eliab and Betsey, Oct. 8, 1817. [[h. Julia F. (Morse)]
  G.R.2.]
Elijah, s. Eliphelet and Johannah, May 6, 1736.
Elijah, s. Asael and Anna, Jan. 18, 1755.
Eliphalet, s. El[i]phalit and Joanah, Oct. 25, 1725.
Eliphalett, s. Henry and Elisabeth, Apr. 13, 1782.
Eliphelet, s. Eliphelet Jr. and Abigail, Feb. 9, 1774.
Eliphelet, s. Eliphelet and Julia, Mar. 31, 1824.
Elisabeth, d. Peter and Sarah, Apr. 28, 1746.

HOLBROOK, Elisha Dewing, s. Eliphelet and Julia, Sept. 1, 1826.
Elizabeth, d. Eliab and Betsey, June 25, 1811.
Elizebeth, d. Peter, Mar. 26, 1720.
Elizebeth, d. Peter and Hannah, Jan. 3, 1723.
Elkanah, s. Peter and Mary, Jan. 21, 1788.
Ella, d. Nathan and Sarah, Mar. 16, 1803.
Ellis, s. Amasa and Sabra, Mar. 9, 1795.
Elmyra, d. Aaron and Polly, May 16, 1832.
Emily, d. Luke and Abigail, May 7, 1812, in Charlton.
Ester, d. Seth and Dinah, Nov. 15, 1780.
Esther, d. Joseph and Grace, Apr. 1, 1739.
Esther, d. Asahael and Anna, Feb. 7, 1764.
Ezekiel, s. Asael and Anna, Mar. 26, 1749.
Flavius, s. Darius and Olive, July 28, 1795.
Gilbert, s. Eliphalet and Julia, Feb. 8, 1818.
Gilbert M., s. Eliab Jr. and Julia, Mar. 31, 1845.
Habijah, s. Asahel and Anna, June 29, 1752.
Handel Alden, s. Joseph W. and Maria, ——, 1842.
Hannah, d. Jesse and Abigail, Oct. 26, 1758.
Hannah, d. Aaron and Hannah, Oct. 16, 1775.
Hannah Elisebeth, d. Eliab Jr. and Julia A., Aug. 23, 1843.
Hannah Maria, d. Amasa and Sabra, Oct. 13, 1811.
Harlows [?] Whiting, s. Eliphalet and Julia, May 22, 1814.
Hellen Angelia, d. Eliab Jr. and Hannah, Apr. 26, 1840.
Henery, s. Eliphelet Jr. and Abigail, Aug. 27, 1756.
Henry, s. Henry and Elisabeth, July 31, 1790.
Henry, s. Eliphalet and Julia, Nov. 18, 1829.
Hiram Pond, s. Eliab Jr. and Julia M., Feb. 15, 1848.
Huldah, d. Jesse and Abigail, Sept. 17, 1754.
Isaac Bates, s. Peter and Mary, Jan. 21, 1792.
James, s. Lt. Nathan and Lidea, Jan. 1, 1781.
James Munroe, s. Sabin and Maria A., Sept. 28, 1843.
James Trask, s. Henry Jr. and Sarah, Dec. 25, 1820.
Jemima, d. Peter and Sarah, Oct. 8, 1747.
Jerusha, d. Luke and Marcy, May 16, 1759.
Jesse, s. Jesse and Abigail, Aug. 7, 1764.
Joel, s. Amariah and Moley, Feb. 2, 1787.
Johanna, d. Eliphelet and Johanna, July 21, 1738.
John, s. John and Hannah, Sept. 24, 1721.
John Whitman, s. Whitman and Nancy W., Nov. 24, 1839.
Jonathan, s. Joseph and Grace, May 31, 1746.
Joseph, s. Joseph and Grace, Oct. 15, 1748.
Joseph, s. Sabin and Mary, Jan. 18, 1817.
Joseph Wight, s. Eliphalet and July, Jan. 18, 1820.

HOLBROOK, Julia, d. Joseph Jr. and Meletiah, Sept. 15, 1784.
Julia, d. Peter and Mary, Nov. 21, 1789.
Julia, d. Joseph and Meletiah, May 7, 1790.
Julia F. (Morse), w. Eliab, July 9, 1817. G.R.2.
Juliaanna, d. Eliphlet and Julia, Nov. 13, 1821.
Kezia, d. Derus [Darius] and Olive, Dec. 1, 1784.
Levi, s. Aaron and Hannah, Feb. 2, 1767.
Lewis, s. Amasa and Sabra, Nov. 15, 1796.
Limon, s. Amariah and Moley, Feb. 26, 1797.
Lois Hutchinson, d. Simeon and Catherine, Dec. 14, 1807.
Lucretia, d. Amos and Lucretia, Aug. 20, 1815.
Lucuetia, d. Jesse and Abigail, July 18, 1766.
Lucy, d. Luke and Marcy, May 25, 1763.
Luke, s. John and Hannah, Mar. 20, 1724.
Luke, s. Seth and Dinah, July 12, 1784.
Lurania, d. Eliab and Betsey, Oct. 31, 1815.
Lyman (see Limon).
Martha, d. Joseph and Mary, Dec. 28, 1726.
Martha, d. Joseph and Mary, May 4, 1732.
Martha, d. Eliphelet Jr. and Abigail, Oct. 11, 1758.
Martin, s. Ezekiel and Sarah, July 11, 1773.
Mary, d. Joseph and Mary, Oct. 13, 1723.
Mary, d. Asael and Anna, July 15, 1745.
Mary, d. Peter and Mary, Feb. 24, 1797.
Mary, d. Saban and Mary, Nov. 5, 1815.
Mary Burdin, d. Henry Jr. and Sarah, Apr. 16, 1817.
Mary Frances [———], w. Amos H., Apr. 27, 1842. G.R.1.
Meletiah, d. Joseph and Grace, Jan. 28, 1755.
Meletiah, d. Joseph Jr. and Meletiah, Aug. 23, 1780.
Meranda, d. Seth and Dinah, Sept. 3, 1794.
Mercy, d. Luke and Mercy, Nov. 11, 1767.
Moses, s. Asahael and Anna, Feb. 10, 1766.
Moses Knapp, s. Cephas and Polly, Jan. 28, 1818.
Naham, s. Lyman and Hypsa L., May 16, 1827.
Nahum, s. Amariah and Moley, Apr. 2, 1781.
Nancy [———], w. Whitman, ——, 1810. G.R.1.
Nancy Polina, d. Whitman and Nancy W., Oct. 8, 1837.
Nathan, s. Asael and Anna, Feb. 14, 1743-4.
Nathan, s. Eliphelet Jr. and Abigail, July 28, 1768.
Nathan, s. Amariah and Moley, Apr. 8, 1794.
Noah, s. Eliphelet and Johahna [Joannah], Dec. 6, 1727.
Olive, d. Eliphelet Jr. and Abigail, Apr. 4, 1754.
Olive, d. Amos and Lucretia, Apr. 26, 1827.
Oliver, s. Peter and Hannah, Jan. 7, 1726-7.

HOLBROOK, Otis, s. Ezekiel and Sarah, Apr. 30, 1778.
Patty, d. Amzi and Sarah, Aug. 9, 1799.
Patty Hill, d. Simeon and Catharine, May 19, 1817.
Persis, d. Seth and Dinah, Oct. 14, 1791.
Persis Kennedy, d. Luke and Abigail, Jan. 22, 1811, in Charlton.
Peruda, d. Eliphelet and Abigail, Mar. 24, 1770.
Peter, s. Peter and Sarah, July 22, 1742.
Peter, s. Eliphelet Jr. and Abigail, Nov. 23, 1762.
Peter, s. Peter and Mary, July 28, 1799.
Phebe, d. Joseph and Grace, Nov. 28, 1743.
Phebe, d. Aaron and Hannah, Jan. 26, 1769.
Pliny, s. Amasa and Sabra, Dec. 14, 1798.
Polly, d. Aaron and Polly, July 17, 1829.
Rachel, d. Luke and Marcy, July 13, 1765.
Rachel, d. Seth and Dinah, Jan. 17, 1777.
Rhoda, d. Aaron and Hannah, May 6, 1778.
Rhoda, d. Amzi and Sarah, Apr. 8, 1791.
Roxanna, d. Seth and Dinah, July 24, 1782.
Saben, Oct. 4, 1813. G.R.1.
Sabin, s. Seth and Dinah, Oct. 19, 1786.
Sabin Jr., s. Sabin and Mary, Sept. 18, 1813.
Sabra, [twin] d. Amasa and Sabra, Aug. 6, 1800.
Sabrina, [twin] d. Amasa and Sabra, Aug. 7, 1800.
Sarah, d. Peter and Sarah, Mar 27, 1739.
Sarah, d. Peter and Sarah, July 24, 1740.
Sarah, d. Stephen and Rachel, Jan. 15, 1765.
Sarah, d. Amzi and Sarah, Mar. 15, 1802.
Sarah Julina, d. Simeon and Catharine, Nov. 13, 1823.
Selvenus, s. Asa and Meletiah, Mar. 8, 1781.
Semeon, s. Peter and Sarah, Oct. 1, 1744.
Sena, d. Luke and Marcy, Jan. 4, 1771.
Seth, s. Eliphalet and Joanna, Feb. 26, 1721.
Seth, s. Joseph and Grace, Nov. 24, 1751.
Seth, s. Eliphelet Jr. and Abigail, July 17, 1765.
Seth, s. Seth and Dinah, July 29, 1789.
Silva, d. Joseph and Meletiah, Aug. 6, 1792.
Simeon, s. Stephen and Rachel, Sept. 1, 1772.
Simeon George, s. Simeon and Catharine, Apr. 14, 1811.
Stephen, s. Peter and Sarah, Apr. 30, 1737.
Stephen, s. Stephen and Rachel, Sept. 29, 1767.
Sumner, s. Ezekiel and Sarah, Jan. 28, 1777.
Supply, s. Sabin and Mary, Sept. 7, 1821.
Sylvia F., d. Lyman and Hypsa L., Sept. 20, 1830.
Timithy, s. Peter and Sarah, Oct. 3, 1751.

HOLBROOK, Tryphena, d. Amariah and Moley, Jan. 17, 1779.
Ursula, d. Jesse Jr. and Clarica, Feb. 5, 1792.
Volentine Rathbun, s. Seth and Dinah, Dec. 14, 1800.
Whitman, s. Amos and Lucretia, Jan. 29, 1811.
William Luke, s. Luke and Abigail, Oct. 10, 1813.

HOOKER (see Huker), Tabitha, d. William and Tabitha, Aug. 6, 1744.

HOOLBROOK (see Holbroke, Holbrook), Abigall, d. Peter and Hanah, May 1, 1728.

HOWARD, George H., ——, 1832. G.R.I.
Henry, Jan. 18, 1804. G.R.I.
Mary E., ——, 1844. G.R.I.
Susan, July 13, 1802. G.R.I.

HUKER (see Hooker), Phillip (Hukcur), s. Wiliam and Tabatha, Nov. 3, 1742.

HUNT, Abagail, d. Edward and Ahagail, Dec. 25, 1724.
Edward, s. Edward and Abagail, May 24, 1727.
Elisebath, d. Edward and Abagail, Oct. 4, 1735.
Elisebath, d. Edward and Abagail, Apr. 15, 1739.
John, s. Edward (Hunts) and Abagail, May 31, 1729.
Mary, d. Edward and Abagail, June 5, 1733.
Saraih, d. Edward and Abagail, Dec. 6, 1721.

HUNTER, Susannah [——], w. Keiver, Sept. 12, 1835. G.R.I.

INGRAHAM, Nathanael (Imgraham), s. Joseph and Mary, Feb. 23, 1720-1.

INMAN, Aaron, s. Francis and Rose, Nov. 29, 1709.
Abya, d. Francis and Rose, Nov. 4, 1712.
Francis, s. Francis and Suzannah, Jan. 11, 1724.
Jeremiah, s. Francis and Susan, Feb. 7, 1719-20.
Joanah, d. Francies and Susanah, June 7, 1729.
Suzannah, d. Francis and Suzanah, May 23, 1722.

JACKSON, Andrew, s. John and Anna, Apr. 27, 1843.

JENNISON, George Washington, s. John and Lucinda, Nov. 30, 1832.

JILLSON, Anna, d. Uriah and Sarah, Oct. 14, 1736.
Apelles, d. Uriah and Sarah, Oct. 31, 1738.
David, s. Nathaniel Jr. and Ruth, Oct. 28, 1735.

JILLSON, Enos, s. Uriah and Sarah, June 25, 1735.
Jonathan, s. Nathaniel Jr. and Ruth, Jan. 29, 1728-9.
Mary, d. Nathaniel Jr. and Ruth, July 11, 1733.
Susanna, d. Nathaniel Jr. and Ruth, Dec. 31, 1730.

JOHNSON (see Jonson), Abigail, [twin] d. Isaac and Abigail, Oct. 7, 1763.
Ezekel, s. Isaac and Susanna, June 25, 1750.
Isaac, s. Isaac and Susanna, Apr. 15, 1745.
Julia Eliza, d. Benjamin F. and Diana S., July 8, 1836.
Lemuel Franklin, s. Benjamin F. and Diana S., Aug. 29, 1834.
Susanna, d. Isaac and Susanna, Mar. 15, 1757.
Timothy, s. Isaac and Susanna, Aug. 21, 1748.
William, [twin] s. Isaac and Abigail, Oct. 7, 1763.
Zuba, d. Nehemiah and Abigail, June 23, 1765.

JONES, Briget, d. David and Hannah, June 18, 1756.
Daniel, s. David and Hannah, Apr. 2, 1759.
Elizabeth, d. John Jr. and Elisabeth, May 30, 1750.
Hannah, d. David and Hannah, May 20, 1764.
John, s. John Jr. and Mary, Oct. 7, 1755.
Mary, d. John Jr. and Mary, Nov. 13, 1752.
Molley, d. David and Hannah, Mar. 28, 1761.

JONSON (see Johnson), Mary, d. Isaac and Susanna, Apr. 27, 1752.
Neamiah, s. Isaac and Susanah, May 4, 1742.
Rachel, d. Isaac and Susanna, Jan. 5, 1754.
Susanah, d. Isaac and Susanah, Dec. 14, 1743.

JOYCE, Edmund Sanford, s. Peter and Sabrina, Jan. 28, 1828.
Hellen Minerva, d. Peter and Sabrina, Aug. 17, 1830.
Henry Clay, s. Peter and Sabrina, May 16, 1834.

KEACH (see Keech), Amos, ——, 1827. G.R.2.

KEECH (see Keach), Warren R., ——, 1847. G.R.2.

KELLEY (see Killey).

KENNEY, Charles, s. Silas and Rhoda, Aug. 14, 1827.
Silas Emmons, s. Silas and Rhoda, Oct. 20, 1825.

KILBURN, Armenda, d. Simeon and Lucy, July 13, 1799.
Herriet, d. Simeon and Lucy, Mar. 4, 1793.
Lois, d. Simeon and Luca, Sept. 1, 1791.
Lovet, s. Simeon and Lucy, May 22, 1796.
Sofa, d. Simeon and Lucy, Aug. 26, 1794.

KILLEY, Adaline S., d. Nathan and Olive, Jan. 23, 1804.
Amos, s. Jeremiah and Rebecca, Mar. 16, 1766.
Hannah, d. Elisha and Lidia, July 15, 1768.
Nathan, s. Elisha and Lydia, Dec. 18, 1769.
Olive Caroline, d. Nathan and Olive, June 15, 1817.
Silva, d. Jeremiah and Rebecca, Apr. 22, 1768.

LAURANCE (see Lawrance, Lawrence), Abbot N., s. Jaireus and Maria B., Apr. 8, 1846.

LAWRANCE (see Laurance, Lawrence), Jarvis, s. Jarvis B. and Maria B., Apr. 22, 1843.

LAWRENCE (see Laurance, Lawrance), Hannah, Dec. 5, 1826.
G.R.1.
Harriot Olive, d. Addison C. and Olive, June 9, 1832.

LAWTEN, Charles W., s. George W. and Synthia, ———.

LEGG, Alford, s. Joshua and Esther, Dec. 29, 1786.
Calton, s. Joshua and Esther, Dec. 20, 1782.
Chapin, s. Joshua and Esther, Nov. 6, 1778.
Rachel, d. Joshua and Esther, Nov. 7, 1780.

LEVINS, Marvin Henry, s. Marvin and Maria, Nov. 12, 1849.

LEWETT (see Liuett).

LILLIE, Henry, s. Henry and Sybil, June 13, 1833.
Sybil Ann, d. Henry and Sybil, Jan. 21, 1830.

LIUETT, Stephen Viol, s. Stephen and Phebe, Apr. 15, 1821.

LOVELL, Edward Buffum, s. Nehemiah G. and Lucy Buffum, Aug. 18, 1841.
Lucy Frances, d. N. G. and Lucy Buffum, Mar. 14, 1844.
Shubael Perkins, s. Rev. Nehemiah G. and Lucy B., Sept. 2, 1846.

LOWELL, Sarah Louisa (L[o]well), d. Ozias M. and Susan A. of Worcester, Feb. 21, 1847.

MAKEPEACE, William, s. William and Mary, Mar. 2, 1795.

MARSH, Abigail, d. John and Abigai[l], Dec. 26, 1720.
Hannah, d. John and Abigail, Mar. 18, 1722.
Hester, d. John and Abigail, June 28, 1726.
John, s. John and Abigail, Oct. 8, 1718.

BELLINGHAM BIRTHS.

MARSH, Mary, d. John and Abigail, Dec. 9, 1716.
Sarah, d. John and Abigail, Mar. 13, 1724.
MASSEY, Catherine P., w. Rev. Joseph T., d. Dea. William Arnold, Apr. 24, 1816, in Charlestown. G.R.2.
George H., ch. Joseph T. and Catharine P., Nov. —, 1841, in Charlestown. G.R.2.
Joseph T., Rev. [h. Catherine P.], June 4, 1808, in Spottsylvania Co., Va. G.R.2.
Louisa L., ch. Joseph T. and Catharine P., June —, 1843, in Middlebury, Va. G.R.2.
McCULLUM, Abbie C., ——, 1805. G.R.1.
MELLEN, Henry, s. Leonard and Elizebeth S., June 17, 1837.
MERIAM, Polly, d. Timothy and Huldah, Aug. 23, 1788.
METCALF, Abba Jane, d. Savel and Nabby, May 9, 1841.
Abigail, d. S[t]ep[he]n and Hephzibah, Apr. 28, 1776.
Anna, d. John and Mary, Apr. 2, 1743.
Bulah, d. Stephen and Hepzibah, Mar. 26, 1762.
Catharine Thayer, d. Savel and Nabby, Nov. 8, 1830.
Frances, d. Jabiz and Elisabeth, Sept. 15, 1776.
Francis, s. Holliss and Abigail, Jan. 28, 1823.
George Latimer, s. Savel and Nabby, Mar. 24, 1844.
Grace, d. John and Mary, June 14, 1749.
Harriet Mary, d. Savel and Nabby, Jan. 11, 1829.
Hephzibah, d. Stephen and Hephzibah, May 27, 1759.
Hephzibah, d. Stephen Esq. and Hephzibah, July 26, 1782.
Hiram Francis, s. Francis and Almira, May 18, 1846.
Hollis, s. Stephen Jr. and Olive, July 13, 1798.
Irving, s. Jabez and Elisabeth, June 8, 1779.
Jabez, s. John and Mary, Apr. 2, 1747.
Jabez, s. Jabez and Elisabeth, July 10, 1781.
John, s. John Jr. and Hannah, July 9, 1788.
John, s. Stephen and Olive, May 11, 1807.
John Cook, s. Savel and Nabby, Dec. 5, 1842.
Jonas, s. Joseph and Mary, Apr. 29, 1799.
Joseph, s. John and Mary, Feb. 1, 1744–5.
Katharine, d. Stephen and Hephzibah, Apr. 27, 1768.
Lemuel, s. Jobez and Elisabeth, Oct. 16, 1783.
Mary, d. Stephen and Hephzibah, Sept. 15, 1764.
Matthew, [twin] s. John and Mary, Dec. 25, 1740.
Mehetable, [twin] d. John and Mary, Dec. 25, 1740.
Obed, s. Samuel and Lois, Dec. 11, 1763.

METCALF, Olive, d. Stephen (Mitcalf) and Olive, Sept. 16, 1809.
Olive, d. Hollis and Abigail, May 26, 1825.
Olive Adalade, d. Savel and Nabby, Aug. 7, 1845.
Olive Almira, d. Francis and Almira, Sept. 10 [? 11], 1847.
Resign, d. Stephen and Hephzibah, Sept. 2, 1771.
Richard Chapman, s. Savel and Nabby, Apr. 20, 1849.
Sarah Mayo, d. Savel and Nabby, Mar. 31, 1837.
Savel, s. Stephen and Olive, Dec. 13, 1804.
Savel Mathew, s. Savel and Nabby, Feb. 23, 1839.
Savell, s. John and Mary, Dec. 16, 1737.
Stephen, s. Stephen and Hephzibah, June 14, 1773.
Stephen, s. Stephen and Olive, June 8, 1802.
———, s. John Jr. and Hannah, Dec. 27, 1786.

MILLER, Lucy Ann, d. James and Lucy, July 5, 1827.

MILLS, Abigall, d. Janathan and Jemimah, June 16, 1731.
Elizebeth, d. Jonthan and Jemima, Nov. 13, 1733.
John, s. Jonathan and Jemima, June 27, 1738.
Jonathan, s. Rev. Jonathan and Jemimah, Sept. 20, 1728.
Sarah, d. Jonathan and Jemima, May 22, 1736.
———, s. Jonathan and Jemimah, July 7, 1730.

MOREY (see Mowry).

MORGAN, Julius, s. William F. and Eliza, June 26, 1834.
William Henry, s. William F. and Eliza, June 28, 1836.

MORSE, Edgar Arthur, s. Henry B. and Sarah N., Feb. 23, 1849.
James Hewins, s. James and Olive, Mar. 26, 1803.
Joel, s. Joel and Abigail, Apr. 2, 1795.
Julia F., w. Eliab Holbrook, July 9, 1817. G.R.2.
Lucy Harding, d. James and Olive, Sept. 12, 1800.

MOWRY, Lewis P., s. Harris J. and Fannie C., July 18, 1847.
G.R.3.

NASON, Alvin Leprelett, s. Luther W. and Marion, Feb. 3, 1844.

NORCROSS, Ellen E., July 11, 1816. G.R.1.
Ellen Gennette, d. Ellis T. and Ellen E., Nov. 19, 1849.
Emma Frances, d. Ellis T. and Ellen E., May 9, 1846.

NUGENT, John, ———, 1833. G.R.1.

ONION, Alcista Lucyett, d. Asa F. and Asena[t]h, Nov. 8, 1825.
Asa F. Jr., s. Asa F. and Asena[t]h, Sept. 11, 1820.
Hannah, d. Asa F. and Asenath, Sept. 12, 1823.

BELLINGHAM BIRTHS.

PAINE, Almina M., d. W[illia]m Jr. and Mary A., Apr. 10, 1845.
PARAY (see Pary, Perry), Eb[e]nezer, s. Ebnezer (Parray) and Abagial, Dec. 25, 1742.
PARKHUST, Nelley, d. Moses and Catharina, Sept. 9, 1790.
PARNELL, Maryett, d. Daniel R. and Mary, Apr. 16, 1818.
PARTERIDGE (see Partrage, Partraidge, Partridge, Patridg, Patridge), Simeon, s. Benjamin Jr. and Mary, Sept. 1, 1766.
PARTRAGE (see Parteridge, Partraidge, Partridge, Patridg, Patridge), Betty, d. Joseph (Partige) and Betty, Dec. 24, 1731.
PARTRAIDGE (see Parteridge, Partrage, Partridge, Patridg, Patridge), Asa, s. Joseph and Eunice, Oct. 23, 1736.
Hannah, d. Joseph and Eunice, Nov. 6, 1733.
PARTRIDGE (see Parteridge, Partrage, Partraidge, Patridg, Patridge), Aaron (Partrid[ge]), s. Benjamin and Sarah, Oct. 28, 1752.
Aaron, s. Job and Deborah, Sept. 24, 1773.
Aaron, s. Aaron and Abigail, May 2, 1806.
Abigail, d. Aaron and Abigail, Apr. 3, 1802.
Althina J. [―――], w. Philip, July 29, 1797. G.R.1.
Amos (Portrage), s. Joseph and Catherine, Dec. 21, 1781.
Amos 2d, s. Amos and Clarissa, July 14, 1820.
Asa, s. Amos and Clarissa, Dec. 28, 1823.
Bathsheba, d. Job and Deborah, Dec. 5, 1784.
Benjamin [dup. (Patiadg)], s. Benjamin (Partridg) and Sary [dup. Sarah], Oct. 26, 1739.
Benjamin, s. Job and Deborah, Apr. 6, 1777.
Benjmin Richardson, s. Joseph and Catherine, Sept. 6, 1787.
Catherine, d. Joseph and Catherine, Aug. 5, 1796.
Charles, s. Amos and Clarissa, Dec. 12, 1827.
Clarissa H., d. Amos and Clarissa, Aug. 5, 1822.
Dana, s. Joseph and Catherine, Oct. 17, 1794.
Deborah, d. Job [and] Deborah, July 15, 1775.
Ede, d. Joseph and Catherine, Feb. 4, 1779.
Elisabeth, d. Joseph and Katharine, Oct. 6, 1783.
Elizebeth, [twin] d. Job and Deborah, July 18, 1770.
Elmira, d. Aaron and Abigail, Apr. 21, 1811.
Experiance, d. Job and Deborah, Sept. 14, 1786.
Frances Maria, d. Allen and Peggy, Dec. 30, 1829.

PARTRIDGE, Hannah, [twin] d. Job and Deborah, July 18, 1770.
Jairus [?], s. Benjamin Jr. and Mary, June 15, 1768.
James, s. James and Abigail, Oct. 20, 1770.
Job, s. Job and Deborah, May 21, 1779 [*sic*, see Moses].
Jonas, s. Job and Deborah, Apr. 27, 1790.
Joseph, s. Benjamin and Sarah, July 24, 1747.
Joseph, s. Joseph and Catherine, Oct. 13, 1785.
Joseph, s. Joseph Jr. and Lucy, Mar. 14, 1815.
Joseph V., Jan. 4, 1839. G.R.2.
Kezia, d. Joseph (Part[ri]dge) and Betty (Pertridge), Jan. 22, 1729–30.
Levi, s. Joseph and Catherine, Apr. 28, 1777.
Liberty, s. Joseph and Catherine, Jan. 13, 1776.
Loas, d. Benj[amin] Jr. and Mary, Apr. 14, 1777.
Lois, d. Benjamin and Sarah, June 24, 1738.
Lucinda, d. Aaron and Abigail, Apr. 5, 1804.
Lucy, d. Joseph Jr. and Lucy, Dec. 11, 1812.
Mary, d. Benj[amin] Jr. and Mary, Apr. 10, 1772.
Melissa [———], w. J. V., Sept. 17, 1839. G.R.2.
Moses, s. Job and Deborah, Sept. 7, 1778 [*sic*, see Job].
Peter, s. Joseph and Eunice, July 17, 1745.
Phillip, s. Joseph and Catherine, Dec. 1, 1792. [Philip, G.R.1.]
Rachel, d. Joseph and Eunice, May 14, 1739.
Rhoda, d. Joseph and Eunice, Oct. 17, 1748.
Rhoda, d. Job and Deborah, Aug. 11, 1781.
Rhoda, d. Aaron and Abigail, June 19, 1809.
Sabrea, d. Benj[amin] Jr. and w., Mar. 13, 1775.
Sarah, d. Benjamin and Sarah, Apr. 10, 174[4].
Sarah, d. Job and Daborah, Aug. 22, 1771.
Semion, s. Benjamin and Sarah, Jan. 2, 1749–50.
Simeon, s. Joseph and Catherine, May 17, 1791.
Simon Peter, s. Joseph and Catherine, Feb. 5, 1790.
Simon Peter, s. Joseph and Catherine, Oct. 19, 1797.
Sophronia M. [———], w. Charles, Nov. 30, 1831. G.R.1.

PARY (see Paray, Perry), Mary, d. Olover (Parray) and Elesebath, Apr. 27, 1742.

PATRIDG (see Parteridge, Partrage, Partraidge, Partridge, Patridge), Job, s. Benjamian and Sarah, Feb. 28, 1741–2.

PATRIDGE (see Parteridge, Partrage, Partraidge, Partridge, Patridg), Daniel Cook, s. Joseph and Lydiaette, Apr. 29, 1840.
Joseph, s. Joseph and Eunice, May 26, 1743.
Joseph Vernon, s. Joseph and Lydiaette, Apr. 29, 1840.

PENEMAN (see Penniman), Daniel, s. Daniel and Deborah, Nov. 28, 1756.
Nathan, s. Daniel and Deborah, July 25, 1762.
Phebe, d. Daniel and Deborah, May 2, 1768.
Silas, s. Daniel and Martha, Aug. 20, 1751.

PENNIMAN (see Peneman), Amos, s. Silas and Huldah, Oct. 9, 1775.
Daniel, s. Nathan and Hannah, June 27, 1805.
Olive, d. Nathan and Mary, June 22, 1792.
Partridge Harding, s. Nathan and Hannah, Aug. 20, 1807.
Polly, d. Nathan and Hannah, Aug. 23, 1812.
Rhene, d. Silas and Huldah, Jan. 27, 1774.
Scammell, s. Silas and Huldah, Oct. 12, 1772.
Silas, s. Silas and Huldah, Aug. 12, 1777, "three months after his fathers Death."
Simeon Partridge, s. Nathan and Mary, Apr. 17, 1794.

PERKINS, Diana, w. Abiram W. Wales, ——, 1846. G.R.1.

PERRY (see Paray, Pary), Abigirl, d. Ebenezer and Abigirl, Sept. 17, 1745.
Amos, s. Ebenezer and Abigail, Sept. 16, 1752.
Arnold, s. David and Mary, Oct. —, 1784.
Asahel, s. Oliver and Elisabeth, June 19, 1744.
Betty, d. David and Mary, June 14, 1787.
David, s. Oliver and Elisabeth, June 14, 1757.
Elisabeth, d. Oliver and Elisabeth, Dec. 27, 1754.
John, s. Oliver and Amy, Apr. 19, 1781.
Joseph, s. Oliver and Elisabeth, Nov. 10, 1746.
Lot, s. Ebenezer (Perrey) and Abigail, Oct. 24, 1750.
Luceny, d. David and Mary, Mar. 4, 1780.
Nahum, s. Oliver and Amey, July 4, 1784.
Nathaniel, s. Ebenezer and Abigail, Nov. 5, 1738.
Noah, s. Oliver and Elisabeth, Mar. 5, 1748-9.
Oliver, s. Oliver and Elisabeth, Mar. 9, 1755.
Oliver, s. Oliver and Amey, Sept. 9, 1782.
Polly, d. David and Mary, Jan. 30, 1782.
Sarah, d. Ebenezer (Pary) and Abagail, May 6, 1741.
Stephen, s. Oliver and Elisabeth, Sept. 27, 1751.
Susanna, d. Ebenezer and Abigail, May 1, 1737.

PHILIPS (see Phillips, Phyleps), Abigial, d. Joshua and Mary, July 28, 1772.
Asa, s. Joshua and Mary, Mar. 14, 1771.

BELLINGHAM BIRTHS.

PHILIPS, Caleb, s. Joshua and Mary, Nov. 22, 1780.
Hannah, d. Joshua and Mary, July 25, 1774.
Hannah, d. Joshua and Mary, Mar. 17, 1785.
Nathan, s. John and Sarah, July 27, 1774.
Sarah, d. Joshua and Mary, Mar. 13, 1783.
Susannah, d. Joshua and Mary, Sept. 12, 1778.

PHILLIPS (see Philips, Phyleps), Amos, s. Joshua and Mary, Aug. 13, 1767.
Caleb, s. Calleb and Susanna, May 9, 1740.
Elias, s. Joshua and Mary, Feb. 27, 1766.
Elisabeth, d. Caleb and Susanna, Oct. 1, 1745.
Esther, d. Joshua and Mary, May 6, 1789.
Hannah, d. Calib and Susanah, June 29, 1734.
John, s. Caleb and Susanna, May 9, 1747.
Joshua, s. Calib and Susannah, Aug. 21, 1735.
Mary, d. Joshua and Mary, Feb. 1, 1769.
Nathaniel, s. Caleb and Susanna, July 5, 1749.
Sarah, d. Caleb and Susanna, Mar. 12, 1751-2.
Susanna, d. Caleb Jr. and Susanna, Dec. 3, 1738.

PHYLEPS (see Philips, Phillips), Nathaniel, s. Caleb Jr. and Susanna, Apr. 29, 1744.

PICKERING (see Pickring), Abagail, d. Daniel J. (b. Blackstone) and Lavina T. (b. Mendon), June 12, 1847.
Anna, d. Simon and Rhoda, Dec. 27, 1791.
Ellefell [?], d. Simon and Rhoda, Apr. 19, 1799.
Ester, d. Samuel and Sarah, Apr. 29, 1772.
Ester, d. Simon and Rhoda, Nov. 13, 1796.
Eunice, d. Samuel (Pickern) and Sarah, June 29, 1777.
Julius Augustus, s. Daniel W. and Elizabeth, Mar. 27, 1830.
Levina, d. Samuel and Sarah, Dec. 8, 1768.
Mary, d. Samuel and Sarah, Aug. 8, 1767.
Newton M., Oct. 18, 1845. G.R.4.
Rebeccah L., d. Asa and Hannah, July 14, 1829.
Rosana, d. Simon and Rhoda, May 17, 1801.
Rosanna, d. Samuel and Sarah, Dec. 5, 1759.
Ruth, d. Samuel and Sarah, Sept. 23, 1774.
Salla, d. Simon and Rhoda, Oct. 12, 1803.
Salle, d. Simon and Rhoda, June 29, 1794.
Samuel, s. Simon and Rhoda, Sept. 15, 1790.
Sarah Angaline, d. Daniel W. and Elizabeth, Apr. 15, 1834.
Simon, s. Samuel and Sarah, July 26, 1764.

PICKERING, Susan [———], w. Wila, Sept. 20, 1811. G.R.4.
Wila [h. Susan], Sept. 4, 1811. G.R.4.

PICKRING (see Pickering), Phebe, d. Jonathan and Elisabeth, Aug. 6, 1763.
Phile D., d. Samuel and Sarah, Oct. 31, 1779.
Sarah, d. Samuel and Sarah, Feb. 21, 1762.

PITTS, Ignatious, s. John and Ruth, May 27, 1750.
John, s. John and Ruth, July 20, 1759.
Michel, s. John and Ruth, May 14, 1755.
Rufus, s. John and Ruth, June 5, 1752.
Ruth, d. John and Ruth, May 11, 1762.

POND, Abigail, d. Oliver and Anna, Sept. 6, 1759.
Benjamin D. [h. Eliza B.], ———, 1805. G.R.1.
Chloe, d. Oliver and Anna, Mar. 10, 1755.
Edene, d. Oliver and Anna, Sept. 1, 1763.
Eliab, s. Eli and Huldah, Dec. 1, 1779.
Eliab M., ———, 1819. G.R.1.
Eliza B. [———], w. Benjamin D., ———, 1804. G.R.1.
Hannah D. [———], w. Alvin, ———, 1814. G.R.2.
Huldah, d. Eli and Huldah, Nov. 18, 1765.
Isabella, ———, 1829. G.R.1.
Jasper, s. Eli and Huldah, Nov. 8, 1781.
Judath, d. Oliver and Anna, Mar. 26, 1753.
Mari, w. Eli, d. Dr. Daniel Bullard and Ruth Wiswell, Aug. 23, 1804. G.R.2.
Oliver C., s. Eli and Mari, May 29 [1836]. G.R.2.
Silvester, s. Oliver and Anna, Aug. 14, 1761.
Susanna, d. Oliver and Anna, Sept. 2, 1757.

PRATT, Amos, s. Joseph and Elizabeth, Nov. 3, 1796.
John, s. Joseph and Elizabeth, May 25, 1789.
Joseph, s. Joseph and Elizabeth, Sept. 13, 1791.
Miletiah, d. Hannah, May 22, 1779.
Nathan, s. Joseph and Elizabeth, Dec. 28, 1793.

PROCTOR, Clara M., d. James A. and Sarah M., Aug. —, 1848. G.R.1.
James Gilmore, s. James A. and Sarah, Dec. 4, 1843.
John Bradford, s. James A. and Sarah M., Oct. 9, 1845.
Lucy A., d. James A. and Sarah, Dec. 6, 1841, in Franklin.

RAZEE, Cyrena, ch. Ellry and Cyrena, Oct. —, 1841. G.R.2.
Lydia, ch. Ellry and Cyrena, Mar. —, 1843. G.R.2.

REMICK, Mary J. [———], w. A. P., ———, 1835. G.R.1.

RHODES (see Roads), Delilah Cook, d. John and Anna, May 13, 1825.
John Nathaniel, s. John and Anna, Aug. 18, 1816.
Mary Ann, d. John and Anna, Nov. 24, 1813.
Orville Cook, s. William O. and Wata, Nov. 1, 1842.
Rachel Gaskill, d. John and Anna, Aug. 24, 1821.
William Orville, s. John and Anna, Mar. 14, 1818.

ROADS (see Rhodes), Poly, d. John and Elizabeth, Nov. 11, 1794.

ROCKET (see Rockwood), Joseph, s. John and Dabaroh, Feb. 14, 1728.

ROCKWOOD (see Rocket), Abby L., d. Horace and Eliza B., June 25, 1844.
Abbygail Mariah, d. Martin Jr. and Lidia C., Feb. 15, 1849.
Ahigail Legg, d. Martin and Abigail, Sept. 25, 1816.
Alce, d. Joseph and w., Mar. 25, 1758.
Alic, d. Daniel and Lovice, Jan. 2, 1794.
Arteman, s. Joseph and Anna, Dec. 23, 1810.
Calvin N., s. Martin and Abigail, Aug. 12, 1830.
Caroline B., d. Martin and Abigail, Apr. 25, 1813.
Cephas, s. John and Eunice, Mar. 12, 1786.
Cephus, s. Joseph and Alce, May 25, 1766.
Daniel, s. Joseph [and] Alce, Feb. 24, 1768.
Deborah, d. Joseph and Alce, June 17, 1754.
Edward Elias, s. Martin Jr. and Julia Maria, Aug. 4, 1839.
Eliza B. [———], w. Horace, Nov. 7, 1810. G.R.2.
Elizabeth (Rockockwood), d. Martin and Abigail, Feb. 27, 1822.
Emily, d. Joseph and Anna, June 2, 1823.
Francis Albert, s. Martin Jr. and Julia Maria, Oct. 21, 1843.
George, ———, 1839. G.R.1.
George Daniels, s. Horace and Eliza, May 10, 1839.
Hannah, d. Levi and Deborah, May 2, 1778.
Henry Martin, s. Martin Jr. and Julia Maria, Mar. 4, 1842.
Horace, s. Martin and Abigail, Aug. 29, 1811.
Jane Helen [———], w. Calvin N., ———, 1828. G.R.2.
John, s. Joseph and Alse, Mar. 19, 1756.
John, s. John and Eunice, Nov. 11, 1780.
John, s. Joseph and Anna, Jan. 25, 1821.
Joseph, s. Joseph and Alce, Apr. 14, 1760.
Joseph, s. Levi and Deborah, Mar. 18, 1780.

BELLINGHAM BIRTHS.

ROCKWOOD, Joseph Munroe, s. Joseph and Anna, July 1, 1818.
Levi, s. Joseph and Alce, Dec. 10, 1751.
Levi, s. Levi and Deborah, May 24, 1782.
Lewis Horace, s. Horace and Eliza, Apr. 26, 1837.
Lucena, d. Joseph and Anna, Oct. 18, 1806.
Maria, d. Joseph and Anna, Oct. 30, 1815.
Martin, s. Levi and Deborah, Mar. 29, 1787.
Martin, s. Martin and Abigail, Sept. 12, 1814.
Mary, d. John and Deborah, July 12, 1725.
Mary Ann, d. Horace and Eliza, Aug. 25, 1841.
Mary Lucinda, d. Martin and Lydia W., Feb. 3, 1847.
Meletiah, d. Joseph and Elce, Apr. 14, 1762.
Nabby Ann, d. Joseph and Anna, May 30, 1826.
Nathan, s. Levi and Deborah, Nov. 4, 1784.
Preston, s. Joseph and Anna, Aug. 2, 1808.
Rachel, d. Levi and Deborah, July 31, 1774.
Reuban, s. Levi and Deborah, Dec. 26, 1790.
Sena E., d. Martin [and] Abigail, Dec. 2, 1819.
Susan, d. Joseph and Anna, May 15, 1813.
Susanna, d. Levi and Debrah, May 21, 1776.
Varnum B., s. Martin and Abigail, Oct. 10, 1824.

SANFORD, William A., s. Giles and Sarah, Jan. 2, 1832.

SAYLES, Almira Ballou, w. Oren, Jan. 22, 1805. G.R.4.
Asa Darling, s. Stephen and Esther, July 10, 1811.
Avilda, d. Daniel Esq., Mar. 4, 1788. G.R.4.
Donerson Berkley, s. Stephen and Esther, Oct. 5, 1813.
Herbert L., s. Oren and Almira, Dec. 1, 1845. G.R.4.
John Osborne, s. Daniel Jr. and Olive, Apr. 10, 1816.
Latimer V., s. Oren and Almira, June 10, 1828. G.R.4.
Lyman, s. Abigail Morse, July 2, 1816.
Olive A., d. Oren and Almira, Nov. 10, 1833. G.R.4.
Oren, Feb. 14, 1802. G.R.4.
Smith O., s. Oren and Almira, June 9, 1839. G.R.4.
Welcome Ballou, s. Daniel Jr. and Olive, July 4, 1813.
Whitman, s. Stephen and Esther, Jan. 15, 1816.

SCAMMELL, Clara Sweetser, d. Samuel L. and Frances A., Nov. 23, 1848.
Hopestill Bethiah, d. John C. and Joanna, Sept. 18, 1816. [Hopestille B., G.R.5.]
Jane Libba, d. John C. and Joanna, Apr. 7, 1818.
John Stearns, s. Samuel L. and Emily, May 26, 1816.
Lucius Lisle, s. John C. and Joanna, Dec. 17, 1819.

BELLINGHAM BIRTHS.

SCAMMELL, Mary Wheeler, d. Samuel L. and Emily, Dec. 23, 1812.
Samuel Leslie, Dr., ———, in Portsmouth, Eng. G.R.5.
Samuel Stearns, s. John C. and Joanna, Nov. 27, 1822.

SCHULTZ, Abigil T., Jan. 11, 1815. G.R.4.

SCHLUSEMEYER, Henrietta [———], w. William, June 11, 1849. G.R.1.

SCOT (see Scott), Charls, s. Salvenus and Mary, July 12, 1739.
Joanna, d. Salvenus and Mary, Nov. 28, 1736.

SCOTT (see Scot), Abigail, d. Samuel and Mary, Mar. 14, 1761.
Abigail, d. Saul and Selah, Mar. 18, 1791.
Abigal, d. Joseph and Elizebath, Oct. 5, 1735.
Adalbert, s. Emory and Waity, Nov. 27, 1828.
Adeliza L., d. Emory and Waity, Mar. 3, 1824.
Albert, Nov. 27, 1828. G.R.4.
Amary, s. Saul and Selah, May 24, 1799.
Anneliza, d. Sullivan and Eliza C., July 4, 1839.
Asa, s. Samuel Jr. and Bethsheba, Oct. 5, 1788.
Bathsheba, d. Sam[ue]ll and Bathsheba, Jan. 17, 1785.
David, s. Silvanes and Mary, May 12, 1729.
David, s. David and Sarah, July 23, 1756.
Edgar Malcom, s. Willard B. and Sarah A., May 20, 1842.
Elisabeth, d. Jonathan and Anna, Dec. 5, 1770.
Elisha, s. Samuel and Bathsheba, Dec. 4, 1779.
Elizebath, d. Joseph and Elizebath, Mar. 9, 1729–30.
Emerline [———], w. John W., June 5, 1818. G.R.2.
Exalaria, d. Saul and Selah, Feb. 16, 1797.
George Moreton, s. Willard B. and Sarah A., Mar. 28, 1839.
Gorge, s. Joseph and Elizeabath, Mar. 14, 1733.
Henry, s. Sam[ue]ll Jr. and Bathsheba, May 14, 1781.
Ichabod, s. Silvanus and Mary, July 7, 1726.
Ichabod, [twin] s. David and Sarah, Nov. 10, 1767.
Israel, s. Sam[ue]ll Jr. and Bathsheba, Mar. 6, 1783.
Jefferson, s. Saul and Selah, Aug. 5, 1806.
Jerusha, d. Saul and Selah, Apr. 9, 1786.
Joanna, d. Samuel and Mary, Jan. 24, 1753.
Joanna, d. David and Sarah, Oct. 25, 1762.
Joanna, d. Samuel and Bathsheba, May 21, 1773.
John, s. Joseph and Elizebath, Mar. 18, 1731.
John, s. Silvanus and Mary, Feb. 14, 1743–4.
John W. [h. Emerline], May 12, 1823. G.R.2.
Jonathan, s. Samuel and Mary, Nov. 13, 1748.

BELLINGHAM BIRTHS.

SCOTT, Joseph, s. Joseph and Elizebath, Sept. 24, 1726.
Leah, d. Joseph and Leah, June 7, 1752.
Leah, d. David and Sarah, Feb. 1, 1765.
Leonard, s. Samuel and Bathsheba, May 18, 1795.
Levina, d. Saul and Selah, Mar. 27, 1793.
Louisa J., d. Emory and Waity, Mar. 31, 1826.
Lucius Monroe, s. Willard B. and Sarah A., Mar. 8, 1834.
Malcom S., s. Emory and Waity, Nov. 5, 1821.
Mary, d. Joseph and Elezebath, Dec. 5, 1722.
Mary, d. David and Sarah, Feb. 26, 1754.
Moley, d. Saul and Selah, Feb. 5, 1784.
Molly, d. Samuel and Mary, Jan. 4, 1756.
Nancy (Capron), w. Elisha, youngest d. Philip Capron and Priscilla, Oct. 20, 1783, in Cumberland, R.I. G.R.3.
Nancy, d. Samuel Jr. and Bethsheba, Apr. 10, 1793.
Nathaniel, s. Samuel and Mary, Apr. 23, 1744.
Olney, s. Saul and Selah, Feb. 7, 1782.
Patience, [twin] d. David and Sarah, Nov. 10, 1767.
Patience, d. Samuel Jr. and Bathsheba, Oct. 1, 1786.
Pollina, d. Samuel and Bathsheba, Apr. 5, 1802.
Rhoda, d. Samuel and Mary, Dec. 19, 1757.
Rylia, s. Saul and Selah, Apr. 4, 1795.
Sabra, d. Samuel and Bathsheba, Jan. 8, 1778.
Samuel, s. Samuel and Mary, Oct. 10, 1750.
Samuel, s. Samuel and Bathsheba, Feb. 11, 1776.
Sam[ue]ll, s. Joseph and Elizebath, Sept. 12, 1724.
Sarah, d. David and Sarah, Sept. 22, 1760.
Sarah [———], w. Willard B., June 14, 1811. G.R.3.
Sary, d. Silvanes and Mary, June 14, 1733.
Saul, s. Samuel and Mary, July 2, 1764.
Saul B., s. Saul and Selah, July 5, 1804.
Selah, d. Saul and Selah, Jan. 4, 1788.
Sellissa, d. Saul and Selah, Sept. 21, 1789.
Silvanes, s. Silvanes (Scoott) and Mary, Feb. 21, 1727.
Thankfull, d. Samuel and Mary, Sept. 21, 1746.
Thankfull, d. Jonath[a]n and Anna, June 24, 1768.
Willard B., s. Saul and Selah, Nov. 16, 1801. [Nov. 14, G.R.3.]
William, s. Samuel and Bathsheba, Sept. 25, 1774.

SEAGRAVES, Francis Eugean, s. John and Almira, Nov. 5, 1843.

SHEA, Ellen, d. Michiel and Abby, Aug. 25, 1848.

SHEARMAN (see Sherman), Abby Ann, d. Elisha and Rhoda, Jan. 30, 1839.
Evaline Merian, d. Elisha and Rhoda, Nov. 28, 1833.

SHEPARD (see Shephard), Abigail, d. Daniel and Deborah, May 13, 1763.
Deborah, d. Daniel and Deborah, Sept. 8, 1770.
Ezra, s. Daniel and Deborah, Apr. 15, 1768.

SHEPHARD (see Shepard), Freelove, d. Daniel and Deborah, May 19, 1765.

SHERBURN (see Sherburne), Abby Jane, d. George and Abigail, May 10, 1841.
George Albert, s. George and Abigail, May 4, 1844.
Inez Lorra, d. George and Abigail, Sept. 8, 1847. [Sherburne, G.R.2.]

SHERBURNE (see Sherburn), Abigail [———], w. Geo[rge], ———, 1810. G.R.2.
Edgar A., s. George and Abigail, Dec. 29, 1849.
George [h. Abigail], Mar. 12, 1804. G.R.2.
Mary Elizebeth, d. George and Abigail, Apr. 4, 1839.

SHERMAN (see Shearman), James Monroe, s. Elisha and Rhoda, Nov. 29, 1836. [[h. Phebe A.] G.R.4.]
Phebe A. [———], w. James M., Mar. 27, 1841. G.R.4.

SHUMWAY, Olive, d. Jabez and Olive, Feb. 28, 1783.

SLAM, Richard, s. Richard (b. Ireland) and Eliza (b. Ireland), Aug. 20, 1847.

SLIE (see Sly), Anne, d. Henery (Sl[i]e) and Lidia, Oct. 17, 1714.
Eliner, d. Henery and Lidia, Apr. 15, 1710.
Joshua, s. Henery and Lidia, May 8, 1719.
Lidia, d. Henery and Lidia, Oct. 16, 1725.
Miles, s. Henery and Lidia, Oct. 6, 1716.

SLOCOM (see Slocomb, Slocum), Albert Galliton, s. Bethuel and Mary, Oct. 16, 1821.
Asa, s. Simon and Esther, Sept. 11, 1780.
Asa G., s. Bethuel and Mary, Dec. 24, 1818.
Bethuel Albee, s. Bethuel and Mary, Mar. 9, 1814. [Slocomb [h. Caroline], G.R.1.]
Charles, s. Bethuel and Mary, May 13, 1816.
Christopher, s. Simon and Esther, Apr. 22, 1788.

SLOCOM, Christopher Columbus, s. Bethuel and Mary, Aug. 6, 1824.
Clarissa H., d. Asa and Clarissa, Oct. 28, 1811.
Esther, [twin] d. Simon and Esther, Apr. 29, 1800.
Horace, s. Simon and Esther, Mar. 22, 1797.
Lewis, s. Simon and Esther, July 21, 1795.
Patty, d. Simon and Esther, June 18, 1793.
Polly, d. Simon and Esther, Mar. 21, 1787.
Polly, d. Simon and Esher, May 21, 1790.
Vesta, [twin] d. Simon and Esther, Apr. 29, 1800.
Vesta, d. Bethuel and Mary, Nov. 22, 1811.

SLOCOMB (see Slocom, Slocum), Caroline [———], w. Bethuel A., Aug. 30, 1815. G.R.I.

SLOCUM (see Slocom, Slocomb), Esther, d. Simon and Esther May 7, 1784.

SLY (see Slie), Henery, s. Henery (Slye) and Lidia, Sept. 29, 1722.

SMITH, Abner, s. Robert Jr. and Levina, May 1, 1780.
Anna H., Nov. 20, 1816. G.R.I.
Augustus, ch. Peletiah and Julia B., June 13, 1840. G.R.I.
Catherine Massey, d. Peletiah Jr. and Julia, Nov. 29, 1843. [ch. Peletiah and Julia B., G.R.I.]
Celia Ann, d. John and Celia Ann, Sept. 7, 1843.
Elesibath, d. James and Sarah, Dec. 25, 1729.
Eliza Jane, d. John and Celia Ann, Apr. 27, 1834.
Emily Olivia, d. John and Celia Ann, Mar. 26, 1837.
Erastus Tylor, s. Samuel and Anna, Apr. 30, 1815.
Esther, d. Matthew and Sarah, Mar. 18, 1753.
Francis R., s. Peletiah Jr. and Julia, Sept. 18, 1830.
Hayward, s. James and Sarah, Dec. 6, 1731.
James New, s. Samuel and Anna, Oct. 31, 1809.
Joanah, d. James and Sarah, Aug. 27, 1738.
Joanah, d. James and Saraih, Apr. 30, 1742.
Joanna, d. Pelletiah and Joanna, Aug. 29, 1803.
John, Jan. 1, 1809. G.R.I.
John Atwood, s. John and Celia Ann, Dec. 29, 1839.
Judith N. [———], w. Reuel, Oct. 3, 1800. G.R.I.
Lemuel, s. Samuel and Anna, Oct. 14, 1811.
Levina, d. Robert and Levina, Apr. 13, 1784.
Levina Bates, d. Pelletiah and Joanna, Aug. 22, 1808.
Lewis Barton, s. Samuel and Anna, Aug. 23, 1817.

SMITH, Margeret, d. Pelletiah and Joanna, Nov. 1, 1797.
Margreret, d. Peletiah and Unice, Nov. 10, 1754.
Margret, d. Robert Jr. and Levina, Mar. 20, 1778.
Mary, d. Matthew and Deborah, Sept. 20, 1775.
Milatiah Wales, d. Peletiah and Joanna, Jan. 17, 1820.
Olive Abigail, d. Peletiah and Joanna, May 22, 1817.
Pelletiah, s. Robert Jr. and Levina, June 25, 1776.
Pelletiah, s. Pelletiah and Joanna, Mar. 25, 1806.
Phebe R. [———], w. Geo[rge] L., ———, 1849. G.R.2.
Reuel, Apr. 23, 1793. G.R.1.
Robart, s. Pelatiah and Unice, Nov. 5, 1752.
Robert, s. Robert Jr. and Levina, Mar. 30, 1782.
Ruel, s. Robert Jr. and Levina, Apr. 23, 1790.
Ruth Alden, d. Peletiah and Joanna, Oct. 4, 1813.
Samuel, Mar. 29, 1788. G.R.1.
Samuel, s. Robert Jr. and Levina, Mar. 28, 1789.
Samuel Rathborne, s. Samuel and Anna, Aug. 24, 1813.
Sarah, d. James and Sarah, May 21, 1734.
Sarah, d. Pelletiah and Joanna, Mar. 22, 1800.
Simon, s. Robert Jr. and Levina, July 1, 1787.
Stephen Benedic, s. Peletiah Jr. and Julia, Mar. 1, 1828.
Victorius, s. James and Sarah, Jan. 22, 1746–7.
Warren A., ch. Peletiah and Julia B., June 17, 1848. G.R.1.
Whitman Bates, s. Peleitiah Jr. and Julia, Apr. 24, 1833.
Zilpha Thayer, d. Peletiah and Joanna, Mar. 22, 1811.

SOUTHLIN, Henry Harrison, s. Charles E. and Lucinda L., Dec. 19, 1843.

SOUTHWICK, Alvira, d. Seth and Deborah, Nov. 25, 1834.
George, s. Seth and Deborah, Mar. 27, 1825.
Lucinda, d. Seth and Deborah, Dec. 20, 1820.
Rufus, s. Seth and Deborah, Mar. 20, 1827.
Ruth, d. Seth and Deborah, Jan. 21, 1830.
Willis, s. Seth and Deborah, June 18, 1819

SPEAR, Benjamin, s. Benjamin and Elizabeth, July 15, 1789.
Benjamin Franklin, s. Benjamin and Elisabeth, Nov. 5, 1802.
Elizabeth, d. Benjamin and Elizabeth, Dec. 22, 1799.
Elvira, d. Benjamin and Elizabeth, May 5, 1794.
Horatio, s. Benjamin and Elizabeth, June 15, 1787.
Laura, d. Benjamin and Elizabeth, Feb. 4, 1797.
Maria, d. Capt. Benjamin and Elizabeth, July 28, 1807.
Pascal Peoli, s. Pascal Peoli and Betsey, Feb. 29, 1812.
Pascalpaoli, s. Benjamin and Elizabeth, Nov. 23, 1785.

SPEAR, Vesta, d. Benjamin and Elizabeth, Jan. 6, 1792.
William Harvey, s. Capt. Benjamin and Elizabeth, Apr. 27, 1805.

STANLEY, Frank, s. Selem A. and Harriet Emily, Oct. 10, 1837.

STAPLE (see Staples), Alles, d. Robert and Allis, Sept. 19, 1725.

STAPLES (see Staple), Marcy, d. Samuel and Rose, May 23, 1718.
Mary, d. Samuel and Rose, Apr. 8, 1721.
Ruth, d. Thomas and Experience, Dec. 4, 1724.
Sarah, d. Samuel and Rose, Nov. 18, 1723.

STEPHENS (see Stevens), Elisabeth, d. Isaac and Marcy, Mar. 26, 1766.
Marcy, d. Isaac and Marcy, Mar. 4, 1768.

STEVENS (see Stephens), Mary, d. Roger and Susanah, Apr. 24, 1729.

STOWE, Walter A., s. Walter D. and Lurania, July 16, 1845.

SUNDERLAND, Frances Elizebeth, d. Daniel and Frances L., Aug. 24, 1843.
———, d. Daniel and Frances L., Dec. 27, 1849.

TABER, Frederick Albert, s. James, Feb. 13, 1849.

TAFT, Frederic Augustus, s. James A. and Elmira, Feb. 8, 1829.
James A. [h. Almira A.], Sept. 17, 1800. G.R.1.
James Enos, s. James A. and Elmira, Apr. 7, 1827.
Sarah Foristall, d. James A. and Elmira, Mar. 7, 1831.

TAGGARD, Mary A., Feb. 20, 1815. G.R.3.

TAINTING, Mary, d. Elisha and Melletiah, Feb. 20, 1804.

THAYER, Abigail, d. Cornelius and Abigail, Apr. 5, 1755.
Abigail, d. Dependance and Hannah, Aug. 31, 1763.
Abigail, d. Elias and Hannah, July 21, 1778.
Abigail, d. Alpheus and Elizabath, Feb. 16, 1810.
Abigail C. [———], w. Manning, Jan. 20, 1802. G.R.2.
Abigall (Thayr), d. Ebenezer and Mary, Apr. 11, 1729.
Abraham, s. Isaac and Miriam, Nov. 20, 1729.
Abraham, s. Isaac and Miriam, Oct. 25, 1734.
Adin (Thaye), s. Thaddeus and Rhobee, Jan. 28, 1784.
Alida, d. Dependance and Hanna, Sept. 25, 1761.

BELLINGHAM BIRTHS. 63

THAYER, Allen, s. Samuel and Maranda, May 11, 1827.
Alpheus, s. Elias and Hannah, Dec. 20, 1764.
Alpheus, s. Alpheus and Elizibath, May 11, 1794.
Alpheus, s. Manning and Abigail, Feb. 12, 1823, "December 6th A.D. 1842. At the request and by the direction of Manning Thayer I add to the name of Alpheus Thayer above recorded Alpheus Dorr Thayer, he being yet under age."
Amos, s. Cornelius and Abigail, Mar. 16, 1760.
Andrew, s. Silas and Lyda, Nov. 26, 1778.
Baruch, s. Ebenezer and Huldah, July 8, 1764.
Bathsheba, d. Isaac and Miriam, Nov. 16, 1738.
Calvin, s. Ebenezer Jr. and Martha, July 7, 1763.
Calvin Cutler, s. Willard and Charlotte, June 21, 1829.
Cephus, s. Calvin and Abigial, Feb. 16, 1789.
Charles, s. Thomson and Charlotte, Jan. 6, 1833.
Charlotte M. [———], w. Horatio, Dec. 30, 1822. G.R.2.
Cilicia Ann, d. Willard and Rhoda, Nov. 24, 1814.
Cornelius, s. Cornelius and Abigail, May 27, 1757.
Cyrene Levina, d. Thomson and Charlotte, Feb. 15, 1831.
Dan, s. Ebenezer and Huldah, May 13, 1767.
Daniel, s. Ezekiel and Huldah, Nov. 19, 1772.
Ebenezer (Tayer), s. Ebenezer and Hannah, Aug. 21, 1737.
Ebenezer, s. Ebenezer and Marthew [Martha], Nov. 29, 1772.
Ebenezer, s. Elias and Hannah, May 20, 1782.
Eleezebath, d. Jonathan and Eleezebath, June 25, 1735.
Eli, s. Ebenezer and Huldah, May 15, 1769.
Elias, s. Ebenezer and Hannah, June 22, 1741.
Elias, s. Elias and Hannah, May 3, 1773.
Elias Jr., s. Elias and Ruth, Oct. 28, 1806.
Elias Nelson, s. Elias and Rut[h], Apr. 3, 1814.
Elisabeth, d. Elias and Hannah, June 15, 1770.
Elizabath, d. Alpheus and Elizabath, May 4, 1806.
Elizabeth J. (Fiske), w. George, Jan. 25, 1842. G.R.2.
Ellen Amelia, d. Manning and Abigail, Mar. 11, 1841.
Ellera, s. Luther and Mary, July 3, 1795.
Elliot W., s. Ezekiel B. and Mary, Apr. 17, 1826.
Ellis, s. Silas and Lyda, Aug. 13, 1769.
Ellis, s. Samuel and Maranda, June 9, 1830.
Esther, d. Ezekiel and Huldah, Sept. 14, 1791, "Three Monts waten eight Days after the Death of the Father."
Eunies, [twin] d. Iiaac and Miriam, Nov. 20, 1730.
Ezekiel, s. Ezekiel and Huldah, Mar. 16, 1777.
Ezekiel Bates, s. Alphe[u]s and Elizabath, Feb. 5, 1799.
Ezra, s. Jonathan and Elezebath, Apr. 28, 1733.

THAYER, Filo, s. Ebenezer and Marthew [Martha], Mar. 18, 1775.
Frances Paulena, d. James P. and Abby A. S., ———[rec. Oct. 10, 1845].
George Henry, s. Thompson and Charlotte, Apr. 10, 1841.
George W., s. Samuel and Maranda, Sept. 28, 1844.
George Washington, s. Marvell and Julia, Feb. 22, 1819.
Hannah, d. Ebenezer and Hannah, Dec. 30, 1734.
Hannah, d. Elias and Hannah, Nov. 11, 1775.
Hannah, d. Ezekiel and Huldah, Apr. 20, 1782.
Hannah A., d. Ezekiel B. and Mary, Apr. 12, 1830.
Hannah Ellis, d. Elias and Ruth, Mar. 19, 1800 [sic, see Ruth Daniels Thayer].
Helena Abby, d. James P. and Abby S., May 6, 1844.
Helena Abby, d. James P. and Susan Ann, May 16, 1849.
Hopstill, d. Jonathan and Elezebath, Mar. 31, 1731.
Horatio, s. Alpheus and Elizabath, Mar. 25, 1803. [[h. Charlotte M.] G.R.2.]
Huldah, d. Ebenezer and Hannah, Sept. 19, 1749.
Huldah, d. Ezekiel and Huldah, May 8, 1788.
Hullda, d. Ebenezer and Mary, Mar. 22, 1724.
Irene, d. Ebenezer and Marthew [Martha], Sept. 16, 1770.
Isabel, d. Ebenezer and Huldah, Feb. 20, 1762.
Jacob, s. Isaac and Miriam, Sept. 4, 1726.
Jacob, s. Isaac and Mary, Nov. 30, 1751.
James Perry, s. Ellery and Abigail, Mar. 1, 1819. [[h. Susan A.] G.R.2.]
Jeru[s]ha, d. Isaac and Mary, Sept. 9, 1756.
John, s. Silas and Lidea, Oct. 13, 1788.
John Albert, s. Ellery and Abigail, Sept. 11, 1829.
John Milton, s. Elias and Ruthe, Jan. 24, 1820.
Jonas, s. Cornelius and Abigill, Apr. 21, 1750.
Jonathan, s. Cornelius and Abigail, Apr. 7, 1753.
Josiah, s. Isaak and Mirriam, Sept. 4, 1721.
Julia Ann, d. Elias and Ruth, Dec. 13, 1808.
Julia Ann, d. Samuel and Maranda, June 10, 1836.
Julian, d. Marvell and Julia, Mar. 21, 1817.
Larnard, s. Ezekiel and Huldah, May 18, 1775.
Leddea (Thayar), d. Ebenezer and Hannah, July 31, 1739.
Levina Kelton, d. Marvil and Julia, Jan. 24, 1810.
Levine, d. Silas and Lyda, May 14, 1776.
Lewis, s. Alpheus and Elizibath, Jan. 22, 1797.
Lewis Lepreleete, s. Lyman W. and Eliza, Feb. 5, 1835.
Lucy Ann, d. Thomson and Charlotte, Dec. 22, 1828.
Luther, s. Ebenezer and Martha, Oct. 6, 1766.

THAYER, Luther, s. Luther and Mary, Jan. 24, 1800.
Lyman Wheelock, s. Elias and Ruth, May 6, 1798.
Mannen, s. Alpheus and Elizibath, Oct. 28, 1791.
Marcy, d. Isaac Jr. and Marcy, Feb. 19, 1750–1.
Martha, d. Elias and Hannah, July 1, 1767.
Martha Ann, d. Manning and Abigail, Feb. 8, 1824.
Marvell Alexander, s. Marvel and Julia, June 15, 1813.
Marvelous, s. Silas and Lidia, Apr. 10, 1783.
Mary, d. Isaac and Mary, June 15, 1753.
Mary, d. Elias and Ruth, Nov. 26, 1804.
Mary Elizabeth, w. Ezekiel B., d. Joshua Wiggin and Mary, June 2, 1809, in Berwick, Me. G.R.2.
Mary Kimball, d. Ellery and Abigail, Apr. 12, 1825.
Mary T. A. [———], w. Gen. John M., ———, 1818. G.R.2.
Mary W., d. Ezekiel B. and Mary, Aug. 26, 1827.
Mathew [? Martha], d. Alpheus and Elizebath, Mar. 11, 1788.
Mercy, d. Isaac and Miriam, May 12, 1732.
Merien Partridge, d. Willard and Charlotte, Sept. 1, 1823.
Mica, s. Jonathan and Elesebath, June 29, 1741.
Miriam, [twin] d. Iiaac and Miriam, Nov. 20, 1730.
Nehemiah, s. Jonathan and Elezebath, Oct. 7, 1738.
Noah, s. Isaac and Miriam, Sept. 16, 1736.
Otis (Thaye), s. Thaddeus and Rhobee, Feb. 18, 1786.
Patty, d. Ezekiel and Huldah, Mar. 22, 1784, in Mendon.
Peter, s. Eb[e]nezear and Mary, Nov. 11, 1731.
Peter, s. Ezekiel and Huldah, Sept. 12, 1779.
Philo Elisha, s. Samuel and Maranda, Mar. 4, 1847.
Rachel, d. Lyman W. and Eliza, Mar. 17, 1834.
Rebecca, d. Isaac and Miriam, Sept. 22, 1737.
Rhoba [———], w. Willard, Aug. 26, 1804. G.R.4.
Rhoda Adams Albee, ———, 1816. G.R.5.
Roda, d. Isaac Jr. and Marcy, May 30, 1749.
Rosanna, ———, 1774. G.R.2.
Ruben, s. Isaac Jr. and Marcy, May 15, 1747.
Ruben, s. Ebenezer and Huldah, Dec. 7, 1759.
Ruel Francis, s. Luther and Uranah, Jan. 25, 1826.
Rufus, s. Calvin and Abigil, Jan. 22, 1787.
Ruth, d. Silas and Lyda, Feb. 14, 1774.
Ruth Daniels, d. Elias and Ruth, July 16, 1800 [*sic*, see Hannah Ellis].
Sarah Wilber, d. Samuel and Maranda, Sept. 13, 1837.
Sewell, s. Marvell and Julia, Mar. 21, 1822.
Silas, s. Ebenezer and Hannah, Nov. 30, 1746.
Silas, s. Silas and Lidia, Apr. 5, 1781.

THAYER, Silas Foster, s. Ellery and Abigail, Sept. 8, 1821.
Silva, d. Silas and Lyda, Sept. 13, 1771.
Susan, d. Elias and Ruth, ——, 1811.
Susan, d. Lyman W. and Rachel, Nov. —, 1823.
Susan A. [———], w. James P., Dec. 16, 1818. G.R.2.
Thadeas, s. Ebenezer Jr. and Martha, Aug. 10, 1760.
Uriah (Thayr), s. Uriah and Rachall, Mar. 16, 1729.
Willard, s. Alpheus and Elizabath, Sept. 27, 1789.
Willard, Apr. 18, 1802. G.R.4.
William Chickering, s. Manning and Abigail, Mar. 26, 1833.
Ziba, s. Dependance and Hannah, Oct. 8, 1754.
Ziba, s. Dependance and Hannah, Oct. 18, 1756.
Zuba, d. Ebenezer and Huldah, Oct. 28, 1757.
———, ch. Willard and Rhoda, Feb. 13, 1817.

THOMAS, Charles R., Apr. —, 1820. G.R.1.

THOMPCON (see Thompson, Thomson, Tompson), Alce, d. Joseph and Mary, Nov. 21, 1727.

THOMPSON (see Thompcon, Thomson, Tompson), Abiall, d. John and Abigall, July 6, 1729.
Abigal, d. Jonathan and Hannah, Sept. 27, 1733.
Abigal, d. Ebenezer and Abigal, May 31, 1736.
Amos, s. Jonathan and Jemima, Nov. 9, 1757.
Anness, d. John and Abigal, Sept. 2, 1734.
Asa, s. Asa and E[s]ther, Jan. 19, 1774.
Benjaman, s. Benjamin and Matha, May 9, 1731.
Danel, s. Joseph and Mary, Dec. 22, 1731.
Deborah, d. Jonathan and Jemima, July 17, 1755.
Dennis "Alias Darling," s. Hannah Thompson, Sept. 6, 1751.
Elezebath, d. Benjamin and Matha, Aug. 31, 1737.
Esther, d. Joseph and Mary, July 23, 1744.
Hanah, d. Jonath[a]n and Hanah, Nov. 28, 1728.
Harriet Frances, d. William and Lydia E., Jan. 5, 1843.
Hulda, d. Ebenezer and Abigal, Apr. 26, 1733.
James Ellis, s. William (b. London Derry, N. H.) and Lydia E. (b. Wrentham), Apr. 6, 1847.
Jason, s. David and Lucy, Apr. 9, 1765.
Jemima, d. Eb[e]nezear and Abigail, Oct. 5, 1730.
John, s. Jonathan and Hannah, June 8, 1744.
Jonana [Joanna], d. Tomothy and Rachel, Jan. 8, 1761.
Jonathan, s. Jonathan and Hannah, Sept. 6, 1731.
Joseph, s. Joseph and Mary, Dec. 10, 1733.
Joseph Jr., ch. Joseph and Abigail, May 30, 1824.

BELLINGHAM BIRTHS.

Thompson, Judy, d. John and Abigal, Apr. 7, 1737.
Marion, ch. Joseph and Abigail, Apr. 14, 1820.
Martha, [twin] d. Benjaman and Martha, Mar. 5, 1728.
Mary, [twin] d. Benjaman and Martha, Mar. 5, 1728.
Mary, d. Joseph and Mary, Nov. 18, 1729.
Mary Isabella, d. William and Lydia E., Feb. 20, 1840.
Mathaw [Martha], d. John Jr. and Abigell, Feb. 2, 1723-4.
Moses, s. Jonathan Jr. and Jemima, Feb. 27, 1763.
Nathan, s. Joseph and Mary, Oct. 8, 1747.
Olive, d. Peter and Martha, Oct. 26, 1744.
Olive, d. Peter and Bethiah, Apr. 19, 1763.
Peter, s. Joseph and Mary, Nov. 18, 1735.
Peter, s. David and Lucy, June 1, 1768.
Phebe, d. John and Abigal, Jan. 10, 1731.
Rhoda, d. Ichabod and Rachel, Apr. 25, 1739.
Samuael, s. Benjaman and Matha, July 20, 1733.
Sarah, d. David and Lucy, Sept. 19, 1763.
Sarah, d. David and Lucy, May 3, 1766.
Seth, s. Ebenezer and Abigall, Sept. 3, 1728.
Tamer, d. Benjaman and Matha, Mar. 10, 1728.
Thimothy, s. Benjaman and Martha, May 15, 1735.

THOMSON (see Thompcon, Thompson, Tompson), Aaron, s. John Jr. and Abigail, May 2, 1739.
Aaron, s. Jonathan and Jemima, May 13, 1766.
Abigail, d. Ichibod and Rachail, May 28, 1741.
Amos, s. Amos and Mary, June 14, 1789.
Baxter, s. Jonathan Jr. and Jemima, Apr. 5, 1761.
Baxter, s. Amos and Mary, Mar. 14, 1791.
Bulah, d. Ebenezer and Sarah, July 17, 1739.
Caleb, s. Jonathan and Hannah, Nov. 5, 1737.
Chloe, d. Joseph and Mary, Aug. 20, 1740.
Cyrus, s. Peter and Martha, May 28, 1751.
Dan, s. Joseph and Lois, Jan. 14, 1774.
David, s. Jonathan and Hanah, Mar. 21, 1740.
David, s. David and Lucy, Jan. 3, 1771.
Eli, s. Joseph and Lois, Nov. 9, 1788.
Elizebeth, d. Aaron and Mary, Oct. 17, 1788.
Esther, d. Joseph and Mary, Aug. 5, 1738.
Esther, d. Asa and Esther, May 30, 1770.
Frelove, d. Caleb and Lydia, June 10, 1776.
Hannah, d. Calib and Lydia, June 3, 1773.
Hannah, d. Calib and Lydia, Oct. 7, 1789.
Jemima, d. Jonathan and Jemima, Mar. 11, 1771.

THOMSON, Joel, s. Calib and Lydia, Feb. 13, 1770.
John, s. Laban and Jerusha, Jan. 8, 1824.
Jonathan, s. Jonathan and Jemima, Dec. 8, 1768.
Joseph, s. Joseph and Lois, Feb. 6, 1780.
Laban, s. Joseph and Lois, Feb. 13, 1784.
Lucy, [twin] d. David and Lucy, Jan. 21, 1775.
Margaret, d. Asa and Esther, July 15, 1767.
Meletiah, [twin] d. David and Lucy, Jan. 21, 1775.
Melinda, d. Cyrus and Keziah, Dec. 29, 1777.
Nahum, s. Jonathan [and] Jemima, May 6, 1778.
Nansa, d. Joseph and Lois, Sept. 15, 1775.
Nathan, s. Cyrus and Keziah, Feb. 6, 1775.
Olive, d. David and Eunice, Dec. 11, 1780.
Peter, s. Peter and Martha, Jan. 27, 1738-9.
Phebe, d. Asa and Esther, Feb. 24, 1772.
Piam, s. Cyrus and Keziah, Aug. 26, 1781.
Polley, d. David and Eunice, Mar. 8, 1786.
Polly, d. Cyrus and Keziah, Nov. 13, 1788.
Rachel, d. Ichabod and Rachel, Dec. 25, 1737.
Rachel, d. Jonathan and Jemima, June 10, 1773.
Rhufus, s. Caleb and Lydia, July 9, 1782, in Mendon.
Ruth, d. Joseph and Mary, Sept. 2, 1742.
Ruth, d. Joseph and Lois, July 2, 1777.
Seth, s. Peter and Bethiah, Dec. 15, 1764.
Seth, s. Joseph and Lois, Jan. 4, 1782.
Silence, d. Calib and Lydia, June 21, 1771.
Simeon, s. David and Lucy, Jan. 2, 1773.
Susanna, d. Calib and Lydia, Oct. 21, 1785.
Warren, s. David and Eunice, Jan. 27, 1778.
William Alonzo, s. William V. and Hannah, June 3, 1835.
Zenus, s. Caleb and Lydia, Mar. 9, 1779, in Milford.
Ziba, s. Joseph and Lois, Apr. 21, 1785.

TILSON, ———, s. Abraham and Hannah E., Nov. 28, 1849.

TINGLEY, Andrew Jackson, [twin] s. Charles W. and Margaret, Feb. 23, 1838.
Charles Morris, s. Charles W. and Margeret, Oct. 23, 1839.
Francis Edwin, s. Charles W. and Margaret, Jan. 24, 1836.
Martin Van Buren, [twin] s. Charles W. and Margaret, Feb. 23, 1838.
Silas Edwin, s. Silas and Rosanna, Aug. 23, 1834.

TOBEY, Polley, d. Silvenus and Ruth, Nov. 9, 1789.

TOBEY, Sally, d. Silvenus and Ruth, July 29, 1792.
Thomas, s. Silvenus and Ruth, Jan. 4, 1788.

TOMPSON (see Thompcon, Thompson, Thomson), Benonie, s. Benjamin and w., May 10, 1727.
Deborah, d. John and Abigail, Apr. 27, 1726.
Eunis, d. Jonthan and Hannah, Nov. 21, 1726.
John, s. John and Abigail, Nov. 15, 1721.
Joseph, s. Joseph and M[a]ry, July 12, 1726.
Moses, s. Ebenezer and Abigail, Mar. 28, 1727.
Timothy, s. Eliezer and Hannah, Dec. 4, 1726.

TOWN, Louis, d. Abial J. and Allis, Feb. 17, 1821.
William Bates, s. Abial J. and Allis, Aug. 24, 1819.

TWICHAL (see Twitchel), Paticence, d. Ben[jamin] and Paticence, Mar. 17, 1772.

TWITCHEL (see Twichal), Morris, s. Ben[jamin] and Patience, Oct. 26, 1774.

UPHAM, Elisabeth [dup. Elisebath], d. John and Patience, Dec. 3, 1761.
Patience, d. John and Patience, July 18, 1768.
Robert, s. John and Sarah, Nov. 9, 1743.

VOSE, Melinda M. (Weeks), w. Alexander [of] Oldtown, Me., June 8, 1806. G.R.2.

WAILS (see Wale, Wales), Abirum Wight, s. John and Abagail, Aug. 16, 1816.

WALDEN, Laban, s. Job and Alpha, June 24, 1798.

WALE (see Wails, Wales), Ruth Condal, d. Amos A. and Rhoda, Oct. 25, 1837.

WALES (see Wails, Wale), Abiram, "Mem Co A 35 Reg M V" [h. Diana Perkins], ——, 1835. G.R.1.
Abiram White, s. Amos A. and Rhoda, Nov. 9, 1835.
Amos Adams, s. John and Abigail, Apr. 30, 1805.
Amos Oscar, s. Amos A. and Rhoda, Jan. 22, 1840.
Bradford N., s. Abiram W. and Olive, Nov. 8, 1845.
Charles A. [h. Ruth], Apr. 25, 1815. G.R.1.
Diana Perkins, w. Abiram W., ——, 1846. G.R.1.
Irving, s. George F. and Abigail, Dec. 10, 1844.
Jonathan, s. John and Abigail, Oct. 28, 1806.

WALES, Joseph Massey, s. Abiram W. and Olive, Mar. 20, 1849.
Nancy, d. John and Abigail, Sept. 18, 1812.
Otis, Apr. 6, 1803. G.R.2.
Ruth [————], w. C. A., May 7, 1823. G.R.1.
Shadrach Atwood, s. George F. and Abigail, Sept. 20, 1846.
————, ch. George F. and Abigail, June 13, 1849.

WALKER, James, s. Matthew and Maryann, Oct. 22, 1824.
Maryann, d. Matthew and Maryann, July 1, 1819, in Walpole.
Samuel, s. Matthew and Maryann, Mar. 10, 1822, in Waterton.

WARE, Albert O., July 9, 1811. G.R.1.
Mehitable [————], w. Albert O., Jan. 19, 1805. G.R.1.
Sarah, d. Massa [Mercy] Hayward, June 11, 1803.

WARFIELD, Dene, d. Samuel and Margere, Dec. 14, 1780.

WEDGE, Anne, d. Daniel and Hannah, Mar. 24, 1776.

WEEKS, Melinda M., w. Alexander Vose [of] Oldtown, Me., June 8, 1806. G.R.2.

WHEELER, Mary Burrill, w. Parker, Apr. 23, 1842. G.R.1.

WHEELOCK, Phebe, d. Timothy and Joanna, Apr. 5, 1765.

WHITAKER, Juba Forster, s. William and Chloe, Jan. 18, 1808.
Marcia Steward, d. William and Chloe, Jan. 8, 1816.
Persia Walker, s. William and Chloe, Oct. 20, 1810.

WHITE, Joseph, s. James and Katharene, May 2, 1755.
Phebe H., d. Leonard and Diana, Feb. 21, 1822.
Sylvenus, s. Leonard and Diana, Jan. 1, 1826.

WHITING, Calib, s. Pelletiah and Hannah, Apr. 14, 1771.
Mary, d. Pelletiah and Hannah, Aug. 22, 1767.
Sarah, d. Pelletiah and Hannah, Aug. 7, 1769.

WHITNEY (see Whitny), Betsey M. G., d. Nelson and Ruth M., Oct. 17, 1844.
Dexter, ————, 1817. G.R.2.
Henry Adalbert, s. Dexter and Adaliza, July 1, 1842.
Herbert Clifton, s. Ethan and Julia A., Oct. 6, 1849.
Ida Alma, d. Ethan and Julia A., Apr. 7, 1847.
Laban, s. Laban and Olive, Jan. 6, 1815.
Lauria Ann, d. Nelson and Ruth M., June 18, 1849.
Lemuel G., s. Laban and Olive, Jan. 4, 1817.

BELLINGHAM BIRTHS. 71

WHITNEY, Lewis Edward, s. Dexter and Adliza, Sept. 12, 1844.
Melissa R., d. Nelson and Ruth M., Jan. 28, 1847.
Reuel, s. Laban and Olive, Dec. 3, 1811.
WHITNY (see Whitney), Adeliza [――――], w. Dexter, ―――, 1812.
  G.R.2.
WHITTAKER (see Whitaker).
WIGGIN, Mary Elizabeth, d. Joshua and Mary, w. Ezekiel B.
  Thayer, June 2, 1809, in Berwick, Me. G.R.2.
WIGHT (see Wights), Abigail, d. Eliab and Jemima, Oct. 11,
  1786.
Abigail, d. Aaron and Abigail, June 13, 1817.
Abigall, d. Joseph and Matha, Mar. 3, 1735.
Abiram, s. Samuel and Mary, May 5, 1763.
Adeline Augusta, d. Seth and Mary Ann, Mar. 18, 1835.
Adison Lealand, s. Seth and Mary Ann, Oct. 12, 1846.
Ahaz, s. Samuel (Wiaht) and Margret, Jan. 30, 1765.
Amherst, s. Eliab and Jemina, June 15, 1791.
Anna Smith, d. Simeon and Margret, June 28, 1772.
Austin, s. Eliab and Jemina, Apr. 6, 1793.
Eliab, s. Elnathan and Abigal, June 29, 1760.
Eliab, s. Eliab and Jemima, July 14, 1798.
Francis Leland, s. Sineca and Betsey, May 29, 1820.
Francis S., s. Seth and Mary Ann, Mar. 28, 1831.
Isabel, d. Elnathan and Abigail, Feb. 1, 1756.
Isabel Louiza, d. Seth and Mary Ann, Aug. 31, 1838.
James, s. Nathon and Jerusha, Jan. 2, 1786.
Jemima, d. Eliab and Jemima, Sept. 8, 1801.
Joseph, s. Joseph and Martha, June 8, 1749.
Jude, d. Abener [and] Jemima, Apr. 21, 1779.
Lucena, d. Nathan and Jerusha, Nov. 28, 1789.
Luis, s. Abner and Jemima, Mar. 15, 1777.
Lusina, d. Samuel and Mery, July 23, 1769.
Maray, d. Joseph and Mathew [Martha], July 8, 1740.
Marcy, d. Samuel and Mary, Jan. 23, 1766.
Margret [――――], wid., of Springfield, ―――, 1685. P.R.1.
Martha Elenor, d. Seth and Mary Ann, Nov. 10, 1836.
Mary Ann Richards, d. Seth and Mary Ann, Oct. 29, 1832.
Nancy, d. Eliab and Jemima, July 25, 1796.
Nathan, s. Joseph and Martha, Jan. 26, 1743-4.
Nathan, s. Elnathan and Ab[i]goil, Aug. 15, 1757.
Nathan, s. Nathan and Jarusha, Jan. 1, 1782.

WIGHT, Patty, d. Eliab and Jemina, June 26, 1788.
Peter, s. Joseph and Martha, Feb. 14, 1737–8.
Peter, s. Samuel and Mary, July 8, 1757.
Polly, d. Abner and Jemima, Feb. 11, 1781.
Presson, s. Nathan and Jerusha, June 21, 1791.
Samuel, s. Joseph (Wite) and Martha, Dec. 25, 1730.
Seneca, s. Eliab and Jemima, June 24, 1784.
Theron, s. Nathan and Jerusha, Mar. 23, 1794.
———, [twin] d. Seth and Mary Ann, Apr. 12, 1845.
———, [twin] d. Seth and Mary Ann, Apr. 12, 1845.

WIGHTS (see Wight), Pliny, s. Nathan and Jarusha, June 2, 1783.

WILCOX, Adeliza S. [———], w. Elijah D., Mar. 3, 1824. G.R.4.
Elijah D. [h. Adeliza S.], Mar. 24, 1824. G.R.4.
Fenner, Nov. 17, 1823. G.R.4.
Ida A., d. Elijah D. and Adliza S., Oct. 18, 1848.
Susan A., Mar. 26, 1831. G.R.4.

WILEY, George, s. James (b. Ireland) and Catharine (b. Ireland), Aug. 9, 1849, in Blackstone.

WILLIAM (see Williams), Urbane, s. Gurdon and Elizabeth, Mar. 29, 1803.

WILLIAMS (see William), Abby Emeline, d. Preston A. and Mary R., Oct. 13, 1849.
Anna Clarissa, d. Abel B. and Harriet, Feb. 21, 1848.
Emma M., d. Amos T. and Charlotte G., May 18, 1847.
Gurdon, s. Gurdon and Elizabeth, Jan. 29, 1802.
Leroy A. (Willi[a]ms), s. Amos T. and Charlotte G., July 18, 1845.
Mary Eliza, d. Preston A. and Mary R., Apr. 11, 1846.

WILLMOUTH, Adelade, d. Apollos and Alcada, Nov. 19, 1844.

WILLSON, Dameris, d. James and Esther, Aug. 31, 1768.
David, s. James and Esther, Jan. 3, 1766.
Esther, d. James and Esther, Sept. 2, 1758.
Hanna, d. James and Esther, Apr. 11, 1761.
Joseph, s. Robert and Martha, Feb. 5, 1737–8.
Peninnah, d. James and Esther, July 20, 1763.
Susanna, d. James and Esther, Apr. 15, 1756.

WISWELL, Lovell [h. Marinda H.], Apr. 10, 1826. G.R.1.

BELLINGHAM BIRTHS. 73

WOODBURY, John R., ——, 1821. G.R.2.

WOODWARD, Mary, d. Ebenezer and Mary, Jan. 18, 1743-4.
Rachel, d. Ebenezer and Mary, Apr. 8, 1742.

WRIGHT, Henry Augustus, s. Jonathan and Susan M., Aug. 6, 1844.
Jonathan, s. Solomon and Polley, May 5, 1819.
Pelmyra, d. Solomon and Polley, Dec. 28, 1826.
Warren, s. Solomon and Polley, Nov. 5, 1821.

UNIDENTIFIED.

——, Abigail, w. John Chickerin, Sept. 12, 1774. G.R.2.
——, Abigail, w. Geo[rge] Sherburne, ——, 1810. G.R.2.
——, Abigail C., w. Manning Thayer, Jan. 20, 1802. G.R.2.
——, Adeliza, w. Dexter Whitny, ——, 1812. G.R.2.
——, Adeliza S., w. Elijah D. Wilcox, Mar. 3, 1824. G.R.4.
——, Althina J., w. Philip Partridge, July 29, 1797. G.R.1.
——, Amy, w. Alvah Aldrich, June 15, 1826. G.R.3.
——, Angeline A., w. Charles Dewing, ——, 1831. G.R.1.
——, Ann, w. George Fish, ——, 1819. G.R.1.
——, Caroline, w. Bethuel A. Slocomb, Aug. 30, 1815. G.R.1.
——, Caroline R., w. Peletiah S. Bates, ——, 1813. G.R.2.
——, Carrie A., w. Elias T. Bates, ——, 1838. G.R.2.
——, Charlotte, w. —— Allen, Apr. 22, 1836. G.R.1.
——, Charlotte M., w. Horatio Thayer, Dec. 30, 1822. G.R.2.
——, Clarissa, w. Valentine R. Coombs, Nov. 16, 1802. G.R.1.
——, E. A., w. Almon Darling, Jan. 27, 1821. G.R.4.
——, Eliza B., w. Benjamin D. Pond, ——, 1804. G.R.1.
——, Eliza B., w. Horace Rockwood, Nov. 7, 1810. G.R.2.
——, Emerline, w. John W. Scott, June 5, 1818. G.R.2.
——, Emily, w. George Ames, Feb. 19, 1838. G.R.1.
——, Emily T., w. Joseph Adams, Nov. 6, 1807. G.R.1.
——, Esther P., w. Pliny Cook, ——, 1796. G.R.2.
——, Hannah, w. William Bowers, Aug. 13, 1779. G.R.2.
——, Hannah A., w. Addison S. Burr, Apr. 12, 1830. G.R.2.
——, Hannah A., w. Alfred O. Darling, Nov. 25, 1834. G.R.4.
——, Hannah D., w. Alvin Pond, ——, 1814. G.R.2.
——, Hellen, w. Albert M. Adams, ——, 1830. G.R.1.
——, Henrietta, w. William Schlusemeyer, June 11, 1849. G.R.1.
——, Ida A., w. James O. Aldrich, Oct. 18, 1848. G.R.4.
——, Jane, w. Geo[rge] W. Hill, ——, 1843. G.R.5.

BELLINGHAM BIRTHS.

———, Jane Helen, w. Calvin N. Rockwood, ———, 1828. G.R.2.
———, Joanna S., w. Jefferson B. Darling, Aug. 29, 1803. G.R.2.
———, Judith N., w. Reuel Smith, Oct. 3, 1800. G.R.1.
———, Laura A., w. Asa Hill, Mar. 10, 1809. G.R.1.
———, Levina, w. George W. Blake, ———, 1812. G.R.2.
———, Louisa Alice, w. Charles P. Hancock, July 11, 1838. G.R.2.
———, Lucia E., w. Samuel Esten, Mar. 25, 1825. G.R.4.
———, Lucy, w. Amos Arnold, Oct. 5, 1808. G.R.4.
———, Lucy C., w. William Grant, Dec. 1, 1812, in Dover. G.R.2.
———, Lydia A., w. Luther T. Hixon, Dec. 19, 1843. G.R.1.
———, Margret, wid., of Springfield, ———, 1685. P.R.1.
———, Marion, w. Valentine Coombs, Jan. 1, 1807. G.R.1.
———, Martha A., w. A. Hezeltine Belcher, Feb. 8, 1824. G.R.2.
———, Mary, w. Zebina Bullard, Aug. 9, 1794. G.R.1.
———, Mary, w. Elijah Dewing, July 3, 1796. G.R.1.
———, Mary, w. Sabin Cushman, Aug. 9, 1800. G.R.2.
———, Mary, w. Samuel Adams, Apr. 5, 1839. G.R.1.
———, Mary Ann, w. Benjamin Foristall, July 3, 1800. G.R.1.
———, Mary Frances, w. Amos H. Holbrook, Apr. 27, 1842. G.R.1.
———, Mary J., w. A. P. Remick, ———, 1835. G.R.1.
———, Mary Jane, w. George Franklin, Apr. 28, 1846. G.R.1.
———, Mary T. A., w. Gen. John M. Thayer, ———, 1818. G.R.2.
———, Mehitable, w. Albert O. Ware, Jan. 19, 1805. G.R.1.
———, Melissa, w. J. V. Partridge, Sept. 17, 1839. G.R.2.
———, Nancy, w. Whitman Holbrook, ———, 1810. G.R.1.
———, Olive, w. Laban Bates, Apr. 12, 1750. G.R.3.
———, Olive A., w. Dea. Benedict, May 22, 1817. G.R.1.
———, Olive W., w. Seneca Burr, ———, 1833. G.R.2.
———, Pamelia A., w. John H. Eaton, ———, 1830. G.R.2.
———, Phebe A., w. James M. Sherman, Mar. 27, 1841. G.R.4.
———, Phebe R., w. Geo[rge] L. Smith, ———, 1849. G.R.2.
———, Phila H., w. Lewis F. Cook, Apr. 15, 1826. G.R.4.
———, Polly, w. Olney Forestall, Sept. 29, 1791. G.R.1.
———, Polly M. R., w. Asa Burr, Mar. 13, 1791. G.R.2.
———, Rhoba, w. Willard Thayer, Aug. 26, 1804. G.R.4.
———, Roxanna, w. Nathan Adams, Apr. 22, 1794. G.R.1.
———, Ruth, w. C. A. Wales, May 7, 1823. G.R.1.
———, Sarah, w. Benjamin Hall, ———, 1775. G.R.3.
———, Sarah, w. Willard B. Scott, June 14, 1811. G.R.3.
———, Sarah A., w. Sullivan Bates, Dec. 25, 1816. G.R.2.

BELLINGHAM BIRTHS.

———, Selissa, w. Asa Hall Esq., Sept. 21, 1789. G.R.3.
———, Sena A., w. Nathan A. Cook, ———, 1828. G.R.4.
———, Sophronia M., w. Charles Partridge, Nov. 30, 1831. G.R.1.
———, Susan, w. Wila Pickering, Sept. 20, 1811. G.R.4.
———, Susan A., w. James P. Thayer, Dec. 16, 1818. G.R.2.
———, Susan E., w. Daniel Bolster, ———, 1823. G.R.2.
———, Susannah, w. Keiver Hunter, Sept. 12, 1835. G.R.1.
———, ———, mother of John H. Eaton, ———, 1808. G.R.2.

BELLINGHAM MARRIAGES.

BELLINGHAM MARRIAGES.

To the year 1850.

ADAMS, Abigail, Mrs., and Moses Daniels, int. Dec. 14, 1766.
Abigail (Adoms) and John Wailes, int. June 10, 1804.
Almira of Medway, and Francis Metcalf, int. Apr. 22, 1845.
Amos and Mrs. Abigal Thayer, int. Nov. 8, 1779.
Amos Jr. and Abigail Holbrook, Nov. 29, 1812.
Betsey of Medway, and Jonas M. Fairbanks, int. Apr. 17, 1824.
Betsy and David Ware, int. Jan. 23, 1806.
Caleb and Meletiah Holbrook, wid., int. Mar. 31, 1799.
Catharine of Medway, and Noah Coombs, int. Mar. 11, 1838.
Chloe (Adoms) and Paul Gould Jr., int. Aug. 4, 1803.
Christopher [of] Medway, and Sally Smith, Apr. 24, 1814.*
Daniel and Christiania Gould, int. Feb. 27, 1803.
Daniel P. of Westborough, and Abby T. Fisher, Oct. 9, 1836.
David and Sally Ames Ayers, Apr. 19, 1827.
Edmund J., 21, s. Joseph and Asenath, and Amanda L. Smith, Nov. 26, 1846.
Electa Sanford and Mason Wails, int. Sept. 19, 1824.
Elizabeth P. and Leonard P. Bullard, May 26, 1842.
Emily, 19, d. Joseph and Asenath, and Samuel Darling 3d, May 27, 1846.
Hipzibah, Mrs., of Medway, and Stephen Metcalf, int. Apr. 16, 1757.
Joel and Priscilla Whiteny, int. Mar. 4, 1801.
Joel (Adoms) and Hannah Wailes, int. Apr. 15, 1804.
John (Adoms) and Perses Wheeler, int. Jan. 10, 1808.
John Q. and Calista Cutter, int. May 4, 1834.
Joseph and Jemima Alden, Feb. 8, 1816.
Joseph 2d and Asenath Partridge, Sept. 15, 1820.
Joseph and Emily Tourtelot, int. Apr. 30, 1843.
Jotham Jr., widr. [int. omits widr.], 35, of Medway, s. Jotham, and Catherine [int. Catharine] B. Foristall, July 1, 1849.
Julia Ann and Thomas Willis Wood, Jan. 21, 1838.

* Intention not recorded.

ADAMS, Levi and Mrs. Olive Gould, int. Oct. 20, 1797.
Maria A. and Joseph W. Holbrook, Dec. 13, 1840.
Mary, Mrs., of Midway, and Daniel Penniman, int. Sept. 21, 1776.
Mary (Adoms) of Medway, and Moses Hill, int. Oct. 8, 1803.
Mary R. and Preston A. Williams, int. Jan. 16, 1842.
Nahum and Susanna Chamberlin [int. Chamberlain], Apr. 15, 1821.
Nancey of Holiston, and Elijah Fairbanks, int. Mar. 29, 1811.
Nathan [int. of Medway] and Roxlany Sprouter, Sept. 12, 1819.
Obadiah and Sarah Partridge, int. June 23, 1744.
Obadiah and Sarah [int. Salla] Ware, Nov. 14, 1805.
Olive, Mrs., and David Daniels, int. Dec. 31, 1770.
Olive [int. adds Mrs.] and John Clark, July 15, 1798.
Oliver W. and Philinda M. Babcock, Aug. 1, 1838.
Peter and Anna Claflin, int. Mar. 1, 1814.
Reuel and Julia Ann Smith, int. Oct. 12, 1833.
Rhoda and William Page [int. Jr.], Mar. 27, 1823.
Roxana of Holliston, and Hiram Kilburn, —— 24 [1842].*
Sabra and Ezekiel Bates Jr., May 30, 1816.
Sally and [int. adds Lt.] Welcom Thayer, May 25, 1819.'
Samuel and Mrs. Chloe Legg, Aug. 14, 1777.
Samuel Jr. and Mercy Clark, Apr. 16, 1809.
Silas and Mrs. Mary Parker, int. July 10, 1768.
Silas and Mrs. Olive Mason [int. wid., omits Mrs.], Aug. 20, 1794.
Silas and Rosanna [int. Rosana] Jones, Nov. 21, 1822.
Triphena and Roswell Bent, Apr. 6, 1842.

ALBEE, Abel of Milford, and Abigail Partridge, int. Nov. 8, 1818.
Abigail, Mrs., of Mendon, and Seth Hall, May 28, 1737.*
Abner of Mendon, and Mrs. Cate Penniman, int. Aug. 20, 1774.
Alpheus of Milford, and Mrs. Susannah Phillips, Mar. 31, 1796.
Beulah, Mrs., and Joseph Ellexander, int. Jan. 15, 1797.
Charlotte M. of Milford, and Horatio Thayer, int. Nov. 5, 1848.
Deborah, Mrs., of Mendon, and Daniel Bullard, int. Oct. 16, 1774.
Elizabeth, wid., and Ellixander Kelley, int. Feb. 2, 1797.
Ezekiel S. [int. of Mendon] and Abigail Thurber, Oct. 23, 1828.
John of Medway, and Huldah Thayer [int. adds wid.], May 9, 1799.
Mary of Holiston, and Bethuel Scolomb, int. Aug. 12, 1810.
Polly of Mendon, and Reuben Rockwood, int. May 2, 1813.
Rebeckah of Shutesbury, and Emory Haywad, int. Sept. 2, 1832.

* Intention not recorded.

ALBEE, Sarah [int. adds wid.] and Samuel Penniman, Sept. 19, 1799.
Sarah of Mendon, and Elijah Bates, int. Apr. 9, 1809.
Susanna and Lendol Staples, Nov. 25, 1810.
Thomas of Mendon, and Jemima Thomson, int. June 2, 1750.
Zurial of Mendon, and Mrs. Anna Penniman, int. Jan. 12, 1776.
———, Adml., and Allythirai Belcom, int. Aug. 6, 1815.

ALDEN (see Aldin), Elijah and [int. adds Mrs.] Polly Foristall, May 17, 1798.
Isaac, widr. [int. Asaac Jr., omits widr.], s. Isaac of Walpole, and Thankful S. Inman, July 20, 1845.
Jemima and Joseph Adams, Feb. 8, 1816.
Joanna, Mrs., and Aaron Lealand, July 24, 1783.
Lucy, Mrs., and Darius Marcum [int. Markham], Dec. 6, 1770.
Noah Jr. and Mrs. Joanna Cook, Sept. 21, 1775.
Ruth, Mrs., and Benjamin Thayer, Dec. 12, 1793.
Zilpha and Benjamin Hayward, June 19, 1803.

ALDIN (see Alden), Lydia, Mrs., and Caleb Thomson, Dec. 21, 1768.

ALDRICH (see Aldridg, Aldridge, Aldrish), Abel and Esther Cook, int. Apr. 6, 1802.
Abigail and Elish [int. Elisha] Kelley Jr., Sept. 19, 1805.
Abner of Mendon, and Elisabeth Cook, int. Nov. 9, 1747.
Ahas of Uxbridge, and Mrs. Joanna Scoot, int. Mar. 22, 1792.
Ahaz of Uxbridge, and Mary Arnold, June 4, 1821.
Alpha, Mrs., and Job Walden, Sept. 14, 1797.
Anne, Mrs., of Cumberland, and Jonathan Scott, int. Nov. 29, 1767.
Artimissa and Paul Fisher, int. Apr. 17, 1802.
Asenith [int. Asenath] and John Harskell [int. Haskell] Jr., Apr. 16, 1812.
Betsey W. and Charles W. Thayer, int. Sept. 28, 1845.
David of Smithfiaeld, and Mrs. Rebekah Pain, int. Apr. 11, 1778.
Enoch of Uxbridge, and Mrs. Sabra Scott, int. Mar. 7, 1798.
Hannah of Northbridge, and Ebenezer Haward, int. Jan. 23, 1808.
Joanna of Uxbridge, and Ziba Cook, int. Dec. 3, 1787.
Joanna, wid., and William Fletcher, int. June 17, 1804.
Joseph and Mrs. Experiance Stockwell, int. Oct. 29, 1762.
Justus of Uxbridge, and Permelia Arnold, int. Dec. 12, 1830.
Lucy of Mendon, and Simeon Kilbon, int. Jan. 23, 1790.
Luther of Mendon, and Sarah Scott, int. Sept. 13, 1788.
Nancy of Uxbridge, and George Colston, int. Feb. 6, 1802.

ALDRICH, Nathaniel, Capt., of Cumberland, and Anna Thayer, int. Sept. 11, 1824.
Ruben Jr. of Smithfield, and Mrs. Sarah Darling, int. Aug. 2, 1788.
Smith of Mendon, and Olive W. Foster, Oct. 29, 1837.

ALDRIDG (see Aldrich, Aldridge, Aldrish), Phinehas [int. Phineas Aldrich] of Mendon, and [int. adds Mrs.] Anna Pain, Mar. 30, 1780.
Rebeckah, Mrs., and Samuel Smith, int. Jan. 2, 1786.

ALDRIDGE (see Aldrich, Aldridg, Aldrish), Levy of Smithfield, and Penellepy Darling, int. Aug. 12, 1786.

ALDRISH (see Aldrich, Aldridg, Aldridge), Amasa of Mendon, and Uranah Pain, int. Mar. 12, 1781.
Ishmell and Mrs. Simthe Speer, int. Jan. 24, 1775.
Levi Jr. of Mendon, and Mrs. Elisebeth Perry, int. Nov. 11, 1774.

ALEXANDER (see Elexander, Ellexander).

ALLEN, Abigail of Sturbridge, and Hollis Metcalf, int. Apr. 6, 1822.
Amos H., Capt., of Franklin, and Eliza C. [int. omits C.] Patt, May 27, 1835.
Catharine A. and William T. Rand, Apr. 4, 1830.
Clarissa [int. Clarisa] and Leonard Onion, Feb. 19, 1823.
Daniel W. of Mendon, and Myra A. Barber, int. Apr. 25, 1830.
Eliza of Medway, and Ellis Holbrook, int. Mar. 18, 1822.
Ellery of Franklin, and Experience Partridge, int. Oct. 15, 1806.
Harriet and John Field, Feb. 8, 1827.
Keziah and Simon Darling Jr., int. Mar. 23, 1833.
Lydia and Jesse Curtis, int. Nov. 10, 1813.
Mary of Medway, and William Fairbanks, int. Apr. 21, 1844.
Mary Ann of Franklin, and Benjamin Foristall, int. Dec. 20, 1823.
Mary M., 17, d. Daniel and Alma, and Dennis Eames, Dec. 9, 1847.
Simeon of Sturbridge, and Mrs. Sarah Puffer, int. Mar. 16, 1766.
William F. of Mendon, and Polley Bates, Jan. 28, 1810.

AMES (see Eames), Ezekiel H. and Mary Lowe, int. July 10, 1814.

ANDERSON, Allen of Pawtucket, and Naomi Fairbanks, Aug. 3, 1844.

APGAR, Mahlon of N. Y. [int. of New York City, N. Y.], and Maria H. Barney, Sept. 4, 1842.

ARMINGTON, Angeline H., 20, d. Geo[rge] W. and Lydia, and Lucius B. Darling, Nov. 4, 1847.

George W. Jr. of N. Providence, R. I., and Julia Ann Bosworth, Mar. 24, 1842.*

ARMITAGE, Mary Ann and William Field, Aug. 16, 1847.

Matilda and James Shaw, May 3, 1847.

ARNELD (see Arnold), Luke of Smithfield, and Lydia Freeman, int. Nov. 5, 1788.

ARNOLD (see Arneld), Ahab of Smithfield, and Mrs. Rosanna Pickirn [int. Pickring], Dec. 20, 1781.

Alfred, 29, of Washington, D. C., s. William and Hannah, and Mary J. Pickering, Sept. 4, 1849.

Annstiess and Sutton Jilson, int. Mar. 4, 1845.

Anstress and Abraham Fletcher, int. Mar. 7, 1830.

Catharine P. of Charlestown, and Rev. Joseph T. Massey, int. July 17, 1836.

Celia Ann of Mendon, and John Smith, Sept. 5, 1830.

Daniel of Cumberland, Providence Co., R. I., and [int. adds Mrs.] Jerusha Cook, Dec. 28, 1798.

Daniel Jr. and Jane Martin, int. Apr. 27, 1834.

Danill Jr. and Miranda Thayer, int. Aug. 26, 1827.

Elisabeth, Mrs., of Smithfild, and Elkanah Speah, int. Sept. 18, 1779.

Eunice, Mrs., and Nethaniel Scott, int. May 11, 1775.

Jacob and Sally Pain, Sept. 12, 1811.

John and Mrs. Mary Scott, int. May 11, 1775.

John and Sena Morey, int. June 29, 1806.

Lewis B. of Cumberland, R. I., and Marietta Kelley, int. Dec. 24, 1837.

Mary, Mrs., and David Tocker, int. Feb. 25, 1770.

Mary, Mrs., and David Perry, int. Feb. 14, 1780.

Mary and Ahaz Aldrich, June 4, 1821.

Nathan of Cumberland, and Mrs. Ester [int. Esther] Darling, Nov. 30, 1786.

Nathan Jr. and Maria G. Bright, int. Jan. 13, 1839.

Orinda and Adams J. Barber, int. Aug. 8, 1823.

Permelia and Justus Aldrich, int. Dec. 12, 1830.

Sarah, Mrs., and David Scott Jr., int. Apr. 21, 1781.

* Intention not recorded.

ATWALL, Saraih and Josiah Cook, int. Nov. 13, 1742.

ATWOOD, Margaret, Mrs., of Mendon, and Isaac Thayer, int. Sept. 23, 1760.
Shadrach, Dr., and Mrs. Ruth M. Pond, int. Nov. 11, 1832.

AUSTIN, Moody and Ann Carter, int. Nov. 18, 1820.

AVERRY, Joseph of Uxbridge, and Abigal Marsh, int. Jan. 21, 1742-3.

AYERS, Sally Ames of Mendon, and David Adams, Apr. 19, 1827.

BABCOCK, Philinda M. and Oliver W. Adams, Aug. 1, 1838.

BACON, Harriet H. of Barre, and Charles Russell, int. Sept. 23, 1838.
James [int. Ens., of Milford] and Mary A. Rhodes [int. Rhoades], Oct. 17, 1837.

BACTHELDER (see Batchelder), Tappan H. of Holliston, and Clarrissa Holbrook, int. Apr. 26, 1840.

BAILEY (see Bayley), Remember of Franklin, and Oliver Pond, June 2, 1807.*

BAITS (see Bates), Elisabath of Smethfell, and Peter Cook, int. Aug. 29, 1741.

BAKER, Joel Jr., 21, of Boston, s. Joel and Diantha A., and Lucy A. Hixon, May 30, 1848.

BALCOM (see Belcom, Bolcom).

BALLEW (see Ballou, Ballow, Belew, Bellew, Bellou, Bellow, Belu, Blew), Stephen of Cumberland, and Mrs. Anna Metcalf, Sept. 11, 1774.

BALLOU (see Ballew, Ballow, Belew, Bellew, Bellou, Bellow, Belu, Blew), Frances A. [of] Milford, and Samuel S. Scammell, int. Nov. 2, 1845.
Hannah [int. Ballow] and Smith Bates, Feb. 5, 1818.
Lorinda, Mrs. [int. omits Mrs.], and Moses Daniels Jr., May 25, 1824.
Mary of Wrentham, and Ahimaaz Darling, int. Sept. 7, 1800.
Rena (B[a]llou) and Clark Jillson, int. Mar. 5, 1815.

* Intention not recorded.

BELLINGHAM MARRIAGES.

BALLOW (see Ballew, Ballou, Belew, Bellew, Bellou, Bellow, Belu, Blew), Parlay, Mrs., of Cumberland, and Nahum Bates, int. May 14, 1797.

BANGS, Maria and Emory Cook, May 10, 1829.

BARBER, Adams J. and Orinda Arnold, int. Aug. 8, 1823.
Bathsheba A. and Capt. Stephen Benedict, Aug. 9, 1830.
Calvin and Chloe Mash, int. Sept. 21, 1800.
Calvin Jr. and Sylvia Kelly, int. Mar. 21, 1830.
Chloe M. and William H. Cumstock, May 11, 1831.
Elial, Lt., and Hannah Thayer, int. Aug. 26, 1827.
Harriet A. of Medway, and Anson B. Davis, int. Nov. 5, 1843.
Mary D. and Joseph Miller, int. Nov. 2, 1834.
Myra A. and Daniel W. Allen, int. Apr. 25, 1830.

BARKLEY, Ellen of Mendon, and George Bates, Apr. 12, 1835.*

BARNEY, Benajah and Caroline Myrtilla Bliss, int. Sept. 6, 1828.
Charlotte of Wrentham, and Avery Cook, Jan. 3, 1819.*
Hannah and Avery Cook, Nov. 26, 1812.
Maria H. and Mahlon Apgar, Sept. 4, 1842.
Mary Ann and William W. Thomas, Nov. 27, 1828.
Simeon of Rehoboth, and Mary Hall, Mar. 3, 1805.

BARRON, Ruth of Providence, R. I., and Thaddeus Cook, int. Apr. 3, 1842.

BARTELETT (see Bartlet, Bartlett), Bani of Cumberland, and Philadelphia Pickering, int. Dec. 6, 1801.

BARTLET (see Bartelett, Bartlett), Jacob and Charity Inmun, int. Aug. 29, 1741.
Phila of Cumberland, R. I., and Harvey Scott, int. Aug. 1, 1805.

BARTLETT (see Bartelett, Bartlet), Eber of Cumberland, and Patience Scott, int. Oct. 12, 1810.

BARTON, Francis of Wrentham, and Sarah J. Fairbanks, int. Mar. 30, 1845.
John N. of Medway, and Nancy Fairbanks, int. Jan. 12, 1845.

BASS, Hannah, Mrs., and Samuel Penniman Jr., Apr. 28, 1796.
Polly and Nathan Ellis, int. Apr. 26, 1801.

* Intention not recorded.

BATCHELDER (see Bacthelder), Lorra S. of Holliston, and Naham L. Holbrook, int. Aug. 27, 1848.
BATES (see Baits), Abigail and Martin Rockwood, Mar. 29, 1810.
Adaline S. and Avery P. Wheeler, int. Feb. 10, 1828.
Albert G. of Smithfield, R. I., and Maria Burr, Dec. 1, 1836.
Allice of Thompson, Conn., and Abial J. Town, int. Feb. 21, 1819.
Andrew A. and Abigail L. Thayer, Nov. 27, 1834.
Asa and Mrs. Cumfort Haven, int. Feb. 21, 1796.
Cynthia A. and Edward C. Craig, May 24, 1832, in Franklin.
Electa B. and Harvey D. Walker, Apr. 2, 1844.
Eli and Mrs. Abigail Kelly, Oct. 9, 1792.
Elijah and Huldah Legg, int. Jan. 27, 1799.
Elijah and Sarah Albee, int. Apr. 9, 1809.
Elisabeth and Alpheus Thayer, Aug. 16, 1787.
Ezekiel and [int. adds Mrs.] Abigail Legg, Apr. 9, 1767.
Ezekiel and Levina Smith [int. adds wid.], Apr. 25, 1799.
Ezekiel Jr. and Cyrena Thayer, int. Apr. 15, 1804.
Ezekiel Jr. and Sabra Adams, May 30, 1816.
Francis D. [int. of Medway] and Julia A. Mowry, Mar. 20, 1839.
Francis D., widr. [int. Esq., omits widr.], 35, s. Elijah and Sarah, and Hannah E. Fairbanks, wid. [int. Mrs., omits wid.], Apr. 3, 1849.
George of Mendon, and Ellen Barkley, Apr. 12, 1835.*
Hannah, Mrs., and Seth Holbrook 2d, Jan. 21, 1798.
Joanna and Varnum J. [int. James] Bates, Dec. 9, 1821.
John and Mrs. Margeret [int. Margret] Smith, Apr. 6, 1797.
John Jr. and Sarah P. Fisher, Oct. 14, 1830.
Joseph and Mrs. Sarah Hayward, int. Oct. 15, 1762.
Julia of Mendon, and Pelletiah Smith Jr., int. July 8, 1827.
Laban Jr. and Chloe Sampson, int. Sept. 9, 1804.
Laban of Mendon, and Mary B. Thayer, Nov. 24, 1825.
Lavina [int. Levina] and George W. Blake, Nov. 7, 1833.
Lorinda and Arnold Bellou, Apr. 11, 1816.
Louisa Ann and Augustus Ellis, Sept. 17, 1834.
Lucretia and Harris [int. Horris] Cook, Oct. 29, 1801.
Lucrette, Mrs., of Mendon, and Elisha Burr, int. Sept. 1, 1765.
Margaret and Dexter Daniels, Dec. 9, 1828.
Mary of Mendon, and Peter Holbrook [int. Holbrok], Apr. 26, 1787.
Mary and Luther Chamberlain, Oct. 23, 1828.

* Intention not recorded.

BATES, Mary A. and Thomas J. Scott, int. Aug. 19, 1827.
Mellen B. and Mary A. Hough, Nov. 9, 1836.
Nahum and Mrs. Parlay Ballow, int. May 14, 1797.
Olive and Aquila Cook, Sept. 20, 1820.
Ollive and Nathan Kelley, int. Apr. 4, 1803.
Otis and Electa Brown, int. Mar. 14, 1806.
Peletiah S. and Caroline B. Rockwood, May 10, 1832, in Franklin.
Perley B. of Mendon, and Alanson Thayer, Mar. 2, 1831.*
Peter and Sybel Hill, int. Oct. 2, 1803.
Polley and William F. Allen, Jan. 28, 1810.
Rhoda and Silas Kenney, Dec. 6, 1824.
Rhoda T., 30, d. Otis and Electa of Boston, and Rev. James Brown, Sept. 25, 1848.
Sally, Mrs., of Mendon, and Nathan Holbrook, May 29, 1793.
Sarah, Mrs., and Benjamin Hall, int. Jan. 22, 1797.
Sena and Stephen Cook, Oct. 20, 1811.
Simon and Jerusha Fairbank, int. Apr. 7, 1805.
Smith and Hannah Ballou [int. Ballow], Feb. 5, 1818.
Sullivan and Sarah A. Burton, int. Dec. 31, 1832.
Varnum J. [int. James] of Mendon, and Joanna Bates, Dec. 9, 1821.
Whitman of Milford, and Lucy Ann Clark, Dec. 13, 1827.

BAXTER, Delivernce and Joseph Pratt Jr., int. Sept. 26, 1761.
Jemima and Jonathan Thomson Jr., Apr. 10, 1754, in Mendon.
Ruth and John Clark, int. Dec. 14, 1751.

BAYLEY (see Bailey), James of Stougthton [int. Stoughton], and Mrs. Susana [int. Susanna] Phillips, June 4, 1760.

BEALS, Olive and Jacob St[e]vens, int. Aug. 23, 1823.

BEASLEY, Edward [int. Beazley] of Franklin, and Charlottee Smith, Feb. 15, 1809.

BELCHER (see Belsher), Bildad B. of Springfield, and Adelphia F. White, int. Dec. 18, 1835.
David and Mrs. Rachel Burr, int. June 7, 1777.

BELCOM (see Bolcom), Allythirai of Duglass, and Adml. ——— Albee, int. Aug. 6, 1815.

BELEW (see Ballew, Ballou, Ballow, Bellew, Bellou, Bellow, Belu, Blew), Hannah of Rantham, and Daved Cook, int. Dec. 4, 1742.

* Intention not recorded.

BELLEW (see Ballew, Ballou, Ballow, Belew, Bellou, Bellow, Belu, Blew), Olive of Wrentham, and Daniel Sayles, int. Apr. 13, 1812.

Sarah, Mrs. (Bllw), and Samuel Pickring, int. Nov. 21, 1758.

BELLOU (see Ballew, Ballou, Ballow, Belew, Bellew, Bellow, Belu, Blew), Alden and Rena Darling, int. Sept. 1, 1816.

Arnold of Cumberland, and Lorinda Bates, Apr. 11, 1816.

Ezekiel and Nella Parkhurst, int. Oct. 1, 1809.

William Jr. of Cumberland, and Rebeckah Wilber, int. Oct. 15, 1809.

BELLOW (see Ballew, Ballou, Ballow, Belew, Bellew, Bellou, Belu, Blew), Jesse of Wrentham, and Mrs. Elisabeth Pitts, int. Dec. 2, 1775.

Selah, Mrs., of Cumberland, and Saul Scott, int. Apr. 19, 1781.

Willard and Sena Gaskin, int. Mar. 10, 1816.

BELSHER (see Belcher), Elisabeth, Mrs., of Wrentham, and Lt. Aaron Holbrook, int. Oct. 11, 1783.

BELU (see Ballew, Ballou, Ballow, Belew, Bellew, Bellou, Bellow, Blew), Mathar of Ranthan, and Nathanaiel Cook, int. Dec. 26, 1741.

BEMDOR, Jack [int. Bembo] and Cloe Meret [int. Chloe Merrite] [negroes], Sept. 26, 1777.

BEMIS (see Bemiss), Lydia and Harvey Grant, int. Sept. 20, 1835.

BEMISS (see Bemis), Theadore S. and Persis Hill, int. Nov. 11, 1838.

BENEDICT, David H. of Pawtucket, R. I., and Olive A. Smith, Mar. 20, 1839.

Stephen, Capt., of Smithfield, R. I., and Bathsheba A. Barber, Aug. 9, 1830.

Thomas S. of Smithfield, R.I., and Ruth A. Smith, Apr. 15, 1835.

BENNETT, Achsah of Mendon, and Isaac L. Cobbett, May 27, 1830.

BENSON, Stephen of Mendon, and Mrs. Mary Holbrook, int. Sept. 16, 1764.

BENT, Roswell and Triphena Adams, Apr. 6, 1842.

BERT, Grace, Mrs., and Joseph Fairbanks, int. Oct. 17 1826.

BILLINGS, William, s. William, and [int. adds Mrs.] Esther Pickering [int. Pickring], Aug. 20, 1789.

BLAKE, Asa and Mrs. Hannah Thayer, int. May 14, 1769.
Chloe of Medway, and Alfred Patridge, int. Mar. 15, 1840.
Eunice, Mrs., of Wrentham, and David Thomson, July 23, 1776.
George W. of Franklin, and Lavina [int. Levina] Bates, Nov. 7, 1833.
Julia Ann and Sewall Smith, int. Aug. 25, 1839.
Lucy, Mrs., of Wrentham, and David Thompson, int. Oct. 23, 1762.
Moley, Mrs., of Uxbridge, and Daniel Bullard, int. Apr. 20, 1776.
Samuel of Wrentham, and Mary Phillips, int. Jan. 2, 1801.

BLEW (see Ballew, Ballou, Ballow, Belew, Bellew, Bellou, Bellow, Belu), Esther of Cumberland, and James Willson, int. July 26, 1754.
Jerusha, Mrs., of Cumberland, and Ezekiel Cook, int. Sept. 27, 1763.
Mary, Mrs., of Cumberland, and Job Darling, int. Dec. 1, 1756.
Priscillia of Cumberland, and William Cook, int. Nov. 10, 1753.

BLINN, Adaline E., 21, d. John and Polly, and William C. Bowers, Sept. 10, 1846.

BLISS, Caroline Myrtilla of Rehoboth, and Benajah Barney, int. Sept. 6, 1828.

BLOOD, Abigail, Mrs., and Elnathan Wight, int. July 12, 1754.
Joseph and Abigal Thompson, Dec. 11, 1735.*
Mary and Samuel Partraidge, Dec. 28, 1736.*
Nathanail of Oxford, and Ruth Hall, int. Nov. 13, 1742.

BOLCOM (see Belcom), Saraih of Uxbridge, and Joseph Thayar, int. Feb. 25, 1741.

BOLSTER (see Boulster).

BOSWORTH (see Bozworth), George W., Rev. [int. omits Rev.], of Medford, and Louisa M. Messenger, Jan. 5, 1842.
Julia A. L. and Ethan Whitney, Nov. 24, 1842.
Julia Ann of Milford, and George W. Armington Jr., Mar. 24, 1842.*
Nathaniel and Mary E. Petter, int. Sept. 24, 1848.

* Intention not recorded.

BOSWORTH, Ruth and Charles A. Wales, int. Apr. 27, 1846.
Statia and Abigail Walker, int. Mar. 3, 1816.
BOULSTER, Daniel of Smithfield, R. I., and Susan E. Thayer, int. Oct. 12, 1845.
BOWERS, Hannah and Silas Stevens, int. Aug. 20, 1837.
William C., 22, s. William and Hannah, and Adaline E. Blinn, Sept. 10, 1846.
BOYDE, Frances, Mrs., of Wrentham, and John Scott, int. July 28, 1765.
BOYLE, Susan of Sukonk, and George Halyburton, int. Mar. 19, 1820.
BOZE, Ruth of Mendon, and Nathaniell Jillson, Aug. 20, 1728, in Providences.*
BOZWORTH (see Bosworth), Ichabod and Mrs. Chloe Cook, int. July 9, 1769.
Joanna, Mrs., of Cumberland, and Silvanus Scott, int. July 10, 1754.
Jonathan [int. Borzwoth] and Susanna Chillson [int. Susannah Chilson], May 9, 1744, in Wrentham.
Philadelpha and Mason Wales, Feb. 25, 1821.*
Sarah, Mrs. [int. Bosworth], and Benjamin Thayer, Oct. 29, 1767.
Stacy and Mrs. Priscilla Lane, int. Sept. 2, 1770.

BRADFORD, Lewis H. of Providence, R. I., and Susan Ann Thayer, Nov. 28, 1830.

BRADLEY, Sylvia Ann, Mrs., of Medway, and Isaac Burdick, int. Nov. 26, 1843.

BRALE (see Braley), Margret, Mrs., of Darthmoth, and Joseph Killey, int. Feb. 2, 1782.

BRALEY (see Brale), Deborah, Mrs., of Franklin, and Selvenus Scott, int. Nov. 23, 1785.
Ezekiel and Lois Walker, int. Nov. 26, 1805.
Gibbs of Holliston, and Levina Lazell, int. Mar. 7, 1833.

BRATTLE, Dick and Lucy Rose, int. Feb. 25, 1785.

BRIDGE, Mary [int. adds Mrs.] of Medway, and John Combs, Apr. 8, 1756.

* Intention not recorded.

BRIGHT, Maria G. of Medway, and Nathan Arnold Jr., int. Jan. 13, 1839.

BROOKS, Rebekah of Walpole, and Ziba Thomson, int. June 4, 1820.

BROWN, Abby of Leicester, and Charles Dayton, int. Dec. 11, 1836.
Amy, "formerly" of Cumberland, and Samuel Savage, int. Nov. 11, 1752.
Electa and Otis Bates, int. Mar. 14, 1806.
Eliza and Seneca Burr, int. June 1, 1828.
James, Rev., 25, of Abington, Pa., s. Caleb and Pheba A., and Rhoda T. Bates, Sept. 25, 1848.
Luci and Joseph Scott, int. Dec. 23, 1752.
Mary B. of Littleton, and Moses F. Greenwood, int. Nov. 12, 1848.
Rhoda and Willard Thayer, May 26, 1813.
Sarah of Attleberough, and Banfield Capron, int. Feb. 2, 1744-5.

BRUCE, Cheselton E. of Medway, and Mrs. Malena Fuller, int. Mar. 5, 1836.

BRYANT, Adeline C. and James Butters, int. Oct. 25, 1840.
Phillip C. of Smithfield, R. I., and Sarah V. Sumner, July 9, 1829.

BUCK, Levinia and Ora Perkins, Apr. 7, 1839.

BUFFAM (see Buffum), Benj[ami]n of Smithfield, and Mrs. Rhoda Scott, int. Feb. 13, 1784.

BUFFUM (see Buffam), Sarah G. of Fall River, and Hon. Nathaniel B. Burdon, Feb. 12, 1843, in Fall River.*

BULLARD, Adaline of Holliston, and Timothy Whiting Jr., int. Apr. 20, 1828.
Bethsheba [int. Bashaba] and Philo Thayer, Aug. 22, 1799.
Daniel and Mrs. Deborah Albee, int. Oct. 16, 1774.
Daniel and Mrs. Moley Blake, int. Apr. 20, 1776.
Daniel and Mrs. Mary Wheloch, int. Sept. 8, 1781.
Daniel and Mary Torry, int. Mar. 13, 1808.
Deborah, Mrs., of Holliston, and Matthew Metcalf, int. Aug. 16, 1767.
Ellis [int. adds R.] and Olive Burr, Sept. 26, 1833.
Ellis and Cynthia Burr, Jan. 1, 1837.

* Intention not recorded.

BULLARD, Fisher (see Fisher Mullard).
Joshua and Mrs. Bethiah Taft, int. Mar. 2, 1782.
Julia of Mendon, and Marvelous Thayer, Mar. 29, 1810.
Leonard P. and Elizabeth P. Adams, May 26, 1842.
Liberty of Medway, and Hannah Holbrook, int. Feb. 25, 1810.
Otis and Polly Pierce, int. Mar. 1, 1821.
Polly and Allen Thayer, Oct. 9, 1806.
Wheelock and Sally Gould, int. Mar. 14, 1804.

BURCHARD, Debias and Ruth Lawton, ——— [rec. before Apr. 27, 1829] [int. Feb. 8, 1829].

BURDICH (see Burdick), Isaac [int. Burdick] of Milford, and Paulina Burr, Nov. 3, 1833.

BURDICK (see Burdich), Isaac and Mrs. Sylvia Ann Bradley, int. Nov. 26, 1843.

BURDON (see Burton), Nathaniel B., Hon., of Fall River, and Sarah G. Buffum, Feb. 12, 1843, in Fall River.*

BURGESS, Charlotte B. and Stephen A. Coombs, int. Apr. 13, 1828.

BURLINGAME, Horrace of Mendon, and Polly Chase, Oct. 11, 1838.

BURNHAM, Andrew of Cumberland, R. I., and Margaret Hitchcock, int. Mar. 6, 1837.

BURR, Abby S. and James P. Thayer, Jan. 5, 1843.
Asa 2d and Polly Ellis, int. Mar. 29, 1801.
Asa and Mary Partridge, int. Apr. 7, 1805.
Asa and Mrs. Polly M. Rice, int. Jan. 14, 1832.
Cynthia and Ellis Bullard, Jan. 1, 1837.
Electa and John M. Cutler, Oct. 21, 1830.
Elisha and Mrs. Lucrette Bates, int. Sept. 1, 1765.
Elisha Jr. and Electa Foristoll, int. Aug. 4, 1803.
Emeline, 27, d. Elisha and Electa, and Preston M. Wood, Feb. 7, 1847.
Ezekiel P., 28, of Mendon, s. Ezekiel and Esther, and Marian C. Smith, Oct. 24, 1849.*
Hannah E. and Rufus Fairbanks, int. Oct. 15, 1836.
Julia A., 22, d. Laban and Maria, and Varnum B. Rockwood, June 1, 1848.
Laban and Nabby [int. Naby] Smith, Mar. 31, 1814.

* Intention not recorded.

BELLINGHAM MARRIAGES. 93

BURR, Laban and Maria Green, int. Aug. 19, 1821.
Liberty and Orrilla Daniels, int. Sept. 16, 1827.
Lucretia and Amos Holbrook, Dec. 1, 1808.
Lucy, wid. [int. Mrs., omits wid.], 29, d. John Chickering and Abagail, and William Grant, Nov. 13, 1844.
Marcus and Love Tibbitts, int. Mar. 10, 1844.
Maria and Albert G. Bates, Dec. 1, 1836.
Olive, Mrs., and Stephen Metcalf Jr., Apr. 26, 1796.
Olive and Ellis [int. adds R.] Bullard, Sept. 26, 1833.
Paulina and Isaac Burdich [int. Burdick], Nov. 3, 1833.
Polly S. and Jonathan V. Thurston, Feb. 20, 1844.
Rachel, Mrs., of Hingham, and David Belcher, int. June 7, 1777.
Sarah, Mrs., and Samuel Darling [int. Jr.], Oct. 31, 1782.
Sarah and Eleazer Ware, May 21, 1807.
Seneca and Eliza Brown, int. June 1, 1828.
Seneca and Lucy Chickering, Apr. 30, 1839.
Sophia and George Edwards, int. Aug. 25, 1828.

BURT (see Bert).

BURTON (see Burdon), Sarah A. of Pawtucket, R. I., and Sullivan Bates, int. Dec. 31, 1832.

BUTTERS, James of Bristol, N. H., and Adeline C. Bryant, int. Oct. 25, 1840.

BUTTERWORTH, Elizabeth [int. Elizabath, wid.] and Capt. Japheth Daniels, Dec. 5, 1798.
Ezube [int. Zuba], Mrs., and Luther Ellis, Apr. 15, 1798.
Nathaniel and Elizebath Hayward, int. Aug. 1, 1761.
Nathanie[l] and Mrs. Elisabeth Holbrook, int. Sept. 14, 1782.
Otis and Mrs. Anna Chery, int. Jan. 28, 1798.
Penelibe of Rehobath, and Samuel Darling, int. Sept. 12, 1741.

CAHOON, Europe of Smithfield, R. I., and Walter D. Stowe, int. Apr. 3, 1847.

CAPRING (see Capron), Charles and Mary Scoot, int. Nov. 6, 1742.

CAPRON (see Capring), Banfield and Sarah Brown, int. Feb. 2, 1744-5.
Elisha of Cumberland, R. I., and Nancy Darling, Dec. 29, 1818.
Leah of Cumberland, Providence Co., and Joseph Scott, int. June 2, 1750.

CAPRON, Maranda S. of Cumberland, R. I., and Elisha Scott Jr., int. Feb. 7, 1841.
Oliver of Cumberland, and Mrs. Esther Freeman, int. Apr. 19, 1757.

CARPENTER, Naman of Attleborough, and Sylvia Freeman, Apr. 30, 1837.

CARTER, Ann of Roxbury, and Moody Austin, int. Nov. 18, 1820.
Cephas and Mary Murphy, int. Sept. 3, 1815.

CASS, Jarvis and Rachel C. Cook, Nov. 28, 1839.

CHACE (see Chase), Isable and Seth Hayward, int. Apr. 6, 1800.

CHAFEY, Pattey (Chasey) of Woodstock, Conn., and Thomas Hemingwey, int. Feb. 12, 1809.

CHAMBERLAIN (see Chamberlin), Leonard of Wrentham, Norfolk Co., and Lydia Sheperdson, Oct. 9, 1823.*
Luther of Providence, R. I., and Mary Bates, Oct. 23, 1828.
Malinda and John Jones, int. July 24, 1821.

CHAMBERLIN (see Chamberlain), Susanna [int. Chamberlain] and Nahum Adams, Apr. 15, 1821.

CHAPEN (see Chapin), Maria and Enoch P. Hastings, Apr. 17, 1839.
Rachel, Mrs., and Joshua Legg, June 13, 1776.

CHAPIN (see Chapen), Daniel of Mendon, and Abigail Corbitt, int. Mar. 30, 1754.
Japheth and Patience Hayward, int. June 24, 1749.
Marcy, Mrs., and Samuel Craggin, Oct. 19, 1769.

CHASE (see Chace), Abigail [int. Chach] and Giles M. Curliff [int. Cunliff], May 1, 1837.
Allen and Mrs. Lidea [int. Lidia] Pratt, May 15, 1796.
Burgess T., widr. [int. omits widr.], 59, and Julia A. Stearns, wid. [int. omits wid.], Aug. 13, 1844.
Joseph and Ann Delight, int. Nov. 20, 1830.
Polly and Horrace Burlingame, Oct. 11, 1838.

CHECKERING (see Chickering), Abigail R. of District of Dover, and Manning Thayer, int. Mar. 16, 1822.

* Intention not recorded.

BELLINGHAM MARRIAGES. 95

CHENEY (see Chinery), Hannah [int. Cheeney], Mrs., of Medfield, and Daniel Wedge, Mar. 14, 1774.

CHERY, Anna, Mrs., of Milford, and Otis Butterworth, int. Jan. 28, 1798.

CHICKERING (see Checkering), Lucy and Seneca Burr, Apr. 30, 1839.
Mary W. of Dover, and Eliab Wight Jr., int. Apr. 22, 1827.

CHILLSON (see Chilson), Elisabeth and John Jones Jr. [int. omits Jr.], May 18, 1749.
John Jr. and Elmira Cook, int. Nov. 29, 1823.
Joseph and Mercey Shutleworth [int. Mercy Shuttleworth], Nov. 23, 1744.
Joseph and Lydia Pratt, Nov. 15, 1747 [int. Sept. 12, 1749, *sic*].
Susanna [int. Susannah Chilson] and Jonathan Bozworth [int. Borzwoth], May 9, 1744, in Wrentham.

CHILSON (see Chillson), Abigail and Stephen Otis Cook, Dec. 6, 1837.
Anna and Joseph Rockwood, int. Feb. 12, 1804.
Asa and Amy Ann Wood, int. Oct. 22, 1843.
Ichabod and Deborah Holbrook, May 8, 1808.
John and Mrs. Abigal [int. Abigial] Draper, Jan. 3, 1782.
John D. and Sabrina E. Tingley, int. Mar. 13, 1849.
Jonathan and Celicia Ann Thayer, Apr. 25, 1834.
Joseph and Mrs. Hannah Pratt, Jan. 25, 1786.
Joshua and Mrs. Margret Wright. Sept. 4, 1783.
Joshua Jr. [int. Chillson] and Levi [int. Levina] Scott, Apr. 3, 1831.
Levi [int. Chillson] and Betsey [int. Betsy] Pratt, Aug. 12, 1823.
Levi and Eliza Streeter, int. Nov. 27, 1834.
Lydia and Amaziah [int. Ameziah] Cushman, May 19, 1816.
Margret and Ahimaaz Darling Jr., int. Apr. 13, 1828.
Martha W. and William E. Hubbard, int. Sept. 20, 1846.
Martin and Levina Scott, Jan. 3, 1819.
Mary, Mrs., and Amos Thomson, Dec. 14, 1785.
Nabby and Capt. [int. omits Capt.] Amos Hill, Dec. 8, 1816.
Nathan and Susanna R. Lewett, int. Oct. 5, 1832.
Orrin and Diadama Cook, int. Feb. 12, 1825.
Paul and Mary Thayer, int. Mar. 9, 1828.
Willard and Huldah Thayer, int. Mar. 25, 1826.

CHINERY (see Cheney), Betsey of Medfield, and Joseph Greenwood, int. Apr. 11, 1813.

CLAFING (see Claflin), Elisebath of Hopkinston, and John Marsh, int. July 4, 1743.

CLAFLIN (see Clafing), Anna of Holliston, and Peter Adams, int. Mar. 1, 1814.

CLARK (see Clerk), Alfred and Polly Wright, Jan. 1, 1840.
Celina, Mrs., of Wrentham, and Benjamin Darling, int. Jan. 30, 1794.
Edy of Cumberland, and Mrs. Moley Draper, int. Sept. 27, 1790.
Elisabeth, Mrs., and Samuel Treeman [Freeman], int. Sept. 22, 1771.
Hellen of Medway, and Thomas D. Richards, int. Aug. 6, 1843.
Joel J. [int. omits J., of Holliston] and Almira E. [int. A.] Forristall, Apr. 22, 1841.
John of Wrentham, and Ruth Baxter, int. Dec. 14, 1751.
John and [int. adds Mrs.] Olive Adams, July 15, 1798.
Lucy Ann and Whitman Bates, Dec. 13, 1827.
Mary S. F., 23, d. Benj[amin] and Lucy, and Albert G. Slocum [int. Slocom], Oct. 20, 1844.
Mercy and Samuel Adams Jr., Apr. 16, 1809.
Paul of Franklin, and Phebe [int. Mrs. Pheba] Penniman, Nov. 30, 1797.
Rachel, Mrs., of Franklin, and Luther Cobb, May 7, 1795.
Rachel [int. Rachael] and Anson Cook, Apr. 20, 1816 [int. Mar. 30, 1817, *sic*].
Rhoda of Sharon, and Fisher Mullard [? Bullard], int. Sept. 6, 1805.
William A. and Mary M. Cook, int. Aug. 29, 1847.

CLERK (see Clark), Hannah, Mrs., of Midway, and John Metcalf Jr., int. Dec. 17, 1785.

COBB, Abigail Lewis of Smithfield, and Peter Daubikin, int. Dec. 25, 1813.
Claracy [int. Clarisse], Mrs., and Thomson Thayer, Mar. 23, 1795.
Luther and Mrs. Rachel Clark, May 7, 1795.
Samuel [int. adds Capt.] of Milford, and [int. adds Mrs.] Keziah Darling, June 3, 1798.
Samuel and Margaret Hayward, int. Jan. 10, 1804.

COBBETT (see Corbett, Corbitt), Isaac L. and Achsah Bennett, May 27, 1830.

COBURN (see Colburn), Levi P. of Hopkinton, and Mary Ann Darling, Nov. 24, 1842.

COLBURN (see Coburn), Angeline A. and Charles Dewing, int. Feb. 4, 1849.
Harriet [int. Harriett] Ellis of Dedham, and [int. adds Rev.] Edward Freeman, Nov. 27, 1834, in Dedham.
Lucretia [int. Colbern] and John Gardner Gilbert, Nov. 8, 1837.
Mariam L. of Milford, and George Law, int. Aug. 8, 1849.

COLSTON (see Colstone), George and Nancy Aldrich, int. Feb. 6, 1802.
William [int. Colson] and Mrs. Mara Shearman, May 20, 1779.

COLSTONE (see Colston), William and Mrs. Sarah Liscomb, int. Aug. 1, 1783.

COLVIN, Mark and Maryann Rawson, int. Sept. 26, 1819.

COMBES (see Combs, Coombs), John Jr. [int. Combs] and Mary Partridge, wid., Apr. 26, 1780.
Sally, Mrs. [int. Mrs. Salley Combs], and Aaron Hill, Dec. 21, 1780.

COMBS (see Combes, Coombs), Elizabeth and Gordin Williams, int. Sept. 13, 1801.
John and [int. adds Mrs.] Mary Bridge, Apr. 8, 1756.
Mary and Elijah Dewing Jr., July 5, 1820.
Miletiah and Elisha Tambling, int. Jan. 2, 1803.
Rufus and Betsy Ide, int. Jan. 4, 1805.
Valentine R. [int. Coombs, of Grafton] and Clarissa [int. Clarrasa] Thayer, Nov. 7, 1826.

CONDEN, Ruth, Mrs., and John Wales, June 9, 1794.

COOK (see Cooke), Abigail and Joseph Thayer, int. Dec. 14, 1751.
Abijah and Roxanna Holbrook, Apr. 9, 1812.
Abijah and Mrs. Roxanna Penniman, int. Nov. 5, 1843.
Abner of Cumberland, and Mrs. Rhoda Thompson, int. Mar. 7, 1757.
Abner Jr. of Wrentham, and Julia B. Cook, int. Oct. 5, 1845.
Adeliza and Dexter Whitney, Sept. 26, 1839.
Albert L. and Olive C. Kelley, Nov. 13, 1839, in Uxbridge.
Albinus and Betsey Scott, Mar. 10, 1313 [*sic*, 1813].
Alfred of Franklin, and Mrs. Vienna [int. Viena, omits Mrs.] Taft, Feb. 20, 1825.
Alpha and William B. Darling, int. Jan. 28, 1832.
Amos of Cumberland, Providence Co., R. I., and Olive Darling, Aug. 15, 1799.

COOK, Anna and John Rhodes, int. Nov. 8, 1812.
Anson of Wrentham, and Rachel [int. Rachael] Clark, Apr. 20, 1816 [int. Mar. 30, 1817, sic].
Aquila and Olive Bates, Sept. 20, 1820.
Arial of Mendon, and Mrs. Crusa Cook, int. Jan. 3, 1796.
Avery of Wrentham, and Hannah Barney, Nov. 26, 1812.
Avery of Wrentham, and Charlotte Barney, Jan. 3, 1819.*
Benjamin and Rachael Gaskel, int. Mar. 9, 1817.
Caleb and Provided Gaskill, int. Sept. 15, 1753.
Charles and Zylpha Hunt, int. Oct. 13, 1844.
Chloe, Mrs., of Cumberland, and Ichabod Bozworth, int. July 9, 1769.
Crusa, Mrs., and Arial Cook, int. Jan. 3, 1796.
Daniel and Elisabeth Scott, Dec. 25, 1746.
Daniel Jr. and Mrs. Charlott [int. Cherlotte] Legg, May 22, 1783.
Daved and Hannah Belew, int. Dec. 4, 1742.
David Jr. and Mrs. Susanna Legg, int. Feb. 15, 1777.
David and Mrs. Elona Holbrook, int. May 18, 1798.
David, "M^{r.} or Deac.," and Molly Sybley, int. Dec. 15, 1815.
David and Elmira Smith, int. Oct. 25, 1846.
Diadama and Orrin Chilson, int. Feb. 12, 1825.
Duty and Hama Mowry, int. Mar. 1, 1818.
Elias 2d and Orinda Gaskill, int. July 17, 1824.
Elias Jr. and Henrietta Pain, Sept. 8, 1827.
Elisabeth and Abner Aldrich, int. Nov. 9, 1747.
Elisabeth, Mrs., and Henry [int. Hennery] Holbrook, Dec. 20, 1780.
Elisha and Mrs. Sally King, int. Mar. 12, 1797.
Elizabath of Wrentham, and Silas Jillson, int. Nov. 6, 1808.
Elmira and John Chillson Jr., int. Nov. 29, 1823.
Elmira of Cumberland, R. I., and Lyman Cook, int. Mar. 13, 1829.
Emory and Maria Bangs, May 10, 1829.
Esther and Abel Aldrich, int. Apr. 6, 1802.
Esther and Joel Crooks, Oct. 1, 1826.
Eunice, Mrs., and Reuben Gillson, int. Aug. 26, 1798.
Eunice and Stephen Lewett, int. Aug. 31, 1833.
Ezekiel and Mrs. Jerusha Blew, int. Sept. 27, 1763.
Ezekiel [int. Ezekeiel] Jr. and Mrs. Joanna Pickering [int. Pickren], May 9, 1791.
Fenner and Myranda Thayer, Apr. 2, 1820.
Galen of Franklin, and Sally Pickering, Oct. 17, 1822.
George and Mrs. Phebe Tillson, int. Oct. 11, 1772.

* Intention not recorded.

BELLINGHAM MARRIAGES.

Cook, Harris [int. Horris] of Wrentham, and Lucretia Bates, Oct. 29, 1801.
Henrietta of Wrentham, and John N. Rhoades, int. Sept. 20, 1840.
Jarves of Cumberland, R. I., and Lucy Smith, int. May 17, 1835.
Jemima and Aaron Thayer, Nov. 23, 1738.*
Jerusha [int. adds Mrs.] and Daniel Arnold, Dec. 28, 1798.
Joanna, Mrs., of Cumberland, and John Hall, int. Feb. 27, 1768.
Joanna, Mrs., and Noah Alden Jr., Sept. 21, 1775.
Joanna, Mrs., and Wing Killy, int. May 6, 1792.
John and Mrs. Alce Rockwood, Nov. 26, 1778.
John 2d and Nancy Wight, Aug. 31, 1817.
Josiah and Saraih Atwall, int. Nov. 13, 1742.
Julia B. and Abner Cook Jr., int. Oct. 5, 1845.
Julia M. and Martin Rockwood [int. Jr.], Oct. 23, 1838.
Lealond [int. Lealon] and Sofferly [int. Soffarly] Smith, Nov. 8, 1815.
Leland [int. Lealand] and Lydia Cook, Dec. 6, 1827.
Levi of Cumberland, and Mrs. Rhoda Darling, Oct. 5, 1797.
Levice, Mrs., of Wrentham, and John Darling Jr., int. May 19, 1781.
Levina [int. Lavine], Mrs., of Wrentham, and Robert [int. Robart] Smith Jr., Mar. 7, 1776.
Levina [int. Levine], Mrs., and Joshua Lazdel, Oct. 8, 1778.
Lloyd H. of Milford, and Abby A. Rockwood, int. Nov. 17, 1849.
Lorinda, d. Albinus, and James B. Mason, Oct. 27, 1836.
Lorinda H. of Wrentham, and Amos D. Crooks, int. Oct. 20, 1849.
Louisa Ann and Milton Cook, int. Mar. 28, 1841.
Lucy and Joseph Partridge [int. Parteridge], Mar. 8, 1812.
Lydia and Leland [int. Lealand] Cook, Dec. 6, 1827.
Lyman and Elmira Cook, int. Mar. 13, 1829.
Lyman A. of Cumberland, R. I., and Levina B. Smith, Sept. 22, 1830.
Margery, Mrs., of Mendon, and Job Darling, int. Mar. 15, 1764.
Martha and Roads Grant, int. July 22, 1804.
Mary, Mrs., and John Goins [int. Gowin], June 14, 1786.
Mary and Albert Hill, May 18, 1831.
Mary M. and William A. Clark, int. Aug. 29, 1847.
Mayo and Sarah Smith, June 13, 1820.
Milton of Wrentham, and Louisa Ann Cook, int. Mar. 28, 1841.
Nabby and Savel Metcalf, int. Dec. 15, 1827.
Nancy [int. Nancey] and Elisha Shearman, Feb. 14, 1811.

* Intention not recorded.

Cook, Nancy J. and Daniel T. W. Darling, int. Feb. 14, 1841.
Nathanaiel and Mathar Belu, int. Dec. 26, 1741.
Noah of Cumberland, and Mrs. Patience Upham, Sept. 8, 1791.
Peter and Elisabath Baits, int. Aug. 29, 1741.
Phebe [of] Smithfeld, and Beriah Grant, int. Jan. 10, 1779.
Pliny and Esther Pickering, Sept. 30, 1825.
Rachel and Stephen Holbrook, int. July 17, 1762.
Rachel C. and Jarvis Cass, Nov. 28, 1839.
Reuben and Ester Holbrook, int. Jan. 6, 1802.
Rhoda and Elisha Shearman [int. Sherman], May 28, 1833.
Sally and Willard Wales, Jan. 1, 1812.
Sarah S., wid. [int. Mrs., omits wid.], 45, d. Peletiah Smith and Joannah, and George W. Ray, widr. [int. omits widr.], Nov. 26, 1846.
Seth of Glocester [int. Gloucester], Providence Co., R. I., and Mrs. Uranah [int. Urania] Cook, May 28, 1795.
Seth and Susan Willcox, int. Sept. 26, 1819.
Seviah, Mrs., of Cumberland, and Nethanel Darling, int. Jan. 9, 1792.
Silas of Cumberland, R. I., and Joanna Shearman [int. Sherman], Mar. 26, 1820.
Silas Jr. and Mrs. Patience Shearman [int. wid., omits Mrs.], Jan. 1, 1822.
Silis [int. Siles] of Cumberland, and Mrs. Joanna [int. Joannan] Darling, Oct. 26, 1775.
Sophia M. and Samuel B. Pickering, int. Aug. 25, 1844.
Stephen of Wrentham, and [int. adds Mrs.] Elisabeth Metcalf, Mar. 16, 1758.
Stephen and Mrs. Joanna Scott, Oct. 20, 1768.
Stephen of Wrentham, and Sena Bates, Oct. 20, 1811.
Stephen Otis and Abigail Chilson, Dec. 6, 1837.
Susanna of Wrentham, and Seth Darling, int. Mar. 9, 1800.
Susanna and Henry Hayward, Nov. 23, 1828.
Thaddeus and Ruth Barron, int. Apr. 3, 1842.
Uranah [int. Urania], Mrs., and Seth Cook, May 28, 1795.
Vienna [int. Viena] and Benjamin B. Taft, Aug. 31, 1820.
Walter and Margery Corbett, Nov. 17, 1726.*
Wata and William O. Rhodes, int. Mar. 28, 1841.
Welcom B. and Rhoda Pickering, int. Feb. 8, 1829.
Whipple of Cumberland, and Mrs. Lucy Darling, int. Sept. 18, 1796.
Whitman V. of Franklin, and Ruth W. Paine, int. Nov. 7, 1835.
William and Priscillia Blew, int. Nov. 10, 1753.

* Intention not recorded.

Cook, W[illia]m W. and Eliza E. Kingman, Dec. 29, 1842.
Ziba and Joanna Aldrich, int. Dec. 3, 1787.

COOKE (see Cook), Nancy, Mrs., of Cumberland, and Benj[amin] Darling, int. Mar. 19, 1785.
Nathan A. and Sena A. Cooke, int. Mar. 9, 1845.
Sena A. of Wrentham, and Nathan A. Cooke, int. Mar. 9, 1845.

COOMBS (see Combes, Combs), Amos and Mary Tower, int. Mar. 4, 1833.
Laurinda S. and William Messenger, int. Mar. 30, 1845.
Noah and Catharine Adams, int. Mar. 11, 1838.
Oded, Capt., and Lorinda Stacy, int. Feb. 19, 1837.
Stephen A. and Miriam B. Woolsom, int. May 3, 1825.
Stephen A. and Charlotte B. Burgess, int. Apr. 13, 1828.

CORBETT (see Cobbett, Corbitt), Bethiah, Mrs., and Samuel Scammel, int. Aug. 18, 1759.
Danail and Mary Holbrook, int. Nov. 4, 1741.
Margery and Walter Cook, Nov. 17, 1726.*
Mehitabel, Mrs., of Mendon, and Cornelius Darling, int. Feb. 23, 1766.
Mehittible and Stephen Tenney, Nov. 2, 1737.*
Meletiah, Mrs., and John Mesenger, int. May 6, 1758.

CORBITT (see Cobbett, Corbett), Abigail and Daniel Chapin, int. Mar. 30, 1754.

COVELL, David and Lucy L. Engley, int. Dec. 17, 1835.

CRAGGIN, Samuel of Mendon, and Mrs. Marcy Chapin, Oct. 19, 1769.

CRAIG, Edward C. and Cynthia A. Bates, May 24, 1832, in Franklin.

CROOK (see Crooks), Jeremiah M. and Amy Ann Haskell, int. Mar. 9, 1841.

CROOKS (see Crook), Amos D. and Lorinda H. Cook, int. Oct. 20, 1849.
Jeremiah of Mendon, and Phebe Darling, Dec. 9, 1787.
Jeremiah Jr. and Anna Durffey, int. Oct. 16, 1815.
Joel and Esther Cook, Oct. 1, 1826.
Sally A. and Osborn Jillson, int. Aug. 27, 1846.

* Intention not recorded.

CUMMINS, Elizabeth B. of Medway, and Capt. John C. Hill, int. Sept. 7, 1833.

CUMSTOCK, William H. and Chloe M. Barber, May 11, 1831.

CURLIFF, Giles M. [int. Cunliff] of Cranston, R. I., and Abigail Chase [int. Chach], May 1, 1837.

CURTIS, Calvin of Sharon, and Mrs. Bethiah [int. Bathiah] Foristall, Apr. 25, 1796.
Jesse of Medway, and Lydia Allen, int. Nov. 10, 1813.
Patience and Dexter B. Rice, int. Feb. 10, 1828.
Thaddeus and Vienna Darling, int. May 10, 1818.

CUSHMAN, Amaziah [int. Chushman] of Kingstun, and Mrs. Martha [int. Marthe] Smith, Feb. 28, 1775.
Amaziah [int. Ameziah] and Lydia Chilson, May 19, 1816.
Appollos [int. Apollas] and Susan [int. Susen] Ripley, Feb. 20, 1816 [int. Dec. 26, 1816, *sic*].
Charles F., 21, s. Sabin and Mary, and Olive M. Holbrook, Nov. 22, 1846.
Cyrena and Nathan Place, int. Mar. 3, 1816.
Cyrena and Ellery A. Razy, int. Sept. 8, 1839.
Lydiaett and Joseph Partridge, int. Nov. 6, 1836.
Martin G. and Seripta M. Taft, int. Jan. 7, 1849.
Mathew Smith and Mrs. Cinthia [int. Cynthia] Holbrook, Mar. 24, 1796.
Saban and Mary Thurber, int. Oct. 31, 1819.

CUTLER, Charlotte of Medway, and Willard Thayer, int. Apr. 9, 1820.
John M. of Holliston, and Electa Burr, Oct. 21, 1830.
Lucinda of Medway, and Amos Hill, int. Dec. 8, 1821.

CUTTER, Calista of Temple, N.H., and John Q. Adams, int. May 4, 1834.

DAKIN, James B. and Mary Perkins, May 23, 1833.

DAMAN, Joseph and Hopstill Thayer, int. Apr. 28, 1750.

DANAIELS (see Danels, Daniel, Daniell, Daniels), Marcy of Mendon, and Davaid Pond, Dec. 19, 1740.*

DANELS (see Danaiels, Daniel, Daniell, Daniels), Mary of Mendon, and Eliezer Hayward, Feb. 15, 1732–3.*

* Intention not recorded.

DANIEL (see Danaiels, Danels, Daniell, Daniels), Harriet Lucas of Mendon, and Billings Mann, int. June 22, 1828.

DANIELL (see Danaiels, Danels, Daniel, Daniels), Christopher C. of Milford, and Zilpha T. Smith, int. Oct. 17, 1831.

DANIELS (see Danaiels, Danels, Daniel, Daniell), Absalom, Dr., and Rachel Southwick, int. Aug. 23, 1829.
David of Mendon, and Mrs. Olive Adams, int. Dec. 31, 1770.
Dexter of Providence, R.I., and Margaret Bates, Dec. 9, 1828.
Diana of Mendon, and Wing Kelly, int. Oct. 6, 1799.
Elizabath, wid., of Shearbon, and Lt. Aaron Holbrook, int. July 24, 1813.
Ellis [int. Daniels Ellis] of Barre, and Laura Spear, Nov. 9, 1820.
Huldah, Mrs., of Mendon, and Silis Penniman, int. Mar. 8, 1772.
Japheth of Holiston, and Mrs. Meletiah Hayward, int. July 30, 1763.
Japheth, Capt., of Holliston, and Elizabeth [int. Elizabath, wid.] Butterworth, Dec. 5, 1798.
Lavina, Mrs., of Medway, and Joseph Fairbanks, int. May 6, 1826.
Moses of Medway, and Mrs. Abigail Adams, int. Dec. 14, 1766.
Moses Jr. of Mendon, and Mrs. [int. omits Mrs.] Lorinda Ballou, May 25, 1824.
Orrilla and Liberty Burr, int. Sept. 16, 1827.
Polly [int. Polley] of Mendon, and Aaron Thomson, Jan. 2, 1788.
Salley, wid., of Dedham, and Amasa Foristall, int. May 4, 1822.
Samuel and Mrs. Elisabeth Wiswall, int. Oct. 2, 1760.
Tyler and Patty Wight, Nov. 16, 1815.

DARLIN (see Darling), Mary and Jonthan Draper Jr., May 29, 1728.*

DARLING (see Darlin), Abigail and Jonathan Draper, int. Apr. 11, 1753.
Ahimaaz and Mary Ballou, int. Sept. 7, 1800.
Ahimaaz Jr. and Margret Chilson, int. Apr. 13, 1828.
Barton and Martha W. Paine, int. Mar. 21, 1830.
Barton and Persis Smith, int. Sept. 27, 1835.
Benj[amin] and Mrs. Nancy Cooke, int. Mar. 19, 1785.
Benjamin and Mrs. Celina Clark, int. Jan. 30, 1794.
Collins C., 32, of Medway, s. Julia of Medway, and Mariam [int. Meriam] P. Thayer, May 29, 1845.
Cornelius and Mrs. Mehitabel Corbett, int. Feb. 23, 1766.

* Intention not recorded.

BELLINGHAM MARRIAGES.

DARLING, Daniel T. W. and Nancy J. Cook, int. Feb. 14, 1841.
Elesibath and Pelletiah Darling, int. Nov. 4, 1743.
Enoch and Lois Thomson, int. Mar. 2, 1750–1.
Ester [int. Esther], Mrs., and Nathan Arnold, Nov. 30, 1786.
Esther and Stephen Sayles, Jan. 11, 1810.
George and Abigail L.' Rockwood, int. Mar. 13, 1836.
Hannah, Mrs., and Daniel [int. David] Jones, June 30, 1796.
Jefferson B. and Joanna Smith, May 27, 1823.
Jerusha, Mrs., and Peter Darling Jr., Jan. 1, 1778.
Joanna [int. Joannan], Mrs., and Silis [int. Siles] Cook, Oct. 26, 1775.
Job and Mrs. Mary Blew, int. Dec. 1, 1756.
Job and Mrs. Margery Cook, int. Mar. 15, 1764.
John and Mrs. Ann Jillson, int. Nov. 7, 1755.
John Jr. and Mrs. Levice Cook, int. May 19, 1781.
Joshua and Martha Wilson, int. Feb. 26, 1762.
Kezia, Mrs., and Richard Darling, int. Jan. 9, 1792.
Keziah [int. adds Mrs.] and [int. adds Capt.] Samuel Cobb, June 3, 1798.
Keziah and Charles S. Landes, int. Oct. 1, 1826.
Lucius B., 20, s. Samuel and Margaret, and Angeline H. Armington, Nov. 4, 1847.
Lucy, Mrs., and Whipple Cook, int. Sept. 18, 1796.
Margeret and Charles W. Tingley, Dec. 24, 1837.
Mariah of Uxbridge, and Leonard White, int. Jan. 2, 1836.
Martha and John Sayles, May 28, 1817.
Mary and Enuch Hill, int. Dec. 26, 1747.
Mary, Mrs., and John Herskal, int. May 19, 1780.
Mary Ann and Levi P. Coburn, Nov. 24, 1842.
Milletiah and Levi Smith, Jan. 14, 1807.
Moses of Cumberland, and Rachel Darling, int. May 11, 1754.
Nancy and Elisha Capron, Dec. 29, 1818.
Nethanel and Mrs. Seviah Cook, int. Jan. 9, 1792.
Olive and Amos Cook, Aug. 15, 1799.
Patta and Darius Fisk, int. Jan. 5, 1789.
Pelletiah and Elesibath Darling, int. Nov. 4, 1743.
Penellepy and Levy Aldridge, int. Aug. 12, 1786.
Penellope, Mrs., and Isarael Wilson, int. Mar. [written in pencil] 31, 1765.
Peter Jr. of Cumberland, and Mrs. Jerusha Darling, Jan. 1, 1778.
Phebe and Jeremiah Crooks, Dec. 9, 1787. [d. Cornelius and Mehitable, P.R. 2.]
Phila [int. Philee], Mrs., and Jesse [int. Jessa] Sumner, Nov. 25, 1790.

DARLING, Rachel and Moses Darling, int. May 11, 1754.
Rachel, Mrs., and Daniel Sheepard, int. Nov. 15, 1772.
Rena of Cumberland, and Alden Bellou, int. Sept. 1, 1816.
Rhoda, Mrs., and Levi Cook, Oct. 5, 1797.
Richard and Mrs. Kezia Darling, int. Jan. 9, 1792.
Ruth and John Pitts, int. Sept. 7, 1747.
Sabra [int. adds Mrs.] and Ebenezer Thayer, June 28, 1798.
Sally and Alanson Thayer, Nov. 1, 1818.
Samuel and Penelibe Butterworth, int. Sept. 12, 1741.
Samuel and Mrs. Esther Slack, int. Dec. 10, 1754.
Samuel and Mrs. Tamasin Ellis, int. Jan. 26, 1760.
Samuel [int. Jr.] and Mrs. Sarah Burr, Oct. 31, 1782.
Samuel Jr. and Margaret Smith, May 28, 1815.
Samuel 3d, 21, of Medway, s. Samuel and Margaret, and Emily Adams, May 27, 1846.
Samuel Jr. and Julia Morse, int. Mar. 29, 1849.
Sarah, Mrs., and Ruben Aldrich Jr., int. Aug. 2, 1788.
Seth and Susanna Cook, int. Mar. 9, 1800.
Simon and Mrs. Peggy Vorce, int. Sept. 2, 1793.
Simon Jr. and Keziah Allen, int. Mar. 23, 1833.
Timothy and Mrs. Rechel [int. Rachel] Trask, Feb. 3, 1794.
Vienna of Providence, and Thaddeus Curtis, int. May 10, 1818.
William B. and Alpha Cook, int. Jan. 28, 1832.
Ziba and Viana Freeman, int. June 22, 1796.

DAUBIKIN, Peter and Abigail Lewis Cobb, int. Dec. 25, 1813.

DAVIS, Anson B. and Harriet A. Barber, int. Nov. 5, 1843.
Ezekiel H. of Upton, and Phebe H. White, int. Nov. 1, 1847.

DAYTON, Charles and Abby Brown, int. Dec. 11, 1836.

DELIGHT, Ann and Joseph Chase, int. Nov. 20, 1830.

DESPER, Joseph of Medway, and Julia Ann Niles, int. Aug. 17, 1849.

DEWING, Betsy and Ebenezer French, int. Feb. 8, 1823.
Charles of Mendon, and Angeline A. Colburn, int. Feb. 4, 1849.
Elijah Jr. and Mary Combs, July 5, 1820.
Julia [int. Dewin] and Eliphalet [int. Eliphelet] Holbrook, Nov. 26, 1812.

DOAK (see Dorr), Nathaniel of Providence, Providence Co., and Mrs. Lucretia Ellis, Nov. 16, 1794, in Franklin.*

* Intention not recorded.

DORR (see Doak), Annot L. and Abel Weatherhead, int. July 11, 1841.

DRAKE, Eliza P. and Elbridge G. Ware, Apr. 10, 1844.
John and Betsy Hendrick, int. May 13, 1826.
John and Mary C. Grant, int. Sept. 11, 1847.

DRAPER, Abigal [int. Abigial], Mrs., and John Chilson, Jan. 3, 1782.
Jonathan of Comberland, and Abigail Darling, int. Apr. 11, 1753.
Jonthan Jr. and Mary Darlin, May 29, 1728.*
Moley, Mrs., and Edy Clark, int. Sept. 27, 1790.
Rachel, Mrs., and Timothy Thompson, int. Jan. 26, 1760.

DUDLEY, Sally B. of Grafton, and John Metcalf, int. Aug. 30, 1829.
Sumner and Elizabeth G. Pond, int. Sept. 24, 1837.

DURFFEY, Anna and Jeremiah Crooks Jr., int. Oct. 16, 1815.

EADS, Sarah, Mrs., [of] Medway, and Peter Frost, int. Apr. 9, 1779.

EAMES (see Ames), Dennis, 23, of Mendon, s. Moses and Nancy, and Mary M. Allen, Dec. 9, 1847.

EARL, Edath of Smithfield, R. I., and William Hoyt, int. Mar. 18, 1827.

EDWARDS, George of Holliston, and Sophiá Burr, int. Aug. 25, 1828.

ELEXANDER (see Ellexander), Elizabeth, Mrs., of Mendon, and William Johnson, int. May 10, 1790.

ELIOT (see Elliott).

ELLEXANDER (see Elexander), Joseph of Milford, and Mrs. Beulah Albee, int. Jan. 15, 1797.

ELLIOT, Sarah J. and Elbe H. Underwood, int. June 22, 1846.

ELLIS, Augustus of Providence, R. I., and Louisa Ann Bates, Sept. 17, 1834.
Betsey and Daniel Lasall, int. Mar. 21, 1802.
Daniels (see Ellis Daniels).
Hannah, Mrs., of Medway, and Ebenezer Hayward, int. Sept. 18, 1762.

* Intention not recorded.

ELLIS, Hannah, Mrs., and Elias Thayer, int. Jan. 27, 1763.
Joseph of Franklin, and Mrs. Abigail Pratt [int. wid., omits Mrs.], Mar. 26, 1795.
Lucretia, Mrs., of Franklin, Norfolk Co., and Nathaniel Doak, Nov. 16, 1794, in Franklin.*
Luther and Mrs. Ezube [int. Zuba] Butterworth, Apr. 15, 1798.
Nathan and Polly Bass, int. Apr. 26, 1801.
Oliver of Medway [int. Midway], and Anna Fisher, Apr. 24, 1787.
Polly and Asa Burr 2d, int. Mar. 29, 1801.
Rosanna and Daniel Thurston, Oct. 3, 1799.
Sabra, Mrs., and Amasa Holbrook, Apr. 3, 1794.
Tamasin, Mrs., of Medway, and Samuel Darling, int. Jan. 26, 1760.
Timothy Jr. of Franklin, and Debarah Partridge, int. July 17, 1803.
Willard of Uxbridge, and Eliza Pierce, int. Aug. 8, 1832.

ENGLEY, Lucy L. of Franklin, and David Covell, int. Dec. 17, 1835.

FAERBANKS (see Fairbank, Fairbanks, Farbank), Joseph of Midway, and Mrs. Mary Metcalf, int. Apr. 5, 1787.

FAIRBANK (see Faerbanks, Fairbanks, Farbank), Jerusha of Franklin, and Simon Bates, int. Apr. 7, 1805.

FAIRBANKS (see Faerbanks, Fairbank, Farbank), Calvin of Holliston, and Lucy Fairbanks, int. Nov. 9, 1817.
Cynthia and Joel Hammond, Aug. 3, 1844.
Elijah and Nancey Adams, int. Mar. 29, 1811.
Grace, Mrs., and John Fairbanks Esq., int. July 19, 1835.
Hannah E., wid. [int. Mrs., omits wid.], 34, of Holliston, d. Asa Burr and Polly, and Francis D. Bates, widr. [int. Esq., omits widr.], Apr. 3, 1849.
John Esq. of Holliston, and Mrs. Grace Fairbanks, int. July 19, 1835.
Jonas M. and Betsey Adams, int. Apr. 17, 1824.
Joseph and Mrs. Lucy Fisher, Oct. 26, 1785.
Joseph and Mrs. Lavina Daniels, int. May 6, 1826.
Joseph and Mrs. Grace Bert, int. Oct. 17, 1826.
Lucy and Calvin Fairbanks, int. Nov. 9, 1817.
Lucy, Mrs., and Baruch Perry, int. Mar. 22, 1829.
Nancy and John N. Barton, int. Jan. 12, 1845.
Naomi and Allen Anderson, Aug. 3, 1844.

* Intention not recorded.

FAIRBANKS, Olive (see Olive Fairbanks Wales).
Rufus of Millbury, and Hannah E. Burr, int. Oct. 15, 1836.
Salla and Robert Smith, int. Dec. 1, 1804.
Sarah J. and Francis Barton, int. Mar. 30, 1845.
William and Mary Allen, int. Apr. 21, 1844.

FARBANK (see Faerbanks, Fairbank, Fairbanks), Deborah, Mrs., of Holliston, and Job Parteridge, int. Sept. 10, 1769.

FARNUM, Warner of Cheshire [int. Chesire], and Isanna A. Fisher, Mar. 19, 1833.

FARRINGTON, Charles H. and Adaline M. Sylvester, int. Mar. 4, 1846.
Eliza A., 28, d. Aaron and Rebecca, and William H. Thompson, Oct. 13, 1847.
Harriet B. and James M. Ober, int. Oct. 26, 1833.
Sylvanus W. and Jane A. Snow, int. Jan. 11, 1846.

FERRIS (see Foris).

FIELD, John of Dedham, and Harriet Allen, Feb. 8, 1827.
William and Mary Ann Armitage, Aug. 16, 1847.

FISH, Seth [int. of Swansey] and Mrs. Esther Thompson [int. Mrs. Ester Thomson], July 2, 1780.

FISHER (see Fitsher), Abby T. and Daniel P. Adams, Oct. 9, 1836.
Abigaile of Franckling, and Jesse Hill, int. Dec. 19, 1789.
Anna and Oliver Ellis, Apr. 24, 1787.
Ebenezer H. of Medway, and Meletiah [int. Miletiah] W. Smith, Aug. 19, 1839.
Isanna A. and Warner Farnum, Mar. 19, 1833.
Levis of Holliston, and [int. adds Mrs.] Hannah Thayer, Oct. 5, 1797.
Lewis L. and Sarah H. Forestall, int. Sept. 27, 1847.
Lois, wid., of Milford, and Lt. Seth Holbrook, May 9, 1827.
Lucy, Mrs., and Joseph Fairbanks, Oct. 26, 1785.
Lydia E. and William Thomson, int. May 17, 1835.
Nancy and Warren Kendell, int. Aug. 3, 1828.
Patience of Wrentham, and John Holbrook, int. Jan. 6, 1746.
Paul and Artimissa Aldrich, int. Apr. 17, 1802.
Rosanna, wid., of Wrentham, and Capt. Aaron Thayer, int. Mar. 7, 1822.

FISHER, Samuel Jr. of Midwey [int. Midway], and Mrs. Lydia
    Harskill, Sept. 14, 1773.
Sarah P. and John Bates Jr., Oct. 14, 1830.

FISK, Darius of Cumberland, and Patta Darling, int. Jan. 5,
    1789.
James J. and Rebekah Prouty, int. Oct. 28, 1832.
Jemima of Upton, and Abner Smith, int. June 1, 1800.
Polley, Mrs., of Cumberland, and Dr. William Whitaker, int.
    Sept. 3, 1775.

FITSHER (see Fisher), Eleazer [int. Fisher] of Woodstock, and
    Mrs. Margret [int. Marget] White, Nov. 26, 1778.

FLECHER (see Fletcher), Hezekiah and Patty Read, int. Mar.
    31, 1811.

FLETCHER (see Flecher), Abraham of Mendon, and Anstress
    Arnold, int. Mar. 7, 1830.
William of Mendon, and Joanna Aldrich, wid., int. June 17, 1804.

FOLET (see Follet), Oliver of Cumberland, R. I., and Levina
    Pickering, int. Dec. 23, 1820.

FOLLET (see Folet), Samuel of Hubbardston, and Mrs. Tamer
    [int. Tamor] Smith, Dec. 17, 1783.

FORESTALL (see Foristall, Foristoll, Forristall), Sarah H. and
    Lewis L. Fisher, int. Sept. 27, 1847.

FORIS, Sarah [int. Farris] of Cumberland, R.L, and Jesse Leach,
    Mar. 29, 1827.

FORISTALL (see Forestall, Foristoll, Forristall), Amasa and
    Salley Daniels, wid., int. May 4, 1822.
Amase and Mrs. Sarah Haven, int. Feb. 10, 1793.
Benjamin and Mary Ann Allen, int. Dec. 20, 1823.
Bethiah [int. Bathiah], Mrs., and Calvin Curtis, Apr. 25, 1796.
Catherine [int. Catharine] B., 32, d. Luther and Susan, and Jotham
    Adams Jr., widr. [int. omits widr.], July 1, 1849.
Elmira and James A. Taft, Apr. 11, 1824.
Harriet D. [int. Forestall], 19, d. Benj[amin] and Mary, and
    Albert Gardner, May 4, 1848.
Jane H. of Holliston, and Calvin N. Rockwood, int. Apr. 13,
    1849.
Lucy, Mrs. [int. omits Mrs.], and Ezekiel Stoddar, Dec. 30, 1784.
Onley and Polly Wood, int. Oct. 23, 1814.

FORISTALL, Polly [int. adds Mrs.] and Elijah Alden, May 17, 1798.
Sally and Amasa Wood, Sept. 30, 1810.

FORISTOLL (see Forestall, Foristall, Forristall), Electa and Elisha Burr Jr., int. Aug. 4, 1803.

FORRISTALL (see Forestall, Foristall, Foristoll), Almira E. [int. A.] and Joel J. [int. omits J.] Clark, Apr. 22, 1841.
Elizabeth (Forister) [int. Mrs. Elisabeth Foristall] and Benjamin Spear, Mar. 29, 1785.
Ezra of Holliston, and [int. adds Mrs.] Bethiah Hayward, Aug. 16, 1764.

FORSTER (see Foster), Barthelomew [int. Bartholomew Foster] of Wrentham, and Mrs. Mary Pratt, Feb. 2, 1775.

FOSTER (see Forster), Betsey [int. Betsy] and John F. Pond, Sept. 27, 1821.
Olive W. and Smith Aldrich, Oct. 29, 1837.
Sally [int. Sallah], Mrs., and Caleb Woodward, Dec. 1, 1785.

FRANKLIN, Frances L. and Daniel Sunderland, Apr. 3, 1842.
Mary Ann of Cumberland, R. I., and George Peck, int. May 13, 1833.

FREEMAN (see Freman), Benjamin and Mrs. Mary Healey, int. Feb. 21, 1756.
Chloe and Dr. William Whitaker, Sept. 4 [int. Oct. 11, *sic*], 1807.
Edward [int. adds Rev.] and Harriet [int. Harriett] Ellis Colburn, Nov. 27, 1834, in Dedham.
Esther, Mrs., and Oliver Capron, int. Apr. 19, 1757.
Fanny and Wilder Whipple, June 26, 1817.
Hipsylante of Mendon, and Lyman Holbrook, int. Dec. 12, 1819.
Lydia and Luke Arneld, int. Nov. 5, 1788.
Otis of Mendon, and Leah Scott, int. May 5, 1788.
Phila T. and [int. adds Lt.] Joseph Wood, Aug. 9, 1830.
Ralph (Treeman) and Mrs. Phebe Thomson, int. Nov. 11, 1764.
Samuel (Treeman) and Mrs. Elisabeth Clark, int. Sept. 22, 1771.
Sylvia and Naman Carpenter, Apr. 30, 1837.
Viana, Mrs., of Cumberland, and Ziba Darling, int. June 22, 1796.

FREMAN (see Freeman), Salsbury and Ruth Haringdon, int. Oct. 16, 1784.

FRENCH, Ebenezer of Boston, and Betsy Dewing, int. Feb. 8, 1823.
Emeline of Milford, and John W. Scott, July 5, 1846.*
Habijah of Mendon, and Johannah Holbrook, Oct. 30, 1735.*

FROST, Peter and Mrs. Sarah Eads, int. Apr. 9, 1779.

FULLER, Esther, Mrs., and Marvellous Hall, int. Sept. 20, 1772.
Harriet of Medway, and Alfred B. White, int. Sept. 22, 1844.
Malena, Mrs., and Cheselton E. Bruce, int. Mar. 5, 1836.

GAMMELL, William, Rev., of Medfield, and Mary Slocom, int. Feb. 27, 1811.

GARDNER, Albert, 30, b. Mendon, of Mendon, s. Thomas and Nancy of Mendon, and Harriet D. Foristall [int. Forestall], May 4, 1848.

GARNSY, Samuel of Medway, and Mary Peck, Dec. 14, 1731.*

GASKEL (see Gaskill), Rachael of Mendon, and Benjamin Cook, int. Mar. 9, 1817.

GASKILL (see Gaskel), Orinda and Elias Cook 2d, int. July 17, 1824.
Provided and Caleb Cook, int. Sept. 15, 1753.

GASKIN, Sena of Cumberland, and Willard Bellow, int. Mar. 10, 1816.

GATCHELL, John G. of Cumberland, R. I., and Mary Warrall [int. Worrall], Feb. 27, 1834.

GATES, Eliza T. of Graften, and Frenk Pike, int. Mar. 2, 1834.

GAY, Timothy of Pawtucket, R. I., and Nancy Green, May 3 [int. July 3, *sic*], 1824.

GETCHELL (see Gatchell).

GIBSON, Thaddeus and Mrs. Elisabeth [int. Elisbeth] Sumner, Feb. 2, 1778.

GILBERT, John Gardner and Lucretia Colburn [int. Colbern], Nov. 8, 1837.

GILLSON (see Jillson, Jilson), Reuben of Cumberland, and Mrs. Eunice Cook, int. Aug. 26, 1798.

* Intention not recorded.

GILMORE, James [int. Gilmoar] of Franklin, and Fanny Hitchcock, Aug. 9, 1843.

GODMON, John [int. Godman] and Mrs. Anne Hayward, Nov. 15, 1769.

GOINS, John [int. Gowin] of Franklin, and Mrs. Mary Cook, June 14, 1786.

GOOGINS, George and Abigail Wight [int. White], Mar. 30, 1843.

GOULD, Christiania of Holliston, and Daniel Adams, int. Feb. 27, 1803.
Jemima and Abraham Hixon, Sept. 30, 1834.
Jerusha and Laban Thomson, May 29, 1823.
Ledia, Mrs., of Holliston, and Henry Kilburn, int. Aug. 20, 1798.
Olive, Mrs., of Holliston, and Levi Adams, int. Oct. 20, 1797.
Paul Jr. of Holliston, and Chloe Adoms [Adams], int. Aug. 4, 1803.
Sally of Mendon, and Wheelock Bullard, int. Mar. 14, 1804.

GOWIN (see Goins).

GRANT, Beriah and Phebe Cook, int. Jan. 10, 1779.
Ezekiel C. and Adaline Shepard Stratton, int. Sept. 28, 1828.
Harvey and Lydia Bemis, int. Sept. 20, 1835.
Lorra and Allen L. Pierce, int. Sept. 12, 1826.
Mary C. of Franklin, and John Drake, int. Sept. 11, 1847.
Roads of Wrentham, and Martha Cook, int. July 22, 1804.
William, 31, s. Nathan and Lucy, and Lucy Burr, wid. [int. Mrs., omits wid.], Nov. 13, 1844.

GREELEY, Enoch and Susannah Lewit, int. May 1, 1814.

GREEN (see Greene), Hannah of Mendon, and Ebenezer Thayer, Apr. 24, 1734.*
Harriot and Dan Thomson, int. Apr. 20, 1817.
Márgrat (Gree[n]) of Mendon, and Benjamin Rockwood, Feb. 12, 1734–5.*
Maria and Laban Burr, int. Aug. 19, 1821.
Nancy and Timothy Gay, May 3 [int. July 3, *sic*], 1824.
Sarah of Mendon, and Ebenezer Thompson, Nov. 2, 1737.*

GREENE (see Green), James J. and Cinthia Pond, int. Oct. 31, 1819.

* Intention not recorded.

GREENWOOD, Joseph and Betsey Chinery, int. Apr. 11, 1813.
Moses F. and Mary B. Brown, int. Nov. 12, 1848.

GRINNELL, Nancy H. and Henry B. Metcalf, int. Mar. 14, 1846.

GUERNSEY (see Garnsey).

GUILD, Betsey [dup. Guilde] of Franklin, and Pascal P. Spear, int. Feb. 27 [dup. Jan. 4], 1811.
Emma, Mrs., of Franklin, and Dea. Daniel Lazell, int. Oct. 27, 1839.

HADLEY, Ebenezer and Mary Kilburn, int. Nov. 20, 1831.
Hulday D., 25, of Blackstone, d. William and Mercy, and Lewis F. Williams, Nov. 30, 1848.*

HALL, Abigal and Ebeneazear Perry, Feb. 10, 1736–7.*
Asa Esq. and Sellissa Scott, June 16, 1831.
Asa 2d and Alathina Parkman, int. Oct. 19, 1834.
Benjamin of Cumberland, and Mrs. Sarah Bates, int. Jan. 22, 1797.
Deborah, Mrs., and Daniel Shepard, int. Nov. 13, 1762.
Eliza and Capt. Lyman W. Thayer, int. Oct. 22, 1831.
John and Mrs. Joanna Cook, int. Feb. 27, 1768.
John of Hopkinton, and Mrs. Briget Jones, Apr. 27, 1786.
John S. of Chatham, Conn., and Martha R. Lovell, Sept. 7, 1841, in Fall River.*
Marvellous and Mrs. Esther Fuller, int. Sept. 20, 1772.
Mary and Simeon Barney, Mar. 3, 1805.
Olive and John Jay Pain, Mar. 3 [int. Mar. 7, *sic*], 1819.
Ruth and Nathanail Blood, int. Nov. 13, 1742.
Seth and Mrs. Abigail Albee, May 28, 1737.*
Seth and Mrs. Martha Thompson, int. Apr. 22, 1757.
Seth, widr. [int. omits widr.], and Elisabeth Spear, wid. [int. omits wid.], Dec. 17, 1761.
Uranah and Jabesh Lyon, June 26, 1729.*
William and Mrs. Molly Selocomb, int. June 14, 1783.
Zurial and Jain Smith, int. Dec. 14, 1742.

HALYBURTON, George and Susan Boyle, int. Mar. 19, 1820.

HAM, William of Providence, R.I., and Nancy Scott, Dec. 14, 1848.*

HAMMOND, Joel of Uxbridge, and Cynthia Fairbanks, Aug. 3, 1844.

* Intention not recorded.

114 BELLINGHAM MARRIAGES.

HANDCOCK, Fanny, Mrs., and Amos Phillips, Nov. 23, 1797.

HARDING, John 3d of Midway, and Mrs. Beaulah Metcalf, int. Sept. 8, 1781.

HARINGDON, Ruth of Cumberland, and Salsbury Freman, int. Oct. 16, 1784.

HARSKELL (see Harskill, Haskell, Herskal), John Jr. [int. Haskell] of Cumberland, and Asenith [int. Asenath] Aldrich, Apr. 16, 1812.

HARSKILL (see Harskell, Haskell, Herskal), Lydia, Mrs., and Samuel Fisher Jr., Sept. 14, 1773.

HART, William, 27, of Mansfield, s. Aden and Roxy A., and Emeline E. Thayer, Nov. 29, 1849.

HASKELL (see Harskell, Harskill, Herskal), Amy Ann of Cumberland, R.I., and Jeremiah M. Crook, int. Mar. 9, 1841.
Samuel Jr. and Amanda Pond, int. Aug. 31, 1817.

HASTINGS, Enoch P. of Milford, and Maria Chapen, Apr. 17, 1839.

HAVEN, Cumfort, Mrs., of Framingham, and Asa Bates, int. Feb. 21, 1796.
Sarah, Mrs., of Framingham, and Amase Foristall, int. Feb. 10, 1793.
Sarah S. of Milford, and Alfred L. Hill, int. Mar. 13, 1847.

HAWARD (see Hayard, Haywad, Hayward), Ebenezer and Hannah Aldrich, int. Jan. 23, 1808.

HAWES (see Horse), Ellen E. and Ellis T. Norcross, int. Aug. 3, 1845.
Jemima of Franklin, and Eliab Wight, int. Oct. 14, 1782.
Nathan of Franklin, and Silvia Winn, Sept. 27, 1827.

HAYARD (see Haward, Haywad, Hayward), Samuel and Mrs. Bethiah Holbrook, int. Oct. 15, 1763.

HAYDEN, Caroline and Henry Lillie [int. Lilie], Sept. 21, 1834.
Charlott [int. Charlotte] of Mendon, and Thomson [int. Thompson] Thayer, Dec. 2, 1824.

HAYWAD (see Haward, Hayard, Hayward), Emory and Rebeckah Albee, int. Sept. 2, 1832.

HAYWARD (see Haward, Hayard, Haywad), Anne, Mrs., and
John Godmon [int. Godman], Nov. 15, 1769.
Barzillai of Bridgewarter [int. Bridgewater], and Hannah Rathborne [int. Rathbone], Dec. 27, 1813.
Benjamin and Zilpha Alden, June 19, 1803.
Bethiah [int. adds Mrs.] and Ezra Forristall, Aug. 16, 1764.
Clarrasa and Joseph Luther, int. Jan. 8, 1827.
David of Mendon, and Joanna Wilson, int. Nov. 17, 1750.
Ebenezer and Mrs. Hannah Ellis, int. Sept. 18, 1762.
Eliezer and Mary Danels, Feb. 15, 1732–3.*
Elisha and [int. adds Mrs.] Elisabeth Parker, Jan. 29, 1766.
Elizebath and Nathaniel Butterworth, int. Aug. 1, 1761.
Ezekiel and Mrs. Hannah Johnson, int. Apr. 26, 1767.
Hannah, Mrs., and Thomas Wheelock, Dec. 28, 1769.
Henry of Mendon, and Susanna Cook, Nov. 23, 1828.
Jemima, Mrs., and Ephraim Parkhirst [int. Epharaim Parkhust], Sept. 31 [*sic*], 1767.
Jerushe [int. Jerusha] and Otis Wales Jr., June 21, 1822.
Margarret of Milford, and Samuel Cobb, int. Jan. 10, 1804.
Melatiah of Midway, and Amos Holbrook, int. Jan. 10, 1773.
Meletiah, Mrs., and Japheth Daniels, int. July 30, 1763.
Patience of Mendon, and Japheth Chapin, int. June 24, 1749.
Phebe, Mrs., and Joshua Laland, int. Oct. 25, 1767.
Samuel and Elizabath Partridg, Mar. 15, 1734.*
Samuel of Mendon, and Alce Holbrook, May 24, 1737.*
Samuel P. of Mendon, and Rachel G. Rhodes, int. Feb. 9, 1845.
Sarah and James Smith, Nov. 21, 1728.*
Sarah, Mrs., and Joseph Bates, int. Oct. 15, 1762.
Seth and Isable Chace, int. Apr. 6, 1800.
Warfield of Mendon, and Mrs. Lydia Thayer, int. Dec. 20, 1760.

HEALEY, Mary, Mrs., of Wrentham, and Benjamin Freeman, int. Feb. 21, 1756.

HEATON, Mary, Mrs., of Wrentham, and Joshua Phillips, int. Mar. 17, 1765.
Nathaniel of Wrentham, and Mrs. Margeret Metcalf, int. Oct. 17, 1765.
Nathaniel of Wrentham, and Sarah Phillips, int. Sept. 9, 1809.

HEMINGWEY, Thomas and Pattey Chasey [Chafey], int. Feb. 12, 1809.

HENDRICK, Betsy and John Drake, int. May 13, 1826.

* Intention not recorded.

HERSKAL (see Harskell, Harskill, Haskell), John [of] Cumberland, and Mrs. Mary Darling, int. May 19, 1780.

HILL (see Hills), Aaron and Mrs. Sally Combes [int. Mrs. Salley Combs], Dec. 21, 1780.
Abida of Mendon, and Henry Tucker, int. May 18, 1831.
Albert of Medway, and Mary Cook, May 18, 1831.
Alfred L. and Sarah S. Haven, int. Mar. 13, 1847.
Amos, Capt. [int. omits Capt.], and Nabby Chilson, Dec. 8, 1816.
Amos and Lucinda Cutler, int. Dec. 8, 1821.
Arnold of Holliston, and Levina Smith, int. Jan. 30, 1803.
Catherine of Medway, and Simeon Holbrook, int. Apr. 6, 1806.
Claricy [int. Cleresy] and Asa Slocom, Apr. 15, 1810.
David and Mrs. Mary [int. Macy] Holbrook, Apr. 21, 1785.
Elizabeth [of] Franklin, and Metcalf White, int. Sept. 11, 1836.
Enoch and Mrs. Mehetabel Metcalf, int. Mar. 9, 1760.
Enuch and Mary Darling, int. Dec. 26, 1747.
Ephraim of Medway, and Mrs. Kezia Partridge, int. Jan. 28, 1758.
Hannah of Sherburn, and Nathan Penniman, int. June 27, 1798.
Henry and Hannah Medcalf, int. Apr. 17, 1824.
Huldah and Paul Dexter Pond, int. Dec. 23, 1807.
Jesse and Abigaile Fisher, int. Dec. 19, 1789.
John C., Capt., and Elizabeth B. Cummins, int. Sept. 7, 1833.
Lois, "Ms." [int. Mrs.], and Ezra Whiston, Sept. 23, 1790.
Moses and Mary Adoms [Adams], int. Oct. 8, 1803.
Moses and Persis Phips, int. Mar. 20, 1808.
Olive, Mrs., of Milford, and Capt. Seth Holbrook, int. Nov. 3, 1833.
Persis of Franklin, and Theodore S. Bemiss, int. Nov. 11, 1838.
Sybel of Mendon, and Peter Bates, int. Oct. 2, 1803.
Uraner of Mendon, and Luther Thayer, int. Aug. 8, 1823.

HILLS (see Hill), Martha C. of Huberstown, Vt., and Jedediah Phipps, Feb. 26, 1835.*
Olive of Wrentham, and Addison C. Lawrence, int. May 7, 1831.

HILTON, Cynthia E. of Wrentham, and Salem Lee, int. May 29, 1833.

HITCHCOCK, Fanny and James Gilmore [int. Gilmoar], Aug. 9, 1843.
Margaret and Andrew Burnham, int. Mar. 6, 1837.

* Intention not recorded.

HIXEN (see Hixon, Hixson), Sarah [int. Hixon] and Silas T. [int. N.] Norcross, Jan. 11, 1821.

HIXON (see Hixen, Hixson), Abraham and Jemima Gould, Sept. 30, 1834.
Isanna E. of Medway, and Daniel Wiley, int. Oct. 21, 1825.
Lucy A., 19, d. Elehew H. and Hannah, and Joel Baker Jr., May 30, 1848.
Partridge and Hannah Vose, Apr. 6, 1843.

HIXSON (see Hixen, Hixon), Clarisa, Mrs. [int. Mrs. Clericy Hixon], of Franklin, and Jesse Holbrook Jr., Jan. 20, 1791.
Ellery and Cynthia Howard, Jan. 1, 1829.

HOLBROOK, Aaron and Hannah Partridge, int. Mar. 4, 1762.
Aaron, Lt., and Mrs. Elisabeth Belsher, int. Oct. 11, 1783.
Aaron and Jemima Thomson, wid., int. July 15, 1804.
Aaron, Lt., and Elizabath Daniels, wid., int. July 24, 1813.
Aaron and Polly Warfield, int. May 11, 1828.
Abi, Mrs., and Joseph Lee, Feb. 12, 1786.
Abigail of Milford, and Warren Lasol, int. Feb. 12, 1804.
Abigail and Amos Adams Jr., Nov. 29, 1812.
Abijah and Mrs. Freelove Pond, int. July 2, 1773.
Adaline and Gilbert Leland, int. Oct. 2, 1842.
Alce and Samuel Hayward, May 24, 1737.*
Amariah and [int. adds Mrs.] Molley Wright, May 13, 1779.
Amariah and Vina Holbrook, Mar. 6, 1806.
Amasa and Mrs. Sabra Ellis, Apr. 3, 1794.
Amos and Melatiah Hayward, int. Jan. 10, 1773.
Amos and Lucretia Burr, Dec. 1, 1808.
Amzi and Sarah Kilburn, int. Feb. 12, 1790.
Anna, Mrs., of Mendon, and Noah Perry, int. May 23, 1773.
Anne, Mrs., and Solomon Prentise, int. July 1, 1770.
Asa and Mrs. Meletiah [int. Melatiah] Rockwood, Nov. 22, 1780.
Asahel, Lt., and Marcy Holbrook, wid., int. June 4, 1779.
Asail and Annah Puffer, int. Feb. 26, 1742–3.
Bethiah, Mrs., and Samuel Hayard, int. Oct. 15, 1763.
Calvin of Milford, and Mrs. Sabra Patridge [int. Partridge], Dec. 13, 1792.
Cephas and Polly Knap, int. July 27, 1817.
Cinthia [int. Cynthia], Mrs., and Mathew Smith Cushman, Mar. 24, 1796.
Clara and Luther Kingsbury, int. Dec. 18, 1803.
Clarrissa and Tappan H. Bacthelder, int. Apr. 26, 1840.

* Intention not recorded.

HOLBROOK, Deborah and Ichabod Chilson, May 8, 1808.
Derias of Mendon, and Olive [int. Mrs. Ollive] Holbrook, Apr. 6, 1780.
Dinah, Mrs., and Seth Holbrook, June 6, 1776.
Ebenezer of Mendon, and Keziah Wight, int. Feb. 12, 1747-8.
Eliab and Betsey Ide, int. Oct. 15, 1809.
Eliab Jr. and Hannah Pickering, Apr. 25, 1839.
Eliab Jr. and Julia F. Morse, int. May 15, 1842.
Eliphalet [int. Eliphelet] and Julia Dewing [int. Dewin], Nov. 26, 1812.
Eliphelet Jr. and Abigail Wight, Nov. 26, 1753, in Mendon.
Elisabeth, Mrs., of Sharburn, and Nathanie[l] Butterworth, int. Sept. 14, 1782.
Ella and Daniel Hunter, int. Oct. 15, 1831.
Ellis and Eliza Allen, int. Mar. 18, 1822.
Elona, Mrs., of Milford, and David Cook, int. May 18, 1798.
Ester and Reuben Cook, int. Jan. 6, 1802.
Esther, Mrs., and Timothy Thayer, int. Jan. 24, 1761.
Ezekiel and Mrs. Sarah Sumner, int. Feb. 21, 1773.
Hannah and Liberty Bullard, int. Feb. 25, 1810.
Henery Jr. and Sally Trask, Nov. 24, 1813.
Henry [int. Hennery] and [int. adds Mrs.] Elisabeth Cook, Dec. 20, 1780.
Henry and Mrs. [int. omits Mrs.] Eunice Patriche [int. Patrick], May 2, 1816.
Horace [int. Horrace] of Milford, and Sarah B. Holbrook, Apr. 28, 1842.
Jesee [int. Jesse] and Abigail Thayer, Mar. 28, 1753, in Mendon.
Jesse Jr. and Mrs. Clarisa Hixson [int. Mrs. Clericy Hixon], Jan. 20, 1791.
Joanna, Mrs., and Timothy Whelock, int. Dec. 30, 1764.
Johannah and Habijah French, Oct. 30, 1735.*
John and Patience Fisher, int. Jan. 6, 1746.
John of Uxbridge, and Lydia Holbrook, int. Dec. 25, 1761.
Jonathan and Mrs. Ann Partridge, int. Sept. 9, 1770.
Joseph W. of Milford, and Maria A. Adams, Dec. 13, 1840.
Lucy, Mrs., and Joel Jinks, int. Dec. 30, 1782.
Luke and Marcy Pond, int. Nov. 24, 1750.
Lurania, 28, d. Eliab and Betsey, and Walter D. Stow [dup. and int. Stowe], Apr. 25, 1844.
Lydia and John Holbrook, int. Dec. 25, 1761.
Lyman and Hipsylante Freeman, int. Dec. 12, 1819.
Marcy, wid., and Lt. Asahel Holbrook, int. June 4, 1779.

* Intention not recorded.

HOLBROOK, Mary and Joseph Tompson, Mar. 18, 1725.*
Mary and Danail Corbett, int. Nov. 4, 1741.
Mary, Mrs., and Nathan Peniman, int. Dec. 15, 1757.
Mary, Mrs., and Stephen Benson, int. Sept. 16, 1764.
Mary [int. Macy], Mrs., and David Hill, Apr. 21, 1785.
Mary and Benjamin F. Johnson, Dec. 20, 1843.
Meletiah, wid., and Caleb Adams, int. Mar. 31, 1799.
Melitiah, Mrs., and Nathan Partridge, June 6, 1776.
Moses and Ruth Puffer, int. Feb. 9, 1743-4.
Naham L. and Lorra S. Batchelder, int. Aug. 27, 1848.
Nahum and Susana Rockwood, int. Feb. 3, 1802.
Nathan and Mrs. Sally Bates, May 29, 1793.
Olive [int. Mrs. Ollive] and Derias Holbrook, Apr. 6, 1780.
Olive M., 19, d. Amos and Lucretia, and Charles F. Cushman, Nov. 22, 1846.
Peter [int. Holbrok] and Mary Bates, Apr. 26, 1787.
Phebe and Calvin Thayer, Aug. 22, 1813.
Phebe, Mrs., and Amos Richardson, int. July 13, 1766.
Phinehas and Mrs. Polle [int. Polly] Wales, Nov. 4, 1795.
Pliny and Martha Perkins, int. May 7, 1826.
Rachal [int. Rachel] and Liberty Partridge, Jan. 31, 1814.
Rachel and Jonathan Thayer, Sept. 4, 1735.*
Roxanna and Abijah Cook, Apr. 9, 1812.
Sabin and Maria A. Phipps, int. Mar. 28, 1841.
Sabrina and Peter Joice [int. Joyce], June 29, 1826.
Sarah and Seth Thayer, int. Mar. 18, 1790.
Sarah and Israel Scott, Oct. 16, 1809.
Sarah B. and Horace [int. Horrace] Holbrook, Apr. 28, 1842.
Senar [?] and Josiah Penneman Jr., int. Mar. 13, 1790.
Seth and Mrs. Dinah Holbrook, June 6, 1776.
Seth 2d and Mrs. Hannah Bates, Jan. 21, 1798.
Seth, Capt., and Olive Fairbanks Wales [? Olive Fairbanks [of] Wales], int. Mar. 26, 1820.
Seth, Lt., and Lois Fisher, wid., Mar. 9 [int. Apr. 5, sic], 1827.
Seth, Capt., and Mrs. Olive Hill, int. Nov. 3, 1833.
Simeon and Mrs. Lowis Hutchenson, int. Apr. 2, 1798.
Simeon and Catherine Hill, int. Apr. 6, 1806.
Stephen and Rachel Cook, int. July 17, 1762.
Stephen Jr. and Mrs. Mary Penniman, int. July 31, 1790.
Theron of Milford, and Nancy Partridge, int. Mar. 4, 1823.
Tryphina and Levi Rockwood, int. July 12, 1801.
Valentine W., widr., 48, of Medway, s. Seth and Dinah, and Roxana Partridge, wid., Dec. 4, 1849.*

* Intention not recorded.

HOLBROOK, Vina and Amariah Holbrook, Mar. 6, 1806.
Whitman and Nancy Wales, int. Nov. 8, 1835.

HORSE (see Hawes), Susanah of Dedham, and Calib Philips, Sept. 12, 1733.*

HORTON, Manly P. of Cumberland, R. I., and Vesta Slocom, May 2, 1833.
Mary M. of Swanzy, and James A. Thayer, int. Mar. 2, 1845.

HOUGH (see How, Hows), Mary A. and Mellen B. Bates, Nov. 9, 1836.

HOW (see Hough, Hows), Caroline P. and Lyric Leamson, int. Mar. 27, 1824.

HOWARD, Andrew J. and Lucinda Thompson [int. Tompson], Aug. 20, 1840.
Cynthia of Upton, and Ellery Hixson, Jan. 1, 1829.
Hannah, wid., of Milford, and Lt. Joshua Phillips, int. Sept. 2, 1805.
Jotham of Milford, and Mary Ann White, Oct. 1, 1829.

HOWS (see Hough, How), Melitiah, Mrs., of Franklin, and John Humphry, Feb. 22, 1789.*

HOYT, William and Edath Earl, int. Mar. 18, 1827.

HUBBARD, William E. of Franklin, and Martha W. Chilson, int. Sept. 20, 1846.

HUMPHRY, John of Franklin, and Mrs. Melitiah Hows, Feb. 22, 1789.*

HUNT, Clark, 23, s. Clark and Cyrena, and Matilda M. Ware, Mar. 1, 1848.
Elizabeth, "Ms." [dup. and int. Mrs. Elizabeth], and Jonathan Pickring [dup. Pickrieng], Feb. 28, 1760.
Zylpha of E. Douglass, and Charles Cook, int. Oct. 13, 1844.

HUNTER, Daniel of Newbraintree, and Ella Holbrook, int. Oct. 15, 1831.

HUNTING, Abigail, Mrs., of Franklin, and Elisha Perry, Apr. 30, 1829.*

HUTCHENSON (see Hutchinson), Lowis, Mrs., of Sutton, and Simeon Holbrook, int. Apr. 2, 1798.

* Intention not recorded.

HUTCHINSON (see Hutchenson), Daniel of Smithfield, R. I., and Ann Southwick, Nov. 1, 1838.

IDE, Betsey of Franklin, and Eliab Holbrook, int. Oct. 15, 1809.
Betsy and Rufus Combs, int. Jan. 4, 1805.

INGRAHAM, Nathaniel and "Ms" Elisabeth Wiswall, int. Feb. 11, 1758.

INMAN (see Inmun), Alpha and Tilson Wood, July 9, 1812.
Thankful S. [int. of Uxbridge] and Isaac Alden, widr. [int. Asaac Alden Jr., omits widr.], July 20, 1845.

INMUN (see Inman), Charity and Jacob Bartlet, int. Aug. 29, 1741.

JENKES (see Jenks, Jinks), Luke of Wrentham, and Mary Willcox, May 27, 1807.*

JENKS (see Jenkes, Jinks), Betsy of Cumberland, R. I., and Jonathan Onion, int. Apr. 21, 1826.
Charles B. [int. Jenkes] and Hannah [int. adds E.] Thayer, Aug. 24, 1817.

JENNISON, John and Lucinda Winch, int. Aug. 29, 1830.

JILLSON (see Gillson, Jilson), Ann, Mrs., of Cumberland, and John Darling, int. Nov. 7, 1755.
Clark of Richmond, N.H., and Rena B[a]llou, int. Mar. 5, 1815.
Luke of Cumberland, and Mrs. Anna Shearman, int. Apr. 5, 1777.
Mercy and William Vorce, int. Apr. 13, 1814.
Nathaniel Jr. of Cumberland, and Mrs. Molly Scott, int. July 11, 1772.
Nathaniell and Ruth Boze, Aug. 20, 1728, in Providences.*
Osborn of Cumberland, R.I., and Sally A. Crooks, int. Aug. 27, 1846.
Silas and Elizabath Cook, int. Nov. 6, 1808.
Waity of Cumberland, R.I., and Emory Scott, int. Mar. 12, 1820.

JILSON (see Gillson, Jillson), Sutton and Annstiess Arnold, int. Mar. 4, 1845.

JINKS (see Jenkes, Jenks), Joel of Wrentham, and Mrs. Lucy Holbrook, int. Dec. 30, 1782.
Lemuel of Cumberland, and Mrs. Hannah Kelly, int. July 22, 1792.

* Intention not recorded.

JOHNSON (see Jonson), Abigil and Israel Phillips, int. July 19, 1785. "Forbid By Israel Phillips July 25, 1785."
Adaline of Worcester, and Nahum Newton, Apr. 20, 1831.*
Alathina of Holiston, and Phillip Partridge, int. Nov. 29, 1821.
Benjamin F. and Diana Smith, int. Sept. 14, 1833.
Benjamin F. and Mary Holbrook, Dec. 20, 1843.
Hannah, Mrs., of Holliston, and Ezekiel Hayward, int. Apr. 26, 1767.
Isaac of Rohaboth, and Susanah Thayar, int. Mar. 7, 1741.
Isaac and Mrs. Abigail Ray, int. Aug. 22, 1762.
Mary, Mrs., of Medwey, and Calvin Stone, int. June 17, 1838.
Millisent of Framingham, and Rev. Calvin Newton, int. Nov. 2, 1828.
Nehemiah and Mrs. Abigail Merrifield, int. Oct. 21, 1764.
William and Mrs. Elizabeth Elexander, int. May 10, 1790.

JOICE, Peter of Duly [int. Joyce of Dudley], and Sabrina Holbrook, June 29, 1826.

JONES, Abigail and Cornelius Thayer, Dec. 24, 1747.
Bathsheba and Benjamin R. Patridge, int. Apr. 27, 1834.
Briget, Mrs., and John Hall, Apr. 27, 1786.
Daniel [int. David] and Mrs. Hannah Darling, June 30, 1796.
David and [int. adds Mrs.] Hannah Pratt, Apr. 25, 1754, in Mendon.
Hannah [int. adds Mrs.] and Joseph Pratt, Jan. 30, 1755, in Mendon.
Hannah, Mrs., and Samuel Scott, June 25, 1826.
John Jr. [int. omits Jr.] and Elisabeth Chillson, May 18, 1749.
John Jr. and Mary Rockwood, wid., int. Sept. 7, 1751.
John of Milford, and Malinda Chamberlain, int. July 24, 1821.
Mary, Mrs., and Benjamin Pickern Jr. [int. Pickirn, omits Jr.], Dec. 1, 1778.
Rosanna [int. Rosana] and Silas Adams, Nov. 21, 1822.
Timothy E. of Franklin, and Eda Partridge, int. Oct. 21, 1831.

JONSON (see Johnson), Abigail, Mrs. [int. Abigil, omits Mrs.], and Benja[min] Pratt [int. Prat] Jr., May 28, 1788.

JOSLIN, Hannah of Cumberland, R.I., and W[illia]m V. Thomson, int. Feb. 7, 1835.

JOYCE (see Joice).

KEITH (see Keth).

* Intention not recorded.

KELLEY (see Kelly, Killey, Killy), Abby and George F. Wales, Mar. 4, 1840.
Elish [int. Elisha] Jr. and Abigail Aldrich, Sept. 19, 1805.
Ellixander of Dummester, Vt., and Elizabeth Albee, wid., int. Feb. 2, 1797.
Margaret and James Pain, int. Oct. 22, 1825.
Marietta and Lewis B. Arnold, int. Dec. 24, 1837.
Nathan and Ollive Bates, int. Apr. 4, 1803.
Olive C. and Albert L. Cook, Nov. 13, 1839, in Uxbridge.

KELLY (see Kelley, Killey, Killy), Abigail, Mrs., and Eli Bates, Oct. 9, 1792.
Abigail, wid., and Ebenezer Thayer, int. Apr. 12, 1835.
Asa of Mendon, and Patience Whitely, int. May 3, 1801.
Francis and Marietta Parkea, int. Mar. 11, 1838.
Hannah, Mrs., and Lemuel Jinks, int. July 22, 1792.
Sylvia of Milford, and Calvin Barber Jr., int. Mar. 21, 1830.
Wing and Diana Daniels, int. Oct. 6, 1799.

KELTON, John of Dorchester, and Levina Thayer, June 29, 1809.

KENDELL, Warren and Nancy Fisher, int. Aug. 3, 1828.

KENNEY, Cyrus of Fairhaven, Vt., and Lydia T. Thompson [int. Thomson], June 24, 1823.
Silas and Rhoda Bates, Dec. 6, 1824.

KENT, Isaac and Mrs. Sarah Wheelock, int. Dec. 31, 1769.

KETH, Abigail of Uxbridge, and Anderson Scott, int. Dec. 23, 1805.

KILBON (see Kilburn), Paulina [int. Kilbin] of Milford, Worcester Co., and Leander Thomas, Apr. 10, 1828.
Simeon and Lucy Aldrich, int. Jan. 23, 1790.

KILBURN (see Kilbon), Henry and Mrs. Ledia Gould, int. Aug. 20, 1798.
Hiram of Milford, and Roxana Adams, —— 24 [1842].*
Mary and Ebenezer Hadley, int. Nov. 20, 1831.
Sarah and Amzi Holbrook, int. Feb. 12, 1790.

KILLEY (see Kelley, Kelly, Killy), Joseph and Mrs. Margret Brale, int. Feb. 2, 1782.

KILLY (see Kelley, Kelly, Killey), Wing and Mrs. Joanna Cook, int. May 6, 1792.

* Intention not recorded.

BELLINGHAM MARRIAGES.

KIMBEL (see Kimbol), Boice Jr. of Milford, and Mrs. Mary Pike, int. Jan. 5, 1782.

KIMBOL (see Kimbel), Mary, Mrs., and Luther Thayer, int. Mar. 16, 1793.

KING, Sally, Mrs., of Mendon, and Elisha Cook, int. Mar. 12, 1797.

KINGMAN, Deborah W. and W[illia]m M. Morse, July 21, 1842.
Eliza E. and W[illia]m W. Cook, Dec. 29, 1842.

KINGSBURY, Luther of Franklin, and Clara Holbrook, int. Dec. 18, 1803.

KNAP (see Knapp), Polly of Franklin, and Cephas Holbrook, int. July 27, 1817.

KNAPP (see Knap), Melvill of Cumberland, R.I., and Prudence Thayer, int. Oct. 1, 1828.

KNIGHT, Lydia and Otis Martin, int. May 24, 1829.

KNOWLTON, Leonard of Mendon, and Nancy D. Smith, int. Sept. 2, 1838.

LACY, Rowena, 22, and George Law, May 6, 1845.

LAIN (see Lane), Hipsibah, Mrs., and Nathaniel Scott, int. May 14, 1783.

LALAND (see Lealand, Lealond, Leland), Joshua of Sharburn, and Mrs. Phebee Hayward, int. Oct. 25, 1767.

LAMSON (see Leamson).

LANDES, Charles S. of Cumberland, R.I., and Keziah Darling, int. Oct. 1, 1826.

LANE (see Lain), Priscilla, Mrs., of Cumberland, and Stacy Bozworth, int. Sept. 2, 1770.

LASALL (see Lasdol, Lasol, Lazdel, Lazell, Leazel, Leazell) Daniel of Mendon, and Betsey Ellis, int. Mar. 21, 1802.
Elias [int. Lazall] and Content Legg, May 26, 1816.

LASDOL (see Lasall, Lasol, Lazdel, Lazell, Leazel, Leazell), Lydia of Mendon, and Only Scott, int. June 10, 1805.

LASOL (see Lasall, Lasdol, Lazdel, Lazell, Leazel, Leazell), Warren and Abigail Holbrook, int. Feb. 12, 1804.

LATHROP (see Lothrop).

LAW, George, 24, s. George and Sally, and Rowena Lacy, May 6, 1845.
George and Mariam L. Colburn, int. Aug. 8, 1849.
Sarah W. and William F. Russell, int. Apr. 3, 1847.

LAWRENCE, Addison C. and Olive Hills, int. May 7, 1831.
Jarvis B. of Franklin, and Maria B. Smith, int. Apr. 26, 1840.

LAWTON, George W. and Cynthea Pond, int. Nov. 1, 1818.
Ruth and Debias Burchard, ———— [rec. before Apr. 27, 1829] [int. Feb. 8, 1829].

LAZDEL (see Lasall, Lasdol, Lasol, Lazell, Leazel, Leazell), Joshua of Mendon, and Mrs. Levina [int. Levine] Cook, Oct. 8, 1778.

LAZELL (see Lasall, Lasdol, Lasol, Lazdel, Leazel, Leazell), Daniel, Dea., and Mrs. Emma Guild, int. Oct. 27, 1839.
Levina and Gibbs Braley, int. Mar. 7, 1833.
Warren and Betsey Walker, May 18, 1820.
Warren 2d of Mendon, and Mrs. [int. omits Mrs.] Sophia C. Thurber, Apr. 4, 1824.

LEACH, Jesse and Sarah Foris [int. Farris], Mar. 29, 1827.

LEALAND (see Laland, Lealond, Leland), Aaron of Holliston, and Mrs. Joanna Alden [int. Aldin], July 24, 1783.
Meriam, Mrs., of Holliston, and Nathan Whiting, Dec. 22, 1791.*

LEALOND (see Laland, Lealand, Leland), Aaron [int. Lealand] of Chester, and Mrs. Eunice Rockwood [int. Eunis, wid., omits Mrs.], June 11, 1788.

LEAMSON, Lyric and Caroline P. How, int. Mar. 27, 1824.

LEAZEL (see Lasall, Lasdol, Lasol, Lazdel, Lazell, Leazell), Isaac of Mendon, and Mrs. Deborah Thomson, int. Mar. 8, 1777.

LEAZELL (see Lasall, Lasdol, Lasol, Lazdel, Lazell, Leazel), Deborah, Mrs., of Mendon, and Levi Rockwood, Feb. 22, 1774.

LEE, Jemima, Mrs., of Wrentham, and Abner Wight, int. Sept. 1, 1776.

* Intention not recorded.

LEE, Joseph and Mrs. Abi Holbrook, Feb. 12, 1786.
Salem and Cynthia E. Hilton, int. May 29, 1833.

LEGG, Abigail [int. adds Mrs.] and Ezekiel Bates, Apr. 9, 1767.
Abigail of Mendon, and Andrew Thayer, int. Feb. 6, 1803.
Abner and Mrs. Lebine Pond, int. July 14, 1781.
Charlott [int. Cherlotte], Mrs., and Daniel Cook Jr., May 22, 1783.
Chloe, Mrs., and Samuel Adams, Aug. 14, 1777.
Content and Elias Lasall [int. Lazall], May 26, 1816.
Huldah of Mendon, and Elijah Bates, int. Jan. 27, 1799.
Jemima of Mendon, and Daniel Thomson, int. Apr. 11, 1761.
Joshua of Wrentham, and Mrs. Rachel Chapen, June 13, 1776.
Susanna, Mrs., and David Cook Jr., int. Feb. 15, 1777.

LELAND (see Laland, Lealand, Lealond), Gilbert of Holliston, and Adaline Holbrook, int. Oct. 2, 1842.

LEWETT (see Lewit), Stephen and Eunice Cook, int. Aug. 31, 1833.
Susanna R. and Nathan Chilson, int. Oct. 5, 1832.

LEWIT (see Lewett), Susannah of Medway, and Enoch Greeley, int. May 1, 1814.

LILLIE, Henry [int. Lilie] and Caroline Hayden, Sept. 21, 1834.

LISCOMB, Sarah, Mrs., of Pomfret, and William Colstone, int. Aug. 1, 1783.

LITTLEFIELD, Ephraim of Milford, and Rhoda Partridge, int. Mar. 6, 1805.

LOTHROP, Nancy of Cumberland, and George Luke, int. Dec. 24, 1810.

LOVELL, Martha R. of Fall River, and John S. Hall, Sept. 7, 1841, in Fall River.*

LOVERING, Joseph of Holliston, and Mrs. Margreret Thayer, int. Dec. 10, 1763.

LOWE, Mary of Fitchburg, and Ezekiel H. Ames, int. July 10, 1814.

LUKE, George and Nancy Lothrop, int. Dec. 24, 1810.

LUTHER, Joseph and Clarrasa Hayward, int. Jan. 8, 1827.

* Intention not recorded.

LYON, Jabesh of Woodstock, and Uranah Hall, June 26, 1729.*

MAKEPEACE, William and Mrs. Mary Whiting, int. Jan. 21, 1794.

MAN (see Mann), Nathan of Wrentham, and "Ms" Abigail Wight, int. May 24, 1764.

MANN (see Man), Billings and Jemima Wight, July 21, 1822.
Billings and Harriet Lucas Daniel, int. June 22, 1828.
Elijah of Mendon, and Mrs. Pedy Slocomb, int. June 6, 1783.
Mary of Medway, and Daniel Richardson Parnel, int. Sept. 3, 1815.
Pheba, Mrs., of Mendon, and Tho[ma]s Pain, int. Apr. 2, 1784.
Thomas S. and Eliza Scott, int. May 12, 1816.

MARCUM, Darius [int. Markham] of Enfield, and Mrs. Lucy Alden, Dec. 6, 1770.

MARSH (see Mash), Abigal and Joseph Averry, int. Jan. 21, 1742–3.
John and Elesebath Clafing, int. July 4, 1743.

MARTIN, Eliza and James M. Staples, int. Jan. 26, 1833.
Jane of Franklin, and Daniel Arnold Jr., int. Apr. 27, 1834.
Otis and Lydia Knight, int. May 24, 1829.

MASH (see Marsh), Chloe of Mendon, and Calvin Barber, int. Sept. 21, 1800.

MASON, James B. of Milford, and Lorinda Cook, Oct. 27, 1836.
Olive, Mrs. [int. wid., omits Mrs.], of Medway, and Silas Adams, Aug. 20, 1794.
Sarah, Mrs., of Cumberland, and Zepheniah Wood, int. Feb. 5, 1782.

MASSEY, Joseph T., Rev., and Catharine P. Arnold, int. July 17, 1836.

McINTIRE, Mary A. of Tuftonborough, N.H., and William Paine Jr., int. Apr. 16, 1843.

McKEEN, Albert of Dunstable, N.H., and Vienna Paine, May 20, 1835.

MEDCALF (see Metcalf), Hannah of Franklin, and Henry Hill, int. Apr. 17, 1824.

* Intention not recorded.

MERET, Cloe [int. Chloe Merrite] of Wrentham, and Jack Bemdor [int. Bembo] [negroes], Sept. 26, 1777.

MERRIFIELD, Abigail, Mrs., and Nehemiah Johnson, int. Oct. 21, 1764.

Silas of Holliston, and Mille Phillips, int. Apr. 5, 1802.

MERRITT (see Meret).

MESENGER (see Messenger), John of Wrentham, and Mrs. Meletiah Corbett, int. May 6, 1758.

MESSENGER (see Mesenger), Eli and Ann Jennette Roberts, int. Aug. 3, 1833.

Eliza Ann of Medwey, and Salsbury Orswell, Dec. 10, 1826.*

Louisa M. and Rev. [int. omits Rev.] George W. Bosworth, Jan. 5, 1842.

William and Laurinda S. Coombs, int. Mar. 30, 1845.

METCALF (see Medcalf), Anna, Mrs., and Stephen Ballew, Sept. 11, 1774.

Beaulah, Mrs., and John Harding 3d, int. Sept. 8, 1781.

Benjamin and Mary Slocom, Aug. 7, 1739.*

Elisabeth [int. adds Mrs.] and Stephen Cook, Mar. 16, 1758.

Francis and Almira Adams, int. Apr. 22, 1845.

Grace, Mrs., and Abiel Pratt, int. Nov. 23, 1777.

Harriet M., 19, d. Savel and Nabby, and George Wyer, Oct. 5, 1848.

Henry B. of Wrentham, and Nancy H. Grinnell, int. Mar. 14, 1846.

Hollis and Abigail Allen, int. Apr. 6, 1822.

Jabiz and Mrs. Elisabeth Tinney, int. Oct. 6, 1775.

Jerusha, Mrs., of Frankling, and Nathan Whight, int. Aug. 20, 1780.

John Jr. and Mrs. Hannah Clerk, int. Dec. 17, 1785.

John and Sally B. Dudley, int. Aug. 30, 1829.

Katharine, Mrs., and Elijah Thayer, int. July 20, 1793.

Maray and Nathan Whitting, int. Mar. 18, 1748-9.

Margeret, Mrs., and Nathaniel Heaton, int. Oct. 17, 1765.

Mary, wid., of Wrentham, and Isaac Thayer, int. Feb. 16, 1750-1.

Mary, Mrs., and Joseph Faerbanks, int. Apr. 5, 1787.

Matthew and Mrs. Deborah Bullard, int. Aug. 16, 1767.

Mehetabel, Mrs., of Medway, and Enoch Hill, int. Mar. 9, 1760.

Mehetabel, Mrs., and Nathaniel Partridge, int. May 17, 1762.

Savel of Medway, and Nabby Cook, int. Dec. 15, 1827.

* Intention not recorded.

METCALF, Stephen and Mrs. Hipzibah Adams, int. Apr. 16, 1757.
Stephen Jr. and Mrs. Olive Burr, Apr. 26, 1796.
Stephen Esq. and Mrs. Sybil Perry, int. Nov. 18, 1836.

MILLER, Anna and Robert Parker, int. Sept. 1, 1805.
Joseph of Mendon, and Mary D. Barber, int. Nov. 2, 1834.
Ruth of Cumberland, and Asa Scott, int. May 2, 1813.

MOORE, Barnard of Medway, and Sabrina S. Willard, int. —— 5, 1841.

MOREY (see Mourey, Mowry), Sena of Smithfield, and John Arnold, int. June 29, 1806.

MORS (see Morse), Betsey of Medway, and Seneca Wight, int. Aug. 24, 1817.

MORSE (see Mors), Julia of Sturbridge, and Samuel Darling Jr., int. Mar. 29, 1849.
Julia F. of Oakham, and Eliab Holbrook Jr., int. May 15, 1842.
Nabby [int. Abigail] and Baxter Thomson, June 9, 1822.
W[illia]m M. and Deborah W. Kingman, July 21, 1842.

MOUREY (see Morey, Mowry), Chloe Ann, Mrs., of Uxbridge, and Capt. Lyman W. Thayer, int. Mar. 19, 1848.

MOWRY (see Morey, Mourey), Hama of Wrentham, and Duty Cook, int. Mar. 1, 1818.
Julia A. and Francis D. Bates, Mar. 20, 1839.

MULLARD, Fisher [? Bullard] and Rhoda Clark, int. Sept. 6, 1805.

MURPHY, Mary of Wrentham, and Cephas Carter, int. Sept. 3, 1815.

NARCROSS (see Norcross), Melita [int. Norcross] and Eli M. [int. Milton] Richardson, Apr. 28, 1814.

NASON, Luther W. and Marion Thompson, Oct. 30, 1843.

NEALSON, Josiah of Mendon, and Mrs. Elisabeth Thayer, int. Apr. 5, 1754.

NEW, Anna of Franklin, and Samuel Smith [int. 2d], Aug. 13, 1809.

NEWEL (see Newell), Bethsheba, Mrs., of Cumberland, and Samuel Scott Jr., int. Jan. 10, 1773.

NEWEL, Patiance [int. Mrs. Patianc] and Will[ia]m Whitely, "on or about" Dec. 10, 1779.

NEWELL (see Newel), Asa and Sela Scott, Dec. 28, 1806.
John and Bathsheba [int. Bethsheba] Scott, Dec. 8, 1805.

NEWTON, Calvin, Rev., and Millisent Johnson, int. Nov. 2, 1828.
Nahum of Shrewsbury, and Adaline Johnson, Apr. 20, 1831.*

NICHERSON, Hepzibath [int. Nickerson] and Reuben Nicherson [int. Nickerson], Oct. 20, 1816.
Reuben [int. Nickerson] and Hepzibath Nicherson [int. Nickerson], Oct. 20, 1816.

NICHOLS (see Nicklos), George [int. Nickols] and Sarah Ann Wilkins, Mar. 16, 1847.

NICKERSON (see Nicherson).

NICKLOS (see Nichols), Abigial, Mrs., of Cumberland, and Lot Perry, int. Jan. 24, 1773.

NILES, Julia Ann and Joseph Desper, int. Aug. 17, 1849.

NORCROSS (see Narcross), Asa [int. Norcress] and [int. adds Mrs.] Silva Thayer, Nov. 16, 1797.
Ellis T. and Ellen E. Hawes, int. Aug. 3, 1845.
Mary [int. Norcroos], Mrs., of Mendon, and David Ward, Mar. 26, 1773.
Silas T. [int. N.] of Franklin, and Sarah Hixen [int. Hixon], Jan. 11, 1821.

OBER, James M. of Wrentham, and Harriet B. Farrington, int. Oct. 26, 1833.

OLIVER, Mary Ann and George D. Pratt, July 7, 1825.

ONEEL, James and Mrs. Rosanna Razey, int. Nov. 26, 1825.

ONION, Asa F. and Asenath Thwing, int. Oct. 31, 1819.
Jonathan and Betsy Jenks, int. Apr. 21, 1826.
Leonard and Clarissa [int. Clarisa] Allen, Feb. 19, 1823.

ORSWELL, Salsbury of N. Providence, and Eliza Ann Messenger, Dec. 10, 1826.*

PAGE, William [int. Jr.] of Windham, Conn., and Rhoda Adams, Mar. 27, 1823.

* Intention not recorded.

PAIN (see Paine), Anna [int. adds Mrs.] and Phinehas Aldridg [int. Phineas Aldrich], Mar. 30, 1780.
Anna and Moses Thayer, int. Feb. 28, 1808.
Henrietta and Elias Cook Jr., Sept. 8, 1827.
James of Mendon, and Margaret Kelley, int. Oct. 22, 1825.
John Jay of Smithfield, R.I., and Olive Hall, Mar. 3 [int. Mar. 7, sic], 1819.
Rebekah, Mrs., and David Aldrich, int. Apr. 11, 1778.
Rufus and Mrs. Nancy Wales, Jan. 12, 1786.
Sally and Jacob Arnold, Sept. 12, 1811.
Suky and Oliver Razey, int. Jan. 26, 1817.
Tho[ma]s and Mrs. Pheba Mann, int. Apr. 2, 1784.
Uranah and Amasa Aldrish, int. Mar. 12, 1781.
William and Ruth Wilber, int. Mar. 25, 1810.
William and Polly Rhodes, int. Dec. 15, 1816.

PAINE (see Pain), Emanuel N. of Blackstone, and Maria Rockwood, int. Dec. 25, 1847.
Emanuel Newton of Mendon, and Susan Rockwood, int. Jan. 28, 1838.
Marietta and Henry Sherburne, Apr. 29, 1823.
Martha W. of Cumberland, R.I., and Barton Darling, int. Mar. 21, 1830.
Ruth W. and Whitman V. Cook, int. Nov. 7, 1835.
Susan Ann, 27, d. William and Polly, and James P. Thayer, Nov. 24, 1846.
Thomas D. of Smithfield, R.I., and Perley C. Thayer, int. Aug. 14, 1834.
Vienna and Albert McKeen, May 20, 1835.
William Jr. and Mary A. McIntire, int. Apr. 16, 1843.

PARKEA (see Parker), Marietta of Mendon, and Francis Kelly, int. Mar. 11, 1838.

PARKER (see Parkea), Elisabeth [int. adds Mrs.] and Elisha Hayward, Jan. 29, 1766.
Mary, Mrs., of Medway, and Silas Adams, int. July 10, 1768.
Robert of Smithfield, R.I., and Anna Miller, int. Sept. 1, 1805.

PARKHIRST (see Parkhurst, Parkis), Ephraim [int. Epharaim Parkhust] of Mendon, and Mrs. Jemima Hayward, Sept. 31 [sic], 1767.

PARKHURST (see Parkhirst, Parkis), Aaron [int. Parkis] and Mrs. Sarah Thomson, Dec. 23, 1790.
Nella and Ezekiel Bellou, int. Oct. 1, 1809.

PARKIS (see Parkhirst, Parkhurst), Kezia, Mrs. [int. Mrs. Lydia Porkis], and Cyrus [int. Syrus] Thomson, Mar. 16, 1774.

PARKMAN, Alathina of Milford, and Asa Hall 2d, int. Oct. 19, 1834.

PARNEL, Daniel Richardson and Mary Mann, int. Sept. 3, 1815.

PARTERIDGE (see Partraidge, Partridg, Partridge, Patridge), Job and Mrs. Deborah Farbank, int. Sept. 10, 1769.

PARTRAIDGE (see Parteridge, Partridg, Partridge, Patridge), Samuel of Wrentham, and Mary Blood, Dec. 28, 1736.*

PARTRIDG (see Parteridge, Partraidge, Partridge, Patridge), Elizabath of Wrantham, and Samuel Hayward, Mar. 15, 1734.*
Esther of Wrantham, [and] Daniel Thayer, Feb. 10, 1734–5.*

PARTRIDGE (see Parteridge, Partraidge, Partridg, Patridge), Aaron and Abigail Pond, int. Mar. 10, 1799.
Abigail and Abel Albee, int. Nov. 8, 1818.
Amos and Mrs. Clarisa [int. Clarissa] Slocom, Nov. 24, 1819.
Ann, Mrs., of Medway, and Jonathan Holbrook, int. Sept. 9, 1770.
Asenath and Joseph Adams 2d, Sept. 15, 1820.
Benjamin Jr. and [int. adds Mrs.] Mary Perry, Oct. 21, 1765.
Benjamin Jr. and Miltiah Pond, int. Dec. 9, 1798.
Debarah and Timothy Ellis Jr., int. July 17, 1803.
Eda and Timothy E. Jones, int. Oct. 21, 1831.
Experience and Ellery Allen, int. Oct. 15, 1806.
Hannah and Aaron Holbrook, int. Mar. 4, 1762.
Job Jr. and Tamer Partridge, int. Mar. 8, 1804.
Joseph and Mrs. Catherine Richardson [int. Katherine Richerson], Apr. 13, 1775.
Joseph [int. Parteridge] and Lucy Cook, Mar. 8, 1812.
Joseph and Lydiaett Cushman, int. Nov. 6, 1836.
Kezia, Mrs., and Ephraim Hill, int. Jan. 28, 1758.
Keziah of Wrantham, and Samuel Thayar, Dec. 24, 1739.*
Liberty of Westminster, and Rachal [int. Rachel] Holbrook, Jan. 31, 1814.
Mary [int. Partrige], wid., and John Combes [int. Combs] Jr., Apr. 26, 1780.

* Intention not recorded.

PARTRIDGE, Mary, Mrs., and Nathan Penneman [int. Penniman], Apr. 3, 1791.
Mary of Medway, and Asa Burr, int. Apr. 7, 1805.
Nancy and Theron Holbrook, int. Mar. 4, 1823.
Nathan of Midwey [int. Midway], and Mrs. Melitiah Holbrook, June 6, 1776.
Nathaniel of Medway, and Mrs. Mehetabel Metcalf, int. May 17, 1762.
Phillip and Alathina Johnson, int. Nov. 29, 1821.
Rhoda and Ephraim Littlefield, int. Mar. 6, 1805.
Roxana, wid., 28, of Medway, d. Artemas Richardson and Deborah, and Valentine W. Holbrook, widr., Dec. 4, 1849.*
Sarah of Wrentham, and Obadiah Adams, int. June 23, 1744.
Sarah, Mrs., and Billy Ware, ———— [int. Dec. 1, 1771].
Sarah [int. adds Mrs.] and Ichabod Pond, Nov. 30, 1797.
Tamer of Medway, and Job Partridge Jr., int. Mar. 8, 1804.

PATRICHE, Eunice, Mrs. [int. Patrick, omits Mrs.], of Holliston, and Henry Holbrook, May 2, 1816.

PATRIDGE (see Parteridge, Partraidge, Partridg, Partridge), Alfred and Chloe Blake, int. Mar. 15, 1840.
Benjamin R. and Bathsheba Jones, int. Apr. 27, 1834.
Sabra [int. Partridge], Mrs., and Calvin Holbrook, Dec. 13, 1792.

PATT, Eliza C. [int. Elizabeth, omits C.] and Capt. Amos H. Allen, May 27, 1835.

PECK, George and Mary Ann Franklin, int. May 13, 1833.
Mary and Samuel Garnsy, Dec. 14, 1731.*

PENIMAN (see Penneman, Penniman), Nathan of Mendon, and Mrs. Mary Holbrook, int. Dec. 15, 1757.

PENNEMAN (see Peniman, Penniman), Josiah Jr. of Mendon, and Senar [?] Holbrook, int. Mar. 13, 1790.
Nathan [int. Penniman] and Mrs. Mary Partridge, Apr. 3, 1791.

PENNIMAN (see Peniman, Penneman), Anna, Mrs., and Zurial Albee, int. Jan. 12, 1776.
Cate, Mrs., and Abner Albee, int. Aug. 20, 1774.
Daniel and Mrs. Mary Adams, int. Sept. 21, 1776.
Daniel and Elizibath Richardson, int. Oct. 20, 1799.
Mary, Mrs., of Uxbridge, and Stephen Holbrook Jr., int. July 31, 1790.

* Intention not recorded.

PENNIMAN, Nathan and Hannah Hill, int. June 27, 1798.
Phebe [int. Mrs. Pheba] and Paul Clark, Nov. 30, 1797.
Roxanna, Mrs., of Franklin, and Abijah Cook, int. Nov. 5, 1843.
Samuel Jr. of Milford, and Mrs. Hannah Bass, Apr. 28, 1796.
Samuel of Milford, and Sarah Albee [int. adds wid.], Sept. 19, 1799.
Silis and Mrs. Huldah Daniels, int. Mar. 8, 1772.

PERKINS, Martha of Surry, N.H., and Pliny Holbrook, int. May 7, 1826.
Mary and James B. Dakin, May 23, 1833.
Ora and Levinia Buck, Apr. 7, 1839.

PERRY (see Pery), Baruch of Holliston, and Mrs. Lucy Fairbanks, int. Mar. 22, 1829.
David and Mrs. Mary Arnold, int. Feb. 14, 1780.
Ebeneazear and Abigal Hall, Feb. 10, 1736–7.*
Elisebeth, Mrs., and Levi Aldrish Jr., int. Nov. 11, 1774.
Elisha of Milford, and Mrs. Abigail Hunting, Apr. 30, 1829.*
Lot and Mrs. Abigial Nicklos, int. Jan. 24, 1773.
Mary [int. adds Mrs.] and Benjamin Partridge Jr., Oct. 21, 1765.
Noah and Mrs. Anna Holbrook, int. May 23, 1773.
Oliver and Elisabeth Streeter, int. Feb. 22, 1752.
Sybil, Mrs., of Milford, and Stephen Metcalf Esq., int. Nov. 18, 1836.

PERY (see Perry), Oliver, s. Oliver, and Amey [int. Mrs. Amy] Pickring, Oct. 8, 1780.

PETTER, Mary E. of Medway, and Nathaniel Bosworth, int. Sept. 24, 1848.

PHELPS, Lydia W., Mrs., of Hopkinton, and Martin Rockwood Jr., int. Mar. 14, 1846.

PHETTIPLACE, Job [int. Phetteplace] of Gloucester, R.I., and Nancy Thomson [int. Thompson], Apr. 1 [?], 1803.

PHILIPS (see Phillips), Calib and Susanah Horse, Sept. 12, 1733.*

PHILLIPS (see Philips), Abagail, Mrs., of Mendon, and Jonathan Scott, int. Nov. 21, 1796.
Amos and Mrs. Fanny Handcock, Nov. 23, 1797.
Hannah, Mrs., and Peletiah Whitting, int. May 20, 1758.

* Intention not recorded.

BELLINGHAM MARRIAGES. 135

PHILLIPS, Israel of Smithfield, and Abigil Johnson, int. July 19, 1785. "Forbid By Israel Phillips July 25, 1785."
John and Mrs. Sarah Pond, int. Jan. 17, 1768.
Joshua and Mrs. Mary Heaton, int. Mar. 17, 1765.
Joshua, Lt., and Hannah Howard, wid., int. Sept. 2, 1805.
Mary and Samuel Blake, int. Jan. 2, 1801.
Mille and Silas Merrifield, int. Apr. 5, 1802.
Sarah, Mrs., and Timothy Rockwood, Dec. 25, 1782.
Sarah and Nathaniel Heaton, int. Sept. 9, 1809.
Susana [int. Susanna], Mrs., and James Bayley, June 4, 1760.
Susannah, Mrs., and Alpheus Albee, Mar. 31, 1796.

PHIPPS (see Phips), Jedediah of Franklin, and Martha C. Hills, Feb. 26, 1835.*
Maria A. of Franklin, and Sabin Holbrook, int. Mar. 28, 1841.

PHIPS (see Phipps), Persis and Moses Hill, int. Mar. 20, 1808.

PICKERING (see Pickern, Pickirn, Pickrin, Pickring), Abigail and Ellery Thayer, Apr. 12, 1818.
Anna and George Washington Taft, int. Oct. 10, 1819.
Esther [int. Pickring, adds Mrs.], d. Samuel (Pickrin), and William Billings, Aug. 20, 1789.
Esther and Pliny Cook, Sept. 30, 1825.
Hannah and Eliab Holbrook Jr., Apr. 25, 1839.
Joanna [int. Pickren], Mrs., of Mendon, and Ezekiel [int. Ezekeiel] Cook Jr., May 9, 1791.
Levina and Oliver Folet, int. Dec. 23, 1820.
Mary J., 25, d. Asa and Hannah, and Alfred Arnold, Sept. 4, 1849.
Peter, Capt., of Mendon, and Phebe Sibley, int. Feb. 24, 1827.
Philadelphia and Bani Bartlett, int. Dec. 6, 1801.
Rhoda and Welcom B. Cook, int. Feb. 8, 1829.
Rossanna and Oliver Raze, int. Aug. 15, 1819.
Sally and Galen Cook, Oct. 17, 1822.
Samuel B. of Mendon, and Sophia M. Cook, int. Aug. 25, 1844.
Simon and Rhoda Willcocks, int. Feb. 10, 1790.
Simon and Elizabeth Whiting, Jan. 26, 1832.

PICKERN (see Pickering, Pickirn, Pickrin, Pickring), Benjamin Jr. [int. Pickirn, omits Jr.] of Mendon, and Mrs. Mary Jones, Dec. 1, 1778.

* Intention not recorded.

PICKIRN (see Pickering, Pickern, Pickrin, Pickring), Rosanna, Mrs. [int. Pickring, omits Mrs.], and Ahab Arnold, Dec. 20, 1781.

PICKRIN (see Pickering, Pickern, Pickirn, Pickring), Sarah, Mrs., and Anthony Raze, int. Apr. 12, 1790.

PICKRING (see Pickering, Pickern, Pickirn, Pickrin), Amey [int. Mrs. Amy] of Mendon, d. Edward, and Oliver Pery, Oct. 8, 1780.
Jonathan [dup. Pickrieng] and "Ms." Elizabeth [dup. and int. Mrs. Elisabeth] Hunt, Feb. 28, 1760.
Samuel of Mendon, and Mrs. Sarah B[e]ll[e]w, int. Nov. 21, 1758.

PIERCE, Allen L. and Lorra Grant, int. Sept. 12, 1826.
Eliza and Willard Ellis, int. Aug. 8, 1832.
Polly of Milford, and Otis Bullard, int. Mar. 1, 1821.

PIKE, Abigil, Mrs., and Calvin Thayer, Apr. 10, 1786.
Frenk and Eliza T. Gates, int. Mar. 2, 1834.
Mary, Mrs., and Boice Kimbel Jr., int. Jan. 5, 1782.
Mary of Woodstock, and Samuel Sessions, int. Jan. 25, 1806.

PITTS, Elisabeth, Mrs., and Jesse Bellow, int. Dec. 2, 1775.
John of Mendon, and Ruth Darling, int. Sept. 7, 1747.

PLACE, Nathan and Cyrena Cushman, int. Mar. 3, 1816.

POND, Abigail of Franklin, and Aaron Partridge, int. Mar. 10, 1799.
Amanda of Franklin, and Samuel Haskell Jr., int. Aug. 31, 1817.
Cinthia of Franklin, and James J. Greene, int. Oct. 31, 1819.
Cynthea of Franklin, and George W. Lawton, int. Nov. 1, 1818.
Davaid of Rantham, and Marcy Danaiels, Dec. 19, 1740.*
Elizabeth G. of New Salem, and Sumner Dudley, int. Sept. 24, 1837.
Freelove, Mrs., of Wrentham, and Abijah Holbrook, int. July 2 1773.
Ichabod of Franklin, and [int. adds Mrs.] Sarah Partridge, Nov. 30, 1797.
John F. of Medway, and Betsey [int. Betsy] Foster, Sept. 27, 1821.
Jonathan of Wrentham, and Mrs. Thankfull ———, int. July 9, 1763.
Lebine, Mrs., of Franklin, and Abner Legg, int. July 14, 1781.
Lovice, Mrs., and Daniel Rockwood, Feb. 18, 1793.

* Intention not recorded.

POND, Marcy of Wrentham, and Luke Holbrook, int. Nov. 24, 1750.
Mary of Medway, and Charles Wight, int. Mar. 7, 1832.
Miltiah of Franklin, and Benjamin Partridge Jr., int. Dec. 9, 1798.
Oliver of Franklin, and Remember Bailey, June 2, 1807.*
Paul Dexter of Franklin, and Huldah Hill, int. Dec. 23, 1807.
Ruth M., Mrs., of Franklin, and Dr. Shadrach Atwood, int. Nov. 11, 1832.
Sarah, Mrs., of Wrentham, and John Phillips, int. Jan. 17, 1768.

PRATT, Abiel of Midway, and Mrs. Grace Metcalf, int. Nov. 23, 1777.
Abigail, Mrs. [int. wid., omits Mrs.], and Joseph Ellis, Mar. 26, 1795.
Benjamin and Mrs. Abigail Puffer, int. Apr. 27, 1763.
Benja[min] Jr. [int. Prat] and Mrs. Abigail [int. Abigil, omits Mrs.] Jonson, May 28, 1788.
Betsey [int. Betsy] and Levi Chilson [int. Chillson], Aug. 12, 1823.
George D. of Newmarket, N.H., and Mary Ann Oliver, July 7, 1825.
Hannah [int. adds Mrs.] and David Jones, Apr. 25, 1754, in Mendon.
Hannah, Mrs., and Joseph Chilson, Jan. 25, 1786.
Joseph and [int. adds Mrs.] Hannah Jones, Jan. 30, 1755, in Mendon.
Joseph Jr. of Oxford, and Delivernce Baxter, int. Sept. 26, 1761.
Joseph and Mrs. Elisabeth [int. Elizabeth] Upham, Jan. 25, 1786.
Lidea [int. Lidia], Mrs., and Allen Chase, May 15, 1796.
Lydia of Dedham, and Joseph Chillson, Nov. 15, 1747 [int. Sept. 12, 1749, *sic*].
Mary, Mrs., and Barthelomew Forster [int. Bartholomew Foster], Feb. 2, 1775.
Patience [int. Patiance] and John Upham, Sept. 2, 1761.

PRENTICE (see Prentise), Jonah of Uxbridge, and Mrs. Elizabeth Smith, int. Aug. 11, 1754.

PRENTISE (see Prentice), Solomon of Hull, and Mrs. Anne Holbrook, int. July 1, 1770.

PROCTOR, James A. of Wrentham, and Sarah M. Smith, Dec. 31, 1840.

* Intention not recorded.

PROUTY, Rebekah of Langdon, N.H., and James J. Fisk, int. Oct. 28, 1832.

PUFFER, Abigail, Mrs., and Benjamin Pratt, int. Apr. 27, 1763.
Annah of Medway, and Asail Holbrook, int. Feb. 26, 1742-3.
Ruth of Medway, and Moses Holbrook, int. Feb. 9, 1743-4.
Sarah, Mrs., and Simeon Allen, int. Mar. 16, 1766.

RAND, William T. of Dedham, and Catharine A. Allen, Apr. 4, 1830.

RASEY (see Raze, Razey, Razy), Rosanna [int. adds Mrs.] and Otis Scott, May 22, 1836.

RATHBORNE, Hannah [int. Rathbone] and Barzillai Hayward, Dec. 27, 1813.

RAWSON, Maryann and Mark Colvin, int. Sept. 26, 1819.

RAY, Abigail, Mrs., of Wrentham, and Isaac Johnson, int. Aug. 22, 1762.
George W., widr. [int. omits widr.], 39, of Medway, s. James and Thankful, and Sarah S. Cook, wid. [int. Mrs., omits wid.], Nov. 26, 1846.

RAZE (see Rasey, Razey, Razy), Anthony of Cumberland, and Mrs. Sarah Pickrin, int. Apr. 12, 1790.
Oliver and Rossanna Pickering, int. Aug. 15, 1819.

RAZEY (see Rasey, Raze, Razy), Oliver and Suky Pain, int. Jan. 26, 1817.
Rosanna, Mrs., and James Oneel, int. Nov. 26, 1825.

RAZY (see Rasey, Raze, Razey), Ellery A. and Cyrena Cushman, int. Sept. 8, 1839.

READ (see Reed), Patty of Wrentham, and Hezekiah Flecher, int. Mar. 31, 1811.
Samuel T. of Worcester, and Abigail Wight, Dec. 16, 1817.

REED (see Read), Habijah of Attelbury, and Lidia Wight, Oct. 14, 1761.

RHOADES (see Rhodes), John N. and Henrietta Cook, int. Sept. 20, 1840.

RHODES (see Rhoades), Emulous, widr., 24, of Wrentham, s. Jonathan and Elmira, and Cindarella Thayer, Aug. 16, 1846.*

* Intention not recorded.

RHODES, John of Wrentham, and Anna Cook, int. Nov. 8, 1812.
Mary A. [int. Rhoades] and [int. adds Ens.] James Bacon, Oct. 17, 1837.
Polly and William Pain, int. Dec. 15, 1816.
Rachel G. and Samuel P. Hayward, int. Feb. 9, 1845.
William O. and Wata Cook, int. Mar. 28, 1841.

RICE, Dexter B. of Mendon, and Patience Curtis, int. Feb. 10, 1828.
Polly M., Mrs., and Asa Burr, int. Jan. 14, 1832.

RICHARDS, Thomas D. and Hellen Clark, int. Aug. 6, 1843.

RICHARDSON, Amos of Medw[a]y, and Mrs. Phebe Holbrook, int. July 13, 1766.
Catherine, Mrs. [int. Katherine Richerson], of Wrentham, and Joseph Partridge, Apr. 13, 1775.
Eli M. [int. Milton] of Franklin, and Melita Narcross [int. Norcross], Apr. 28, 1814.
Elizibath and Daniel Penniman, int. Oct. 20, 1799.

RIDER, Polley of Medway, and Solomon Wright, int. Nov. 6, 1814.

RIPLEY, Susan [int. Susen] and Appollos [int. Apollas] Cushman, Feb. 20, 1816 [int. Dec. 26, 1816, *sic*].

ROBERTS, Ann Jennette of Smithfield, R.I., and Eli Messenger, int. Aug. 3, 1833.

ROBINSON, Elijah of Attelborough, and Mrs. Sarah Smith, int. Nov. 30, 1754.

ROCKWOOD, Abby A. and Lloyd H. Cook, int. Nov. 17, 1849.
Abigail L. and George Darling, int. Mar. 13, 1836.
Alce, Mrs., and John Cook, Nov. 26, 1778.
Benjamin and Margrat Gree[n], Feb. 12, 1734-5.*
Calvin N. and Jane H. Foristall, int. Apr. 13, 1849.
Caroline B. and Peletiah S. Bates, May 10, 1832, in Franklin.
Daniel and Mrs. Lovice Pond, Feb. 18, 1793.
Elizabeth, 24, d. Martin and Abigail, and Silas F. Thayer, May 4, 1846.
Eunice, Mrs. [int. Eunis, wid., omits Mrs.], and Aaron Lealond [int. Lealand], June 11, 1788.
Horace [int. of Medway] and Eliza B. Smith, Feb. 12, 1835.

* Intention not recorded.

Rockwood, John and [int. adds Mrs.] Eunice Smith, Apr. 27, 1780.
Joseph Jr. of Mendon, and Alce Thomson, int. Mar. 10, 1749-50.
Joseph and Anna Chilson, int. Feb. 12, 1804.
Levi and Mrs. Deborah Leazell, Feb. 22, 1774.
Levi and Tryphina Holbrook, int. July 12, 1801.
Lewis L. of Upton, and Meleta B. Windsor, int. Dec. 6, 1840.
Maria and Emanuel N. Paine, int. Dec. 25, 1847.
Martin and Abigail Bates, Mar. 29, 1810.
Martin [int. Jr.] and Julia M. Cook, Oct. 23, 1838.
Martin Jr. and Mrs. Lydia W. Phelps, int. Mar. 14, 1846.
Mary, wid., of Oxford, and John Jones Jr., int. Sept. 7, 1751.
Meletiah [int. Melatiah], Mrs., and Asa Holbrook, Nov. 22, 1780.
Newell and Ann S. Winter, int. Mar. 3, 1823.
Rachel, Mrs., and Levi Thomson, int. Jan. 7, 1797.
Reuben and Polly Albee, int. May 2, 1813.
Susan and Emanuel Newton Paine, int. Jan. 28, 1838.
Susana and Moses Teney, Nov. 1, 1733.*
Susana of Franklin, and Nahum Holbrook, int. Feb. 3, 1802.
Timothy of Franklin, and Mrs. Sarah Phillips, Dec. 25, 1782.
Varnum B., 23, s. Martin and Abigail, and Julia A. Burr, June 1, 1848.

ROSE, Lucy of Milford, and Dick Brattle, int. Feb. 25, 1785.

RUSSELL, Charles and Harriet H. Bacon, int. Sept. 23, 1838.
William F. of Mendon, and Sarah W. Law, int. Apr. 3, 1847.

SALES (see Salis, Sayles), Selah of Franklin, and William Scott, int. Apr. 27, 1800.

SALIS (see Sales, Sayles), Smith of Smithfield, and Mrs. Abigal Scott, int. Mar. 19, 1780.

SALLY, Margaret and Seth Sherman, int. Oct. 21, 1820.

SAMPSON, Chloe of Pelham, and Laban Bates Jr., int. Sept. 9, 1804.

SAVAGE, Samuel and Amy Brown, int. Nov. 11, 1752.

SAYLES (see Sales, Salis), Daniel and Olive Bellew, int. Apr. 13, 1812.
John of Franklin, and Martha Darling, May 28, 1817.
Stephen of Franklin, and Esther Darling, Jan. 11, 1810.

* Intention not recorded.

BELLINGHAM MARRIAGES. 141

SCAMMEL (see Scammell, Scammill), Samuel of Mendon, and Mrs. Bethiah Corbett, int. Aug. 18, 1759.

SCAMMELL (see Scammel, Scammill), Bethiah and John Wheeler, Mar. 29, 1812.
Jane L. and Rev. George N. Townsend, Aug. 10, 1842.
John C. and Joanna Sternes, int. Oct. 23, 1815.
Mary and John Wheeler, Apr. 4, 1807.
Samuel L. and Emela Stearns, int. July 7, 1811.
Samuel S. and Frances A. Ballou, int. Nov. 2, 1845.

SCAMMILL (see Scammel, Scammell), Hopestill [int. Scammell] and Otis Thayer, May 17, 1807.

SCOLOMB (see Selocomb, Slocom, Slocomb, Slocum), Bethuel and Mary Albee, int. Aug. 12, 1810.

SCOOT (see Scott), Joanna, Mrs., and Ahas Aldrich, int. Mar. 22, 1792.
Mary and Charles Capring, int. Nov. 6, 1742.

SCOTT (see Scoot), Abigail, Mrs., and Ahab Wilkinson, int. Apr. 5, 1755.
Abigal, Mrs., and Smith Salis, int. Mar. 19, 1780.
Anderson and Abigail Keth, int. Dec. 23, 1805.
Asa and Ruth Miller, int. May 2, 1813.
Bathsheba [int. Bethsheba] and John Newell, Dec. 8, 1805.
Betsey of Franklin, and Albinus Cook, Mar. 10, 1313 [*sic*, 1813].
Catharine and Alanson Sessions, int. Mar. 20, 1805.
David Jr. and Mrs. Sarah Arnold, int. Apr. 21, 1781.
Elisabeth and Daniel Cook, Dec. 25, 1746.
Elisha Jr. and Maranda S. Capron, int. Feb. 7, 1841.
Eliza of Cumberland, and Thomas S. Mann, int. May 12, 1816.
Eliza C. of Mendon, and Sullivan Scott, Feb. 7, 1838, in Providence, R.I.
Emory and Waity Jillson, int. Mar. 12, 1820.
Harvey and Phila Bartlet, int. Aug. 1, 1805.
Israel and Sarah Holbrook, Oct. 16, 1809.
Isreal of Providence, R.I., and Patty Slocom, int. July 6, 1828.
Jefferson and Alice Worrall, Feb. 21, 1830.
Jerusha and Dorrington Seagraves [int. Seagreaves], Nov. 22, 1804.
Joanna, Mrs., and Stephen Cook, Oct. 20, 1768.
John and Mrs. Frances Boyde, int. July 28, 1765.
John W. of Milford, and Emeline French, July 5, 1846.*
Jonathan and Mrs. Anne Aldrich, int. Nov. 29, 1767.

* Intention not recorded.

BELLINGHAM MARRIAGES.

SCOTT, Jonathan and Abagail Phillips, int. Nov. 21, 1796.
Joseph and Leah Capron, int. June 2, 1750.
Joseph and Luci Brown, int. Dec. 23, 1752.
Leah and Otis Freeman, int. May 5, 1788.
Levi [int. Levina] and Joshua Chilson [int. Chillson] Jr., Apr. 3, 1831.
Levina and Martin Chilson, Jan. 3, 1819.
Mary, Mrs., and John Arnold, int. May 11, 1775.
Mary and John Seagraves Jr., Mar. 21, 1805.
Molly, Mrs., and Nathaniel Jillson Jr., int. July 11, 1772.
Nancy of Providence, R.I., and William Ham, Dec. 14, 1848.*
Nathaniel and Mrs. Hipsibah Lain, int. May 14, 1783.
Nethaniel and Mrs. Eunice Arnold, int. May 11, 1775.
Only and Lydia Lasdol, int. June 10, 1805.
Otis and [int. adds Mrs.] Rosanna Rasey, May 22, 1836.
Patience and Eber Bartlett, int. Oct. 12, 1810.
Rhoda, Mrs., and Benj[ami]n Buffam, int. Feb. 13, 1784.
Sabra, Mrs., and Enoch Aldrich, int. Mar. 7, 1798.
Samuel and Maray Thomson, int. Mar. 14, 1743.
Samuel Jr. and Mrs. Bethsheba Newel, int. Jan. 10, 1773.
Samuel and Mrs. Hannah Jones, June 25, 1826.
Sarah and Luther Aldrich, int. Sept. 13, 1788.
Saul and Mrs. Selah Bellow, int. Apr. 19, 1781.
Sela and Asa Newell, Dec. 28, 1806.
Sellissa and Asa Hall Esq., June 16, 1831.
Selvenus and Mrs. Deborah Braley, int. Nov. 23, 1785.
Silvanus and Mrs. Joanna Bozworth, int. July 10, 1754.
Sullivan and Eliza C. Scott, Feb. 7, 1838, in Providence, R.I.
Thomas J. and Mary A. Bates, int. Aug. 19, 1827.
Vienna and Juba F. Whitaker, int. Oct. 10, 1830.
Willard Ballou and Sarah Amanda Taggard, int. Apr. 18, 1830.
William and Selah Sales, int. Apr. 27, 1800.
William Jr. and Sally Snow, int. Nov. 8, 1834.

SEAGRAVES, Dorrington [int. Seagreaves] of Uxbridge, and Jerusha Scott, Nov. 22, 1804.
John Jr. of Uxbridge, and Mary Scott, Mar. 21, 1805.

SELOCOMB (see Scolomb, Slocom, Slocomb, Slocum), Molly, Mrs., of Franklin, and William Hall, int. June 14, 1783.

SESSIONS, Alanson of N. Providence, R.I., and Catharine Scott, int. Mar. 20, 1805.
Samuel and Mary Pike, int. Jan. 25, 1806.

* Intention not recorded.

SHAIRMEN (see Shearman, Sherman), Elisha and Levina Willburt, int. Dec. 11, 1802.

SHAW, James and Matilda Armitage, May 3, 1847.

SHEARMAN (see Shairmen, Sherman), Anna, Mrs., and Luke Jillson, int. Apr. 5, 1777.
Elisha and Nancy [int. Nancey] Cook, Feb. 14, 1811.
Elisha [int. Sherman] of Cumberland, R.I., and Rhoda Cook, May 28, 1833.
Joanna [int. Sherman] and Silas Cook, Mar. 26, 1820.
Mara, Mrs., and William Colston [int. Colson], May 20, 1779.
Maranda of Foxborough, and Sam[ue]l Thayer, int. Oct. 27, 1826.
Patience, Mrs. [int. wid., omits Mrs.], and Silas Cook Jr., Jan. 1, 1822.
Rhobby [int. Rhoba] and Willard Thayer 2d [int. omits 2d], Sept. 29, 1822.
Seth and Nabby H. Shepherd, int. Dec. 8, 1826.

SHEEPARD (see Shepard, Shepherd), Daniel and Mrs. Rachel Darling, int. Nov. 15, 1772.

SHEPARD (see Sheepard, Shepherd), Daniel and Mrs. Deborah Hall, int. Nov. 13, 1762.

SHEPERDSON, Lydia of Wrentham, Norfolk Co., and Leonard Chamberlain, Oct. 9, 1823.*

SHEPHERD (see Sheepard, Shepard), Nabby H. of Foxborough, and Seth Shearman, int. Dec. 8, 1826.

SHERBURN (see Sherburne), George of Wrentham, and Abigail Thayer, int. May 5, 1833.

SHERBURNE (see Sherburn), Henry of Wrentham, and Marietta Paine, Apr. 29, 1823.

SHERMAN (see Shairmen, Shearman), John of Shrewsbury, and Cloe Thayer, June 25, 1761.
Seth and Margaret Sally, int. Oct. 21, 1820.

SHUTLEWORTH, Mercey [int. Mercy Shuttleworth] and Joseph Chillson, Nov. 23, 1744.

SIBLEY (see Sybley), Phebe and Capt. Peter Pickering, int. Feb. 24, 1827.

* Intention not recorded.

SLACK, Esther, Mrs., of Cumberland, and Samuel Darling, int. Dec. 10, 1754.

SLOCOM (see Scolomb, Selocomb, Slocomb, Slocum), Asa and Claricy [int. Cleresy] Hill, Apr. 15, 1810.
Clarisa [int. Clarissa], Mrs., and Amos Partridge, Nov. 24, 1819.
Mary of Wrentham, and Benjamin Metcalf, Aug. 7, 1739.*
Mary and Rev. William Gammell, int. Feb. 27, 1811.
Patty and Isreal Scott, int. July 6, 1828.
Vesta and Manly P. Horton, May 2, 1833.

SLOCOMB (see Scolomb, Selocomb, Slocom, Slocum), Pedy, Mrs., and Elijah Mann, int. June 6, 1783.

SLOCUM (see Scolomb, Selocomb, Slocom, Slocomb), Albert G. [int. Slocom], 23, of Cumberland, R.I., s. Bethuel and Mary, and Mary S. F. Clark, Oct. 20, 1844.

SMITH, Abner and Jemima Fisk, int. June 1, 1800.
Amanda L., 21, d. Robert and Sally, and Edmund J. Adams, Nov. 26, 1846.
Benjamin and Mrs. Sarah Smith, int. Jan. 19, 1836.
Charlottee and Edward Beasley [int. Beazley], Feb. 15, 1809.
Diana and Benjamin F. Johnson, int. Sept. 14, 1833.
Eliza B. and Horace Rockwood, Feb. 12, 1835.
Elizabeth, Mrs., and Jonah Prentice, int. Aug. 11, 1754.
Elmira of Blackston, and David Cook, int. Oct. 25, 1846.
Eunice [int. adds Mrs.] and John Rockwood, Apr. 27, 1780.
Jain and Zurial Hall, int. Dec. 14, 1742.
James and Sarah Hayward, Nov. 21, 1728.*
Joanna and Jefferson B. Darling, May 27, 1823.
John and Celia Ann Arnold, Sept. 5, 1830.
Julia Ann and Reuel Adams, int. Oct. 12, 1833.
Levi of District of Holland, and Milletiah Darling, Jan. 14, 1807.
Levina [int. adds wid.] and Ezekiel Bates, Apr. 25, 1799.
Levina and Arnold Hill, int. Jan. 30, 1803.
Levina B. and Lyman A. Cook, Sept. 22, 1830.
Lucy and Jarves Cook, int. May 17, 1835.
Margaret and Samuel Darling Jr., May 28, 1815.
Margeret [int. Margret], Mrs., and John Bates, Apr. 6, 1797.
Margret, Mrs., and Simeon Wight, Mar. 18, 1772.
Maria B. and Jarvis B. Lawrence, int. Apr. 26, 1840.
Marian C., 23, of Mendon, d. W[illia]m and Hannah, and Ezekiel P. Burr, Oct. 24, 1849.*

* Intention not recorded.

SMITH, Martha [int. Marthe], Mrs., and Amaziah Cushman, Feb. 28, 1775.
Meletiah [int. Miletiah] W. and Ebenezer H. Fisher, Aug. 19, 1839.
Nabby [int. Naby] and Laban Burr, Mar. 31, 1814.
Nancy D. and Leonard Knowlton, int. Sept. 2, 1838.
Olive A. and David H. Benedict, Mar. 20, 1839.
Pelatiah and Unice Thoite, June 23, 1752, in Medway.
Peletiah and Mrs. Joanna Thayer, int. Nov. 6, 1796.
Pelletiah Jr. and Julia Bates, int. July 8, 1827.
Persis of Cumberland, R.I., and Barton Darling, int. Sept. 27, 1835.
Robart Jr. and Mrs. Rhoda Taft, int. May 29, 1774.
Robert [int. Robart] Jr. and Mrs. Levina [int. Lavine] Cook, Mar. 7, 1776.
Robert and Salla Fairbanks, int. Dec. 1, 1804.
Rhoba, Mrs., and Thadius Thayer, int. Nov. 13, 1783.
Ruth A. and Thomas S. Benedict, Apr. 15, 1835.
Sally and Christopher Adams, Apr. 24, 1814.*
Samuel of Mendon, and Mrs. Rebeckah Aldridg, int. Jan. 2, 1786.
Samuel [int. 2d] and Anna New, Aug. 13, 1809.
Sarah, Mrs., and Elijah Robinson, int. Nov. 30, 1754.
Sarah and Mayo Cook, June 13, 1820.
Sarah, Mrs., and Benjamin Smith, int. Jan. 19, 1836.
Sarah M. and James A. Proctor, Dec. 31, 1840.
Sewall of Medway, and Julia Ann Blake, int. Aug. 25, 1839.
Sofferly [int. Soffarly] and Lealond [int. Lealon] Cook, Nov. 8, 1815.
Tamer [int. Tamor], Mrs., and Samuel Follet, Dec. 17, 1783.
Zilpha T. and Christopher C. Daniell, int. Oct. 17, 1831.

SNELL, Henry C., widr. [int. omits widr.], 41, of Medway, and Eliza Thayer, May 1, 1844 [int. Apr. 13, 1845, *sic*].

SNOW, Jane A. of Hopkinton, and Sylvanus W. Farrington, int. Jan. 11, 1846.
Sally of Smithfield, R.I., and William Scott Jr., int. Nov. 8, 1834.

SOUTHWICK, Ann and Daniel Hutchinson, Nov. 1, 1838.
Rachel of Mendon, and Dr. Absalom Daniels, int. Aug. 23, 1829.
Seth of Mendon, and Alpha Wallden, int. May 10, 1801.

* Intention not recorded.

SPEAH (see Spear, Speer), Elkanah and Mrs. Elisabeth Arnold, int. Sept. 18, 1779.

SPEAR (see Speah, Speer), Benjamin and Mrs. Elizabeth Forister [Forristall] [int. Mrs. Elisabeth Foristall], Mar. 29, 1785.
Charles of Milford, and Sabra D. White, int. Oct. 5, 1845.
Elisabeth, wid. [int. omits wid.], of Cumberland, and Seth Hall, widr. [int. omits widr.], Dec. 17, 1761.
Elisabeth [int. Elizabeth] and Jasper Wiswall [int. Wiswell], Apr. 29, 1821.
Laura and Ellis Daniels [int. Daniels Ellis], Nov. 9, 1820.
Pascal P. and Betsey Guild [dup. Giulde], int. Feb. 27 [dup. Jan. 4], 1811.

SPEER (see Speah, Spear), Simthe, Mrs., and Ishmell Aldrish, int. Jan. 24, 1775.

SPROUTER, Roxlany and Nathan Adams, Sept. 12, 1819.

STACY, Lorinda of Halifax, Vt., and Capt. Oded Coombs, int. Feb. 19, 1837.

STAPLES, James M. and Eliza Martin, int. Jan. 26, 1833.
Lendol of Mendon, and Susanna Albee, Nov. 25, 1810.
Ruth, Mrs., of Mendon, and Elias Thayer Jr., int. July 30, 1797.

STEARNS (see Sternes), Emela of Milford, and Samuel L. Scammell, int. July 7, 1811.
Julia A., wid. [int. omits wid.], 39, and Burgess T. Chase, Aug. 13, 1844.

STERNES (see Stearns), Joanna of Milford, and John C. Scammell, int. Oct. 23, 1815.

STEVENS, Jacob (St[e]vens) of Fiskkill, N.Y., and Olive Beals, int. Aug. 23, 1823.
Silas and Hannah Bowers, int. Aug. 20, 1837.

STOCKWELL, Experiance, Mrs., of Oxford, and Joseph Aldrich, int. Oct. 29, 1762.

STODDAR, Ezekiel of Upton, and Mrs. [int. omits Mrs.] Lucy Foristall, Dec. 30, 1784.

STONE, Calvin and Mrs. Mary Johnson, int. June 17, 1838.

STOW (see Stowe), Walter D. [dup. and int. Stowe], 28, s. Walter and Cyntha of Dover, and Lurania Holbrook, Apr. 25, 1844.

STOWE (see Stow), Walter D. and Europe Cahoon, int. Apr. 3, 1847.

STRATTON, Adaline Shepard of Foxborough, and Ezekiel C. Grant, int. Sept. 28, 1828.

STREETER, Eliza of Smithfield, R.I., and Levi Chilson, int. Nov. 27, 1834.
Elizabeth of Cumberland, and Oliver Perry, int. Feb. 22, 1752.

SUMNER, Elisabeth [int. Elisbeth], Mrs., and Thaddeus Gibson, Feb. 2, 1778.
Jesse [int. Jessa] of Milford, and Mrs. Phila [int. Philee] Darling, Nov. 25, 1790.
Sarah, Mrs., of Mendon, and Ezekiel Holbrook, int. Feb. 21, 1773.
Sarah V. and Phillip C. Bryant, July 9, 1829.

SUNDERLAND, Daniel and Frances L. Franklin, Apr. 3, 1842.

SYBLEY (see Sibley), Molly of Mendon, and "M^r or Deac." David Cook, int. Dec. 15, 1815.

SYLVESTER, Adaline M. of Boston, and Charles H. Farrington, int. Mar. 4, 1846.

TAFT, Benjamin B. and Vienna [int. Viena] Cook, Aug. 31, 1820.
Bethiah, Mrs., of Milford, and Joshua Bullard, int. Mar. 2, 1782.
Charles A. of Milton, and Levina K. Thayer, int. Jan. 2, 1832.
George of Mendon, and Irena [int. Mrs. Irene] Thayer, Oct. 12, 1797.
George Washington and Anna Pickering, int. Oct. 10, 1819.
James A. and Elmira Foristall, Apr. 11, 1824.
Reachel and Uriah Thaire, Feb. 8, 1727–8.*
Rhoda, Mrs., of Uxbridge, and Robart Smith Jr., int. May 29, 1774.
Seripta M. of Blackstone, and Martin G. Cushman, int. Jan. 7, 1849.
Vienna, Mrs. [int. Viena, omits Mrs.], and Alfred Cook, Feb. 20, 1825.

TAGGARD, Sarah Amanda of Hillsborough, N.H., and Willard Ballou Scott, int. Apr. 18, 1830.

TAMBLING, Elisha and Miletiah Combs, int. Jan. 2, 1803.

* Intention not recorded.

BELLINGHAM MARRIAGES.

TENEY (see Tenney, Tinney), Moses and Susana Rockwood, Nov. 1, 1733.*

TENNEY (see Teney, Tinney), Stephen and Mehittible Corbett, Nov. 2, 1737.*

THAER (see Thaire, Thayar, Thayer), Elisabeth, Mrs. [int. Mrs. Elizabeth Thayer], and Caleb Thayer, Apr. 7, 1791.

THAIRE (see Thaer, Thayar, Thayer), Eunice (see Unice Thoite).
Uriah and Reachel Taft, Feb. 8, 1727-8.*

THAYAR (see Thaer, Thaire, Thayer), Joseph and Saraih Bolcom, int. Feb. 25, 1741.
Samuel of Mendon, and Keziah Partridge, Dec. 24, 1739.*
Susanah and Isaac Johnson, int. Mar. 7, 1741.

THAYER (see Thaer, Thaire, Thayar), Aaron of Mendon, and Jemima Cook, Nov. 23, 1738.*
Aaron, Capt., and Rosanna Fisher, wid., int. Mar. 7, 1822.
Abigail and Jesee [int. Jesse] Holbrook, Mar. 28, 1753, in Mendon.
Abigail and Laban Thurber, May 16, 1799.
Abigail and George Sherburn, int. May 5, 1833.
Abigail L. and Andrew A. Bates, Nov. 27, 1834.
Abigal, Mrs., of Mendon, and Amos Adams, int. Nov. 8, 1779.
Alanson and Sally Darling, Nov. 1, 1818.
Alanson of Pawtucket, and Perley B. Bates, Mar. 2, 1831.*
Allen of Mendon, and Polly Bullard, Oct. 9, 1806.
Alpheus and Elisabeth Bates, Aug. 16, 1787.
Alpheus Jr. and Catherine Thayer, Apr. 19, 1818.
Andrew and Abigail Legg, int. Feb. 6, 1803.
Anna and Capt. Nathaniel Aldrich, int. Sept. 11, 1824.
Benjamin of Mendon, and Mrs. Sarah Bozworth [int. Bosworth], Oct. 29, 1767.
Benjamin of Mendon, and Mrs. Ruth Alden, Dec. 12, 1793.
Bethiah [int. adds Mrs.] and Peter Thomson [int. Thompson], Apr. 17, 1760.
Caleb of Mendon, and Mrs. Elisabeth Thaer [int. Mrs. Elizabeth Thayer], Apr. 7, 1791.
Calvin and Mrs. Abigil Pike, Apr. 10, 1786.
Calvin of New Salum [int. New Salem], and Phebe Holbrook, Aug. 22, 1813.
Catherine and Alpheus Thayer Jr., Apr. 19, 1818.
Celicia Ann and Jonathan Chilson, Apr. 25, 1834.

* Intention not recorded.

THAYER, Charles W. and Betsey W. Aldrich, int. Sept. 28, 1845.
Cindarella, 25, of Cumberland, R.I., d. Laban and Joanna, and Emulous Rhodes, widr., Aug. 16, 1846.*
Clarissa [int. Clarrasa] and Valentine R. Combs [int. Coombs], Nov. 7, 1826.
Cloe and John Sherman, June 25, 1761.
Cornelius and Abigail Jones, Dec. 24, 1747.
Cyrena of Mendon, and Ezekiel Bates Jr., int. Apr. 15, 1804.
Daniel [and] Esther Partridg, Feb. 10, 1734–5.*
Dependence of Wrentham, and Hanna Thomson, int. Dec. 30, 1752.
Ebenezer and Hannah Green, Apr. 24, 1734.*
Ebenezer of Mendon, and Mrs. Huldah Thompson, int. June 22, 1754.
Ebenezer and Mrs. Martha Thayer, int. Dec. 23, 1758.
Ebenezer and [int. adds Mrs.] Sabra Darling, June 28, 1798.
Ebenezer and Abigail Kelly, wid., int. Apr. 12, 1835.
Elias and Mrs. Hannah Ellis, int. Jan. 27, 1763.
Elias Jr. and Mrs. Ruth Staples, int. July 30, 1797.
Elijah of Mendon, and Mrs. Katharine Metcalf, int. July 20, 1793.
Elisabeth, Mrs., and Josiah Nealson, int. Apr. 5, 1754.
Eliza, 39, d. Alpheus and Betsey, and Henry C. Snell, widr. [int. omits widr.], May 1, 1844 [int. Apr. 13, 1845, *sic*].
Ellery and Abigail Pickering, Apr. 12, 1818.
Emeline E., 24, d. Sylvenus and Olive, and William Hart, Nov. 29, 1849.
Ezekiel and Mrs. Huldah Thayer, int. June 30, 1771.
Hannah, Mrs., and Asa Blake, int. May 14, 1769.
Hannah [int. adds Mrs.] and Lewis Fisher, Oct. 5, 1797.
Hannah [int. adds E.] and Charles B. Jenks [int. Jenkes], Aug. 24, 1817.
Hannah of Mendon, and Lt. Elial Barber, int. Aug. 26, 1827.
Hopstill and Joseph Daman, int. Apr. 28, 1750.
Horatio and Charlotte M. Albee, int. Nov. 5, 1848.
Huldah, Mrs., and Ezekiel Thayer, int. June 30, 1771.
Huldah [int. adds wid.] and John Albee, May 9, 1799.
Huldah of Mendon, and Willard Chilson, int. Mar. 25, 1826.
Irena [int. Mrs. Irene] and George Taft, Oct. 12, 1797.
Isaac and Mary Metcalf, wid., int. Feb. 16, 1750–1.
Isaac and Mrs. Margaret Atwood, int. Sept. 23, 1760.
Isaac Jr. and Marcy Thayer, int. Sept. 14, 1739.
James A. and Mary M. Horton, int. Mar. 2, 1845.

* Intention not recorded.

BELLINGHAM MARRIAGES.

THAYER, James P. of Mendon, and Abby S. Burr, Jan. 5, 1843.
James P., widr. [int. omits widr.], 27, s. Ellery and Abigail, and Susan Ann Paine, Nov. 24, 1846.
Jerusha, Mrs., and John Green White, Oct. 8, 1775.
Joanna, Mrs., of Mendon, and Peletiah Smith, int. Nov. 6, 1796.
Jonathan of Mendon, and Rachel Holbrook, Sept. 4, 1735.*
Joseph of Mendon, and Abigail Cook, int. Dec. 14, 1751.
Levina and John Kelton, June 29, 1809.
Levina K. and Charles A. Taft, int. Jan. 2, 1832.
Lois, Mrs., of Mendon, and Micah Thayer, int. Oct. 8, 1763.
Luther and Mrs. Mary Kimbol, int. Mar. 16, 1793.
Luther and Uraner Hill, int. Aug. 8, 1823.
Lydia, Mrs., and Warfield Hayward, int. Dec. 20, 1760.
Lydia, Mrs., of Mendon, and Silas Thayer, int. July 17, 1768.
Lyman W. and Rachel T. Thayer, Apr. 24, 1822.
Lyman W., Capt., and Eliza Hall, int. Oct. 22, 1831.
Lyman W., Capt., and Mrs. Chloe Ann Mourey, int. Mar. 19, 1848.
Manning and Abigail R. Checkering, int. Mar. 16, 1822.
Marcy of Mendon, and Issac Thayer, int. Sept. 14, 1739.
Margreret, Mrs., and Joseph Lovering, int. Dec. 10, 1763.
Mariam [int. Meriam] P., 21, d. Willard and Charlotte, and Collins C. Darling, May 29, 1845.
Martha (Thayr) and Peter Thompson, Feb. 5, 1729-3[0].*
Martha, Mrs., of Mendon, and Ebenezer Thayer, int. Dec. 23, 1758.
Marvelous and Julia Bullard, Mar. 29, 1810.
Mary of Mendon, and Paul Chilson, int. Mar. 9, 1828.
Mary B. and Laban Bates, Nov. 24, 1825.
Micah and Mrs. Lois Thayer, int. Oct. 8, 1763.
Miranda of Mendon, and Danill Arnold Jr., int. Aug. 26, 1827.
Moses and Anna Pain, int. Feb. 28, 1808.
Myranda and Fenner Cook, Apr. 2, 1820.
Otis of Milford, and Hopestill Scammill [int. Scammell], May 17, 1807.
Perley C. and Thomas D. Paine, int. Aug. 14, 1834.
Philo and Bethsheba [int. Bashaba] Bullard, Aug. 22, 1799.
Prudence and Melvill Knapp, int. Oct. 1, 1828.
Rachel T. and Lyman W. Thayer, Apr. 24, 1822.
Ruth, Mrs., and Joel Thomson, int. Nov. 7, 1794.
Sam[ue]l and Maranda Shearman, int. Oct. 27, 1826.
Seth of Milford, and Sarah Holbrook, int. Mar. 18, 1790.
Silas and Mrs. Lydia Thayer, int. July 17, 1768.

* Intention not recorded.

THAYER, Silas F., 24, of Dedham, s. Ellery and Abigail, and Elizabeth Rockwood, May 4, 1846.
Silva [int. adds Mrs.] and Asa Norcross [int. Norcress], Nov. 16, 1797.
Susan Ann and Lewis H. Bradford, Nov. 28, 1830.
Susan E. and Daniel Boulster, int. Oct. 12, 1845.
Thadius and Mrs. Rhoba Smith, int. Nov. 13, 1783.
Thomson and Mrs. Claracy [int. Clarisse] Cobb, Mar. 23, 1795.
Thomson [int. Thompson] and Charlott [int. Charlotte] Hayden, Dec. 2, 1824.
Timothy of Mendon, and Mrs. Esther Holbrook, int. Jan. 24, 1761.
Welcom [int. adds Lt.] of Mendon, and Sally Adams, May 25, 1819.
Willard and Rhoda Brown, May 26, 1813.
Willard and Charlotte Cutler, int. Apr. 9, 1820.
Willard 2d [int. omits 2d] and Rhobby [int. Rhoba] Shearman, Sept. 29, 1822.
William [int. adds W.] and Sarah Worrall, July 5, 1829.

THOITE [? Thaire], Unice and Pelatiah Smith, June 23, 1752, in Medway.

THOMAS, Leander and Paulina Kilbon [int. Kilbin], Apr. 10, 1828.
William W. of Medway, and Mary Ann Barney, Nov. 27, 1828.

THOMPSON (see Thomson, Tompson), Abigal and Joseph Blood, Dec. 11, 1735.*
David and Mrs. Lucy Blake, int. Oct. 23, 1762.
Ebenezer and Sarah Green, Nov. 2, 1737.*
Esther, Mrs. [int. Mrs. Ester Thomson], and Seth Fish, July 2, 1780.
Huldah, Mrs., and Ebenezer Thayer, int. June 22, 1754.
Ichabod and Rachel Thompson, Jan. 27, 1736–7.*
Jonathan and Mrs. Sarah Thompson, int. Oct. 2, 1762.
Lucinda [int. Tompson] and Andrew J. Howard, Aug. 20, 1840.
Lydia T. [int. Thomson] and Cyrus Kenney, June 24, 1823.
Marion and Luther W. Nason, Oct. 30, 1843.
Martha, Mrs., and Seth Hall, int. Apr. 22, 1757.
Mary [int. Thomson] and Samuel Wight, Oct. 18, 1752.
Peter and Martha Thayr, Feb. 5, 1729–3[0].*
Rachel and Ichabod Thompson, Jan. 27, 1736–7.*
Rhoda, Mrs., and Abner Cook, int. Mar. 7, 1757.

* Intention not recorded.

THOMPSON, Sarah, Mrs., of Dedham, and Jonathan Thompson, int. Oct. 2, 1762.
Timothy of Smithfield, and Mrs. Rachel Draper, int. Jan. 26, 1760.
William H., 24, of Hopkinton, s. Eliab and Lydia, and Eliza A. Farrington, Oct. 13, 1847.

THOMSON (see Thompson, Tompson), Aaron and Polly [int. Polley] Daniels, Jan. 2, 1788.
Alce and Joseph Rockwood Jr., int. Mar. 10, 1749–50.
Amos and Mrs. Mary Chilson, Dec. 14, 1785.
Baxter and Nabby [int. Abigail] Morse, June 9, 1822.
Caleb and Mrs. Lydia Aldin, Dec. 21, 1768.
Cyrus [int. Syrus] and Mrs. Kezia Parkis [int. Mrs. Lydia Porkis], . Mar. 16, 1774.
Dan and Harriot Green, int. Apr. 20, 1817.
Daniel and Jemima Legg, int. Apr. 11, 1761.
David and Mrs. Eunice Blake, July 23, 1776.
Deborah, Mrs., and Isaac Leazel, int. Mar. 8, 1777.
Hanna and Dependence Thayer, int. Dec. 30, 1752.
Jemima and Thomas Albee, int. June 2, 1750.
Jemima, wid., and Lt. Aaron Holbrook, int. July 15, 1804.
Joel and Mrs. Ruth Thayer, int. Nov. 7, 1794.
Jonathan Jr. and Jemima Baxter, Apr. 10, 1754, in Mendon.
Joseph and Mrs. Lois Whelock, July 29, 1773.
Joseph and Abigail Warfield, int. Dec. 18, 1815.
Laban and Jerusha Gould, May 29, 1823.
Levi of Partridgefield, and Mrs. Rachel Rockwood, int. Jan. 7, 1797.
Lois "a Trationt parson," and Enoch Darling, int. Mar. 2, 1750–1.
Maray of Mendon, and Samuel Scott, int. Mar. 14, 1743.
Nancy [int. Thompson] and Job Phettiplace [int. Phetteplace], Apr. 1 [?], 1803.
Peter [int. Thompson] and [int. adds Mrs.] Bethiah Thayer, Apr. 17, 1760.
Phebe, Mrs., of Mendon, and Ralph Treeman [Freeman], int. Nov. 11, 1764.
Sarah, Mrs., and Aaron Parkhurst [int. Parkis], Dec. 23, 1790.
William of Medway, and Lydia E. Fisher, int. May 17, 1835.
W[illia]m V. and Hannah Joslin, int. Feb. 7, 1835.
Ziba and Rebekah Brooks, int. June 4, 1820.

THURBER, Abigail and Ezekiel S. Albee, Oct. 23, 1828.
Laban of Mendon, and Abigail Thayer, May 16, 1799.

THURBER, Mary of Mendon, and Saban Cushman, int. Oct. 31, 1819.
Sophia C., Mrs. [int. omits Mrs.], and Warren Lazell 2d, Apr. 4, 1824.

THURSTON, Daniel of Grafton, and Rosanna Ellis, Oct. 3, 1799.
Jonathan V. of Grafton, and Polly S. Burr, Feb 20, 1844.

THWING, Asenath of Uxbridge, and Asa F. Onion, int. Oct. 31, 1819.

TIBBITTS, Love of Salisbury, and Marcus Burr, int. Mar. 10, 1844.

TILLSON, Phebe, Mrs., of Cumberland, and George Cook, int. Oct. 11, 1772.

TINGLEY, Charles W. and Margeret Darling, Dec. 24, 1837.
Sabrina E. of Wrentham, and John D. Chilson, int. Mar. 13, 1849.

TINNEY (see Teney, Tenney), Elisabeth, Mrs., of Mendon, and Jabiz Metcalf, int. Oct. 6, 1775.

TOCKER (see Tucker), David of Cumberland, and Mrs. Mary Arnold, int. Feb. 25, 1770.

TOMPSON (see Thompson, Thomson), Joseph and Mary Holbrook, Mar. 18, 1725.*

TORRY, Mary of Mendon, and Daniel Bullard, int. Mar. 13, 1808.

TOURTELOT, Emily of Mendon, and Joseph Adams, int. Apr. 30, 1843.

TOWER, Mary and Amos Coombs, int. Mar. 4, 1833.

TOWN, Abial J. and Allice Bates, int. Feb. 21, 1819.

TOWNSEND, George N., Rev., of Hopkinton, and Jane L. Scammell, Aug. 10, 1842.

TRASK, Rechel [int. Rachel], Mrs., and Timothy Darling, Feb. 3, 1794.
Sally and Henery Holbrook Jr., Nov. 24, 1813.

TUCKER (see Tocker), Henry and Abida Hill, int. May 18, 1831.

* Intention not recorded.

UNDERWOOD, Elbe H. and Sarah J. Elliot, int. June 22, 1846.

UPHAM, Elisabeth [int. Elizabeth], Mrs., and Joseph Pratt, Jan. 25, 1786.
John and Patience [int. Patiance] Pratt, Sept. 2, 1761.
Patience, Mrs., and Noah Cook, Sept. 8, 1791.

VORCE (see Vose), Peggy, Mrs., of Wrentham, and Simon Darling, int. Sept. 2, 1793.
William and Mercy Jillson, int. Apr. 13, 1814.

VOSE (see Vorce), Hannah and Partridge Hixon, Apr. 6, 1843.

WAILES (see Wails, Wales), Hannah of Milford, and Joel Adoms [Adams], int. Apr. 15, 1804.
John of Franklin, and Abigail Adoms [Adams], int. June 10, 1804.

WAILS (see Wailes, Wales), Mason of Franklin, and Electa Sanford Adams, int. Sept. 19, 1824.

WALDEN (see Wallden), Job and Mrs. Alpha Aldrich, Sept. 14, 1797.

WALDO, Laban and Olive Wilcox, int. Mar. 2, 1817.

WALES (see Wailes, Wails), Abiram W. and Olive Ware, int. Oct. 21, 1838.
Charles A. of Franklin, and Ruth Bosworth, int. Apr. 27, 1846.
George F. of Franklin, and Abby Kelley, Mar. 4, 1840.
John of Franklin, and Mrs. Ruth Conden, June 9, 1794.
Jonathan of Woonsoket Falls [int. of Cumberland], R.I., and Marcia S. [int. Steward] Whitaker, May 11, 1831.
Mason of Franklin, Norfolk Co., and Philadelpha Bozworth, Feb. 25, 1821.*
Nancy, Mrs., of Franklin, and Rufus Pain, Jan. 12, 1786.
Nancy and Whitman Holbrook, int. Nov. 8, 1835.
Olive Fairbanks [? Olive Fairbanks [of] Wales] and Capt. Seth Holbrook, int. Mar. 26, 1820.
Otis Jr. of Franklin, and Jerushe [int. Jerusha] Hayward, June 21, 1822.
Polle [int. Polly], Mrs., of Franklin, and Phinehas Holbrook, Nov. 4, 1795.
Polly H. of Franklin, and Sabin Ware, Feb. 1, 1838.*
Willard of Franklin, and Sally Cook, Jan. 1, 1812.

* Intention not recorded.

WALKER, Abigail of Hopkinton, and Statia Bosworth, int. Mar. 3, 1816.
Betsey of Hopkinton, and Warren Lazell, May 18, 1820.
Harvey D. of Millbury, and Electa B. Bates, Apr. 2, 1844.
Lois of Hopkinton, and Ezekiel Braley, int. Nov. 26, 1805.

WALLDEN (see Walden), Alpha and Seth Southwick, int. May 10, 1801.

WARD, David and Mrs. Mary Norcross [int. Norcroos], Mar. 26, 1773.

WARE, Billy of Wrentham, and Mrs. Sarah Partridge, ———— [int. Dec. 1, 1771].
David of Franklin, and Betsy Adams, int. Jan. 23, 1806.
Elbridge G. of Franklin, and Eliza P. Drake, Apr. 10, 1844.
Eleazer of Franklin, and Sarah Burr, May 21, 1807.
Eli of Wrentham, and Mrs. Tamer Wight, int. May 19, 1771.
Matilda M., 19, of Franklin, d. David and Betsey, and Clark Hunt, Mar. 1, 1848.
Olive of Franklin, and Abiram W. Wales, int. Oct. 21, 1838.
Sabin of Franklin, and Polly H. Wales, Feb. 1, 1838.*
Sarah [int. Salla] of Franklin, and Obadiah Adams, Nov. 14, 1805.

WARFIELD, Abigail of Milford, and Joseph Thomson, int. Dec. 18, 1815.
Polly of Milford, and Aaron Holbrook, int. May 11, 1828.

WARRALL (see Worrall), Mary [int. Worrall] and John G. Gatchell, Feb. 27, 1834.

WEATHERHEAD, Abel of Franklin, and Annot L. Dorr, int. July 11, 1841.

WEDGE, Daniel and Mrs. Hannah Cheney [int. Cheeney], Mar. 14, 1774.

WEELOCK (see Wheelock, Wheloch, Whelock), Jonathan of Mendon, and Martha Wight, May 22, 1735.*

WHEAT (see Wheet).

WHEELER, Avery P. of Mendon, and Adaline S. Bates, int. Feb. 10, 1828.
John of Cambridge, and Mary Scammell, Apr. 4, 1807.

* Intention not recorded.

WHEELER, John of Cambridge, and Bethiah Scammell, Mar. 29, 1812.
Perses of Franklin, and John Adoms [Adams], int. Jan. 10, 1808.
WHEELOCK (see Weelock, Wheloch, Whelock), Sarah, Mrs., of Mendon, and Isaac Kent, int. Dec. 31, 1769.
Thomas of Mendon, and Mrs. Hannah Hayward, Dec. 28, 1769.
WHEET, Anna, Mrs., and Israel Whipel, int. Dec. 1, 1781.
WHELOCH (see Weelock, Wheelock, Whelock), Mary, Mrs., of Mendon, and Daniel Bullard, int. Sept. 8, 1781.
WHELOCK (see Weelock, Wheelock, Wheloch), Lois, Mrs., of Mendon, and Joseph Thomson, July 29, 1773.
Timothy of Mendon, and Mrs. Joanna Holbrook, int. Dec. 30, 1764.
WHIGHT (see White, Wight), Nathan and Mrs. Jerusha Metcalf, int. Aug. 20, 1780.
WHIPEL (see Whipple), Israel of Cumberland, and Mrs. Anna Wheet, int. Dec. 1, 1781.
WHIPPLE (see Whipel), Wilder of Cumberland, and Fanny Freeman, June 26, 1817.
WHISTON, Ezra of Framingham, and "Ms." [int. Mrs.] Lois Hill, Sept. 23, 1790.
WHITAKER, Juba F. and Vienna Scott, int. Oct. 10, 1830.
Marcia S. [int. Steward] and Jonathan Wales, May 11, 1831.
William, Dr., and Mrs. Polley Fisk, int. Sept. 3, 1775.
William, Dr., and Chloe Freeman, Sept. 4 [int. Oct. 11, *sic*], 1807.
WHITE (see Whight, Wight), Adelphia F. and Bildad B. Belcher, int. Dec. 18, 1835.
Alfred B. and Harriet Fuller, int. Sept. 22, 1844.
John Green and Mrs. [int. omits Mrs.] Jerusha Thayer, Oct. 8, 1775.
Leonard and Mariah Darling, int. Jan. 2, 1836.
Margret [int. Marget], Mrs., and Eleazer Fitsher [int. Fisher], Nov. 26, 1778.
Mary Ann and Jotham Howard, Oct. 1, 1829.
Metcalf and Elizabeth Hill, int. Sept. 11, 1836.
Phebe H. and Ezekiel H. Davis, int. Nov. 1, 1847.
Sabra D. and Charles Spear, int. Oct. 5, 1845.

WHITELY, Patiance and Asa Kelly, int. May 3, 1801.
Will[ia]m [int. of Mendon] and Patiance [int. Mrs. Patianc] Newel, "on or about" Dec. 10, 1779.

WHITENY (see Whitney), Priscilla of Medway, and Joel Adams, Mar. 4, 1801.

WHITING (see Whitting), Elizabeth of Franklin, and Simon Pickering, Jan. 26, 1832.
Mary, Mrs., of Franklin, and William Makepeace, int. Jan. 21, 1794.
Nathan of Medway, and Mrs. Meriam Lealand, Dec. 22, 1791.*
Timothy Jr. and Adaline Bullard, int. Apr. 20, 1828.

WHITNEY (see Whiteny), Dexter and Adeliza Cook, Sept. 26, 1839.
Ethan and Julia A. L. Bosworth, Nov. 24, 1842.

WHITTING (see Whiting), Nathan of Medway, and Maray Metcalf, int. Mar. 18, 1748–9.
Peletiah of Dedham, and Mrs. Hannah Phillips, int. May 20, 1758.

WIGGENS, Susan M. of Mendon, and Jonathan Wright, int. Apr. 3, 1842.

WIGHT (see Whight, White), Abigail and Eliphelet Holbrook Jr., Nov. 26, 1753, in Mendon.
Abigail, "Ms," and Nathan Man, int. May 24, 1764.
Abigail and Samuel T. Read, Dec. 16, 1817.
Abigail and George Googins, Mar. 30, 1843.
Abner and Mrs. Jemima Lee, int. Sept. 1, 1776.
Charles and Mary Pond, int. Mar. 7, 1832.
Eliab and Mrs. Jemima Hawes, int. Oct. 14, 1782.
Eliab Jr. and Mary W. Chickering, int. Apr. 22, 1827.
Elnathan and Mrs. Abigail Blood, int. July 12, 1754.
Jemima and Billings Mann, July 21, 1822.
Keziah and Ebenezer Holbrook, int. Feb. 12, 1747–8.
Lidia and Habijah Reed, Oct. 14, 1761.
Martha and Jonathan Weelock, May 22, 1735.*
Nancy and John Cook 2d, Aug. 31, 1817.
Patty and Tyler Daniels, Nov. 16, 1815.
Samuel and Mary Thompson [int. Thomson], Oct. 18, 1752.
Seneca and Betsey Mors, int. Aug. 24, 1817.

* Intention not recorded.

WIGHT, Simeon of Midway, and Mrs. Margret Smith, Mar. 18, 1772.
Tamer, Mrs., and Eli Ware, int. May 19, 1771.

WILBER, Rebeckah and William Bellou Jr., int. Oct. 15, 1809.
Ruth of Franklin, and William Pain, int. Mar. 25, 1810.

WILCOX (see Willcocks, Willcox), Jeraul O. and Phebe J. Wilkinson, int. Aug. 12, 1849.
Olive of Cumberland, and Laban Waldo, int. Mar. 2, 1817.

WILEY, Daniel and Isanna E. Hixon, int. Oct. 21, 1825.

WILKINS, Sarah Ann and George Nichols [int. Nickols], Mar. 16, 1847.

WILKINSON, Ahab of Smithfield, and Mrs. Abigail Scott, int. Apr. 5, 1755.
Phebe J. of Cumberland, R.I., and Jeraul O. Wilcox, int. Aug. 12, 1849.

WILLARD, Sabrina S. and Barnard Moore, int. —— 5, 1841.

WILLBURT, Levina of Smithfield, R.I., and Elisha Shairmen, int. Dec. 11, 1802.

WILLCOCKS (see Wilcox, Willcox), Rhoda and Simon Pickering, int. Feb. 10, 1790.

WILLCOX (see Wilcox, Willcocks), Mary of Wrentham, and Luke Jenkes, May 27, 1807.*
Susan of Mendon, and Seth Cook, int. Sept. 26, 1819.

WILLIAMS, Gordin and Elizabeth Combs, int. Sept. 13, 1801.
Lewis F., 29, of Medway, s. William and Betsey, and Hulday D. Hadley, Nov. 30, 1848.*
Preston A. and Mary R. Adams, int. Jan. 16, 1842.

WILLSON (see Wilson), James and Esther Blew, int. July 26, 1754.

WILSON (see Willson), Isarael of Mendon, and Mrs. Penellope Darling, int. Mar. [written in pencil] 31, 1765.
Joanna and David Hayward, int. Nov. 17, 1750.
Martha and Joshua Darling, int. Feb. 26, 1762.

* Intention not recorded.

WINCH, Lucinda of Framingham, and John Jennison, int. Aug. 29, 1830.

WINDSOR, Meleta B. and Lewis L. Rockwood, int. Dec. 6, 1840.

WINN, Silvia and Nathan Hawes, Sept. 27, 1827.

WINTER, Ann S. of Medway, and Newell Rockwood, int. Mar. 3, 1823.

WISWALL, Elisabeth, "Ms," and Nathaniel Ingraham, int. Feb. 11, 1758.
Elisabeth, Mrs., and Samuel Daniels, int. Oct. 2, 1760.
Jasper [int. Wiswell] of Milford, and Elisabeth Spear, Apr. 29, 1821.

WOOD, Amasa of Sutton, and Sally Foristall, Sept. 30, 1810.
Amy Ann of Cumberland, R.I., and Asa Chilson, int. Oct. 22, 1843.
Joseph [int. adds Lt.] of Smithfield, R.I., and Phila T. Freeman, Aug. 9, 1830.
Polly of Upton, and Onley Foristall, int. Oct. 23, 1814.
Preston M., 34, of Blackstone, s. Ruben and Anna, and Emeline Burr, Feb. 7, 1847.
Thomas Willis and Julia Ann Adams, Jan. 21, 1838.
Tilson of Cumberland, and Alpha Inman, July 9, 1812.
Zepheniah and Mrs. Sarah Mason, int. Feb. 5, 1782.

WOODWARD, Caleb and Mrs. Sally [int. Sallah] Foster, Dec. 1, 1785.

WOOLSOM, Miriam B. of Hopkinton, and Stephen A. Coombs, int. May 3, 1825.

WORRALL (see Warrall), Alice and Jefferson Scott, Feb. 21, 1830.
Sarah of Smithfield, R.I., and William [int. adds W.] Thayer, July 5, 1829.

WRIGHT, Jonathan and Susan M. Wiggens, int. Apr. 3, 1842.
Margret, Mrs., of Mendon, and Joshua Chilson, Sept. 4, 1783.
Molley [int. adds Mrs.] of Frankling, and Amariah Holbrook, May 13, 1779.
Polly and Alfred Clark, Jan. 1, 1840.
Solomon and Polley Rider, int. Nov. 6, 1814.

WYER, George of Biddeford, Me., and Harriet M. Metcalf, Oct. 5, 1848.

UNIDENTIFIED.

———, Thankfull, Mrs., and Jonathan Pond, int. July 9, 1763.

BELLINGHAM DEATHS.

BELLINGHAM DEATHS.

To the year 1850.

ADAM (see Adams, Addoms), ———, ch. Naums, meazils, "buried" May — [1836]. P.R.I.
———, ch. Naums, meazils, "buried" May — [1836]. P.R.I.

ADAMS (see Adam, Addoms), Abigail, w. Amos, Feb. 1, 1846, a. 85. G.R.I. [Abigill, wid., P.R.I.]
Amos, June 10, 1817, a. 58. G.R.I. [June 19, P.R.I.]
Asa, Sept. 19 [1793]. P.R.I.
Asenath, w. Joseph, Aug. 2, 1841. [a. 43, G.R.I.]
Bathsheba, w. Eliakem, Aug. 24, 1800, a. 41. G.R.I.
Cloe, wid., Aug. 4 [1811]. P.R.I.
Elenor, Sept. 25 [1825], a. 16. P.R.I.
Eliakem, Gen., Nov. 30, 1807, a. 51. G.R.I.
Elisha, s. Obediah and Sarah, Jan. 23, 1746.
Emeline M., d. Amos and Abigail, consumption, Dec. 25, 1849, a. 19 y. 2 m. 6 d.
Gilbert, s. Joseph and Jemima, typhus feever, Dec. 16, 1848, a. 20. [Gilbut, s. Capt. Joseph, P.R.I.]
Hannah, d. Sam, Nov. 28 [1791]. P.R.I.
Joel, Oct. 19 [1839]. P.R.I.
Marcy, wid., cancer, Mar. 25, 1847, a. 72.
Marget, d. Silus, Nov. 12 [1791]. P.R.I.
Mary, Jan. 13, 1793, a. 45. G.R.I. [w. Silas, June 13, P.R.I.]
Meletiah, w. Calap, May 19, 1848, a. 86. P.R.I.
Mercy, w. Samuel, Mar. 12, 1847, a. 72. G.R.I. [Marcy Adames, Mar. 13, P.R.I.]
Moses, Nov. 5 [1808]. P.R.I.
Naham, Jan. 26, 1836, a. 44. G.R.I. [Naum, P.R.I.]
Nance, d. Amos and Abigil, Sept. 13, 1788.
Nancy, Apr. 15, 1788. G.R.I.
Obadiah, Jan. 2, 1803, a. 83. G.R.I. [Obediah, a. 84 or 85, P.R.I.]
Polly, Dec. 21 [1812]. P.R.I.
Rebeca, Sept. 12, 1814, a. 18 d. G.R.I.

ADAMS, Rebeckah, d. Samuel Jr. and Mercy, Sept. 30, 1813.
Ruth, Jan. 25, 1834, a. 10 m. G.R.1.
Samuel, July 11, 1840, a. 84. G.R.1. [a. 85, P.R.1.]
Samuel, Sept. 13 [dup. Sept. 18], 1843, a. 61 y. 8 m. 16 d. [Samuel Jr., Sept. 13, a. 61, G.R.1.] [a. 62, P.R.1.]
Sarah, wid. Obadiah, Apr. 27, 1817, a. 93. G.R.1. [a. 94, P.R.1.]
Sarah S., d. Joseph and Asenath, consumpsion, Mar. 10, 1847, a. 17 y. 2 m. 26 d. [Mar. 10, G.R.1.] [Mar. 11, a. 17, P.R.1.]
Sena, w. Joseph, Aug. 2, 1841, a. 41. P.R.1.
Silas, Sept. 18 [1798]. P.R.1.
Warren, May 31, 1832, a. 6. G.R.1.
———, ch. Samuel, Dec. 25 [1796]. P.R.1.
———, ch. Samuel, Nov. 12 [1798]. P.R.1.
———, w. Joel, Mar. 23 [1813]. P.R.1.
———, ch. Samuel, Oct. 1 [1813]. P.R.1.
———, ch. Joseph, Oct. 29 [1817]. P.R.1.
———, ch. Nathan, Mar. 13, 1820. P.R.1.
———, ch. Silurs, Feb. 17 [1823]. P.R.1.
———, twin ch. Joseph, Oct. — [1823]. P.R.1.
———, twin ch. Joseph, Sept. 8 [1825]. P.R.1.
———, ch. Silas, June — [1832]. P.R.1.
———, ch. Silas, June — [1832]. P.R.1.
———, ch. Dexter, smallpox, "buried" June 8 [1836]. P.R.1.
———, ch. Dixter, Jan. 31, 1839. P.R.1.
———, ch. Silus, worms, Feb. 16 [1840], a. 3. P.R.1.

ADDOMS (see Adam, Adams), ———, ch. Amous, Sept. 15, 1788. P.R.1.

ALBA (see Albea, Albee, Allbe, Allbee), Alven, s. Nathan dec'd, Mar. 28 [1795]. P.R.1.
Gidean, Dea. [?], of Milford, Oct. 18 [1799]. P.R.1.
Welcom, s. Nathan dec'd, Mar. 22, 1795. P.R.1.

ALBEA (see Alba, Albee, Allbe, Allbee), Nathan, Feb. 16, 1792. P.R.1.

ALBEE (see Alba, Albea, Allbe, Allbee), Allven, s. Nathon and Elisabeth, Feb. 9, 1785. [Allbe, ch. Nathen, P.R.1.]
Alpheus, Aug. 5, 1806. [Aug. 5, in 80th y., G.R.3.] [Alpha, Aug. 4, P.R.1.]
Harriet N., Sept. 8, 1839, a. 21. G.R.5. [Hariet Allbe, P.R.1.]
Hipzibah, d. Peter and Rhoda, Oct. 4, 1775. [Albe, Oct. 5, P.R.1.]
John, Aug. 18, 1839, a. 56. G.R.5. [Allbe, 1838, P.R.1.]
Lucinda, Oct. —, 1823. C.R.

ALDEN (see Aldon, Alldan), Gerusha, d. Noah, Oct. 18 [1798].
P.R.1.
Jemima, d. Noah Jr. and Joanna, Oct. 17, 1788. [Aldon, P.R.1.]
Joanna, wid., Feb. 15 [1804]. P.R.1. [wid. Rev. Noah, a. 79,
G.R.2.]
Joanna, w. Dea. Noah, Sept. 21, 1824, a. 71. G.R.2. [Aldin,
P.R.1.]
Joseph, twin s. Joseph and Jemima, Oct. 21, 1823, a. 3 d. G.R.2.
Lorra, d. Noah, Oct. 8 [1798]. P.R.1.
Lyde, Feb. 25, 1821, a. 39. P.R.1.
Nancy, b. Ireland, w. Isaac, Jan. 28, 1845, a. 38 y. 6 m. 27 d.
Noah, s. Noah Jr. and Joanna, Nov. 1, 1788. [Aldon, P.R.1.]
Noah, Elder, May 5, 1797. [Rev. Noah, May 6, C.R.] [May 5, in 72d y., "and 43 of his Public Ministry 31 of which he spent in this place," G.R.2.]
Noah, twin s. Joseph and Jemima, Sept. 28, 1825, a. 1 y. 10 m.
G.R.2.
Samuel, s. Elisha and Irene, July 4, 1775. [s. Elisher, P.R.1.]
Zilpha, d. Noah and Joanna, July 31, 1775. [d. Rev. Noah, a. 9 y. 4 m. 3 w., P.R.1.]

ALDON (see Alden, Alldan), ———, second ch. Noah Jr., Oct. 26, 1788. P.R.1.

ALDRICH (see Aldridge), Abigail, d. Calvin and Joannah, Nov. 15, 1796, a. 5 y. 6 m. 1 d. G.R.3.
Amey, w. Laban, Dec. 8, 1816, in 60th y. G.R.3. [Aldridge, w. Laben, Dec. 9, P.R.1.]
Anna, w. Capt. Phineas, Oct. 4, 1792, in 33d y. G.R.3.
Basheaby, d. Justus and Permelia, Nov. 23, 1834, a. 2 y. 10 m. 22 d. G.R.3.
David, Mar. 15, 1771, in 86th y. G.R.3.
Hannah, w. D., Feb. 20, 1732, in 44th y. G.R.3.
Joanna M. [?], d. Leaben, Oct. 16 [1805]. P.R.1.
Laban, Dec. 19, 1816, in 63d y. G.R.3. [Leaben Aldridge, P.R.1.]
Levi, ch. Levi and Abigail, Nov. 25, 1752, a. 6 m. 25 d. G.R.3.
Levi, Capt., Dec. 22, 1795, in 66th y. G.R.3. [of Mendan, a. 66, P.R.1.]
Lois, w. Rufus, Mar. 10, 1771, in 28th y. G.R.3.
Lucy, ch. Levi and Abigail, June 12, 1766, a. 2 m. 2 d. G.R.3.
Mehitabel, w. David, Mar. 30, 1774, in 87th y. G.R.3.
Phineas, Capt., Apr. 25, 1821, in 64th y. G.R.3.
Simeon, s. Abner and Elisabeth, July 18, 1768.

ALDRICH, Susannah, w. Rufus, Apr. 23, 1775, in 28th y. G.R.3.
―――, ch. Rufus and Susannah, Apr. 23, 1775. G.R.3.

ALDRIDGE (see Aldrich), ―――, ch. Leaben, July 29 [1825]. P.R.1.

ALLBE (see Alba, Albea, Allbee), Elijah of Milford, Jan. 5 [1835]. P.R.1.
Mary, wid., of Mellfurd, Dec. 25, 1782. P.R.1.
Ruth, wid., Mar. 14 [1832]. P.R.1.
Sairy, w. Capt. John of Mendon, June 7, 1788. P.R.1.

ALLBEE (see Alba, Albea, Albee, Allbe), Lucretia, d. Peter and Rodah, Apr. 7, 1777. [Lucrete Albe, P.R.1.]

ALLDAN (see Alden, Aldon), Noah, Dea., May 4 [1832], a. 77, in Wilbraham. P.R.1.

ALLEN, Asa, s. Samuel and Polly, Oct. 23, 1820.
Experiance, w. Ellery, Oct. 8, 1841, a. 55. G.R.1.
John of Franklen, July 24, 1815, a. 67. P.R.1.
Rebacah, Apr. 2, 1759, in 75th y. [Rebecca, wid. James, a. 75, G.R.1.]
Reuel, [twin] s. Samuel and Polly, Nov. 28, 1824.
Ruby Polk, Oct. 28, 1820, a. 9 hrs. G.R.1.
Rufus, [twin] s. Samuel and Polly, Nov. 28, 1824.
―――, w. John, May 12 [1802]. P.R.1.

AMIDON, Phillip, "Corl," of Mendam, Mar. 19 [1802]. P.R.1.

ARMBY, Silas, Feb. 5, 1848. C.R.

ARMINGTON, ―――, ch. ―――, Oct. 8 [?] [1846]. P.R.1.

ARNAL (see Arnel, Arnol, Arnold, Arnorl), ―――, ch. John, May 2, 1776. P.R.1.
―――, ch. ――― Sr., Nov. 22 [1840], "at the factory." P.R.1.
―――, ch. Noah, Sept. 1 [1847]. P.R.1.

ARNEL (see Arnal, Arnol, Arnold, Arnorl), ―――, ch. Daniel, June 6 [1817]. P.R.1.
―――, ch. Nathan, July 14 [1824]. P.R.1.
―――, w. Nathan Esq., Dec. 5 [1825]. P.R.1.

ARNOL (see Arnal, Arnel, Arnold, Arnorl), John, Aug. 19 [1839], a. 66, "at the poor hous." P.R.1.
―――, ch. Noah, Nov. — [1845]. P.R.1.

BELLINGHAM DEATHS. 167

ARNOLD (see Arnal, Arnel, Arnol, Arnorl), Andrew, s. Daniel Jr. and Jane, Jan. 20, 1844. [Dec. 13, 1843, a. 5 m. 13 d., G.R.3.]
Henry Clay, s. Noah J. and Mary W., Nov. 2, 1845, a. 2 m. 26d.
Jacob, Apr. 11, 1841, in 64th y. G.R.3. [Arnol, P.R.1.]
Maranda, w. Daniel Jr., Mar. 10, 1832, a. 27. G.R.3. [Arnal, P.R.1.]

ARNORL (see Arnal, Arnel, Arnol, Arnold), ———, w. John, July 1 [1817]. P.R.1.

BALLOU (see Blue).

BARBER, Daniel A., s. Adams J. and Orinda, June 16, 1826. [a. 1, G.R.3.] [a. 1 y. 6 m., P.R.1.]
Elizabeth A., w. Adams J., Mar. 3, 1820. G.R.3.
Orinda, w. Adams J., fever, Oct. 21, 1849, a. 44 y. 8 m. 14 d. [d. Daniel Arnold and Jerusha, a. 45 y. 8 m. 14 d., G.R.3.]
[? Barber] ——— (Barb[torn]), w. "old mr" Hamblat, Dec. 25 [1824], a. 6[torn]. P.R.1.

BARNA, ———, ch. Simen, Mar. 3, 1810. P.R.1.

BARTLET (see Bartlett), ———, w. Ebar, May 18 [1833]. P.R.1.

BARTLETT (see Bartlet), Phebe, Nov. 3, 1844, a. 18.

BATES (see Batte, Batts), Abigail, w. Ezekiel, Dec. 18, 1797. [a. 53, G.R.2.] [Abigeal Beats, w. Ezekel, P.R.1.]
Abigail, w. Capt. Eli, Aug. 17, 1825, in 54th y. G.R.3.
Abigail, d. Laban, Oct. 2, 1842. [d. Laban and Olive, in 54th y., G.R.3.] [Abigile Batts, sister of Naum, a. 55, P.R.1.]
Albert G., m., s. Elijah and Sarah A., mortification, Jan. 10, 1848, a. 36 y. 4 m. 11 d. [a. 36 y. 6 m. 11 d., G.R.2.] [Alburt Batts, a. 35, P.R.1.]
Amory, s. Ezekiel and Abigail, Oct. 20, 1798, a. 7 m. G.R.2.
Ann Almy, d. Elijah and Sarah, June 25, 1836, a. 17 y. 1 m. G.R.2. [An Ama Batts, d. Eligah, June 24, a. 17, P.R.1.]
Coumfoart, w. Asa (Beates), Oct. 12 [1798]. P.R.1.
Electa, Mrs., Apr. 22, 1841. C.R. [w. Otis, a. 57, G.R.2.]
Eli, Capt., July 3, 1817, in 48th y. G.R.3. [July 2, P.R.1.]
Eli W., s. Capt. Eli and Abigail, Oct. 6, 1822, a. 22. G.R.3. [Eli Batts, P.R.1.]
Elijah, Sept. 26, 1841. [Batts, P.R.1.] [a. 61, G.R.2. P.R.1.]
Elijah [dup. s. Elijah], Mar. 12, 1844, a. 28 y. 11 m. 18 d. [s. Elijah and Ann Sarah, a. 29, G.R.2.] [Elijah Batts Jr., a. 29, P.R.1.]

BATES, Emmere, s. Ezekel, Oct. 20 [1798]. P.R.I.
Ezekiel, s. Ezekiel and Abigial, Oct. 29, 1776. [Batts Jr., Oct. 30, P.R.I.]
Ezekiel, Sept. 5, 1816. [a. 79, G.R.2.] [Ezekel Batts, Sept. 4, a. 78, P.R.I.]
Francis Augustus, s. Francis D. and Julia A., Feb. 25, 1843. [a. 1 y. 11 m. 15 d., G.R.2.] [Francis Gustis Batts, P.R.I.]
Francis D., s. Ezekiel and Cyrena, May 5, 1808, a. 3 y. 3 m. 4 d. G.R.2. [ch. Ezekel Jr., P.R.I.]
George, s. Capt. Eli, Apr. 7, 1829, in 36th y. G.R.3.
Henry A., s. Mellen and Mary A., Apr. 10, 1840, a. 2 y. 1 m. 17 d. G.R.2. [Batts, ch. Millins, scolt, Apr. 9, a. 2, P.R.I.]
Isaac, Aug. 21, 1787, a. 83. G.R.2. [Batts, of Mendon, Aug. 14, P.R.I.]
John Esq., m., s. Ezekiel and Abigail, July 3, 1848, a. 75 y. 1 m. 13 d. [a. 75, P.R.I.]
Joseph, Apr. 1, 1793, in 60th y. G.R.2. [Batts, of Mendam, P.R.I.]
Julia A., b. Plainfield, Conn., w. Francis D., Nov. 22, 1847, a. 32 y. 5 m. 6 d.
Laban Esq., Apr. 7, 1832. [s. Isaac and Mary, May 7, G.R.3.] [Batts, May 7, P.R.I.]
Levinia, w. Ezekiel, Aug. 16, 1841. [Levina, Aug. 23, a. 83, G.R.2.] [Lovina Batts, wid., Aug. 23, a. 83, P.R.I.]
Lucreete, d. Ezekiel and Abigial, Oct. 8, 1776. [Lucretia, d. Ezekiel and Abigail, a. 7, G.R.I.] [Lucretet Batts, d. Ezekil, P.R.I.]
Lucy Ann, d. Laban and Mary B., Aug. 23, 1838, a. 1 y. 4 m. G.R.2. [Batts, P.R.I.]
Martha, w. Isaac, Apr. 7, 1786, a. 82. G.R.2. [Batts, w. Isaac of Mendon, P.R.I.]
Mary Thayer, d. Laban and Mary B., Apr. 2, 1833, a. 4 y. 1 m. 24 d. G.R.2. [Batts, P.R.I.]
Nahum, Jan. 22, 1847, a. 71. G.R.2. [Batts, Jan. 23, a. 73, P.R.I.]
Olive, w. Laban, Aug. 10, 1834. G.R.3.
Peter, s. Laban and Olive, Sept. 27, 1776. [Batts, s. Laben, P.R.I.]
Sarah, w. Joseph, Mar. 4, 1777, a. 33. G.R.I. [Batts, w. Joseph of Mendon, P.R.I.]
Sarah A., d. Elijah and Sarah, Oct. 17, 1829, a. 1 y. 9 m. G.R.2.
Sarah A., wid., b. Mendon, d. Levi Albee and Temperence, intussusception, Feb. 24, 1847, a. 57 y. 2 m. 7 d. [w. Elijah, 1817, a. 57 y. 2 m. 10 d., G.R.2.] [Batts, 1847, a. 57, P.R.I.]

BATES, Sarah E., d. Elijah and Sarah, Oct. 28, 1819, a. 2 y. 1 m. 28 d. G.R.2. [Batts, P.R.1.]
Smith, s. Laban and Olive, Jan. 5, 1788. [1787, G.R.3.]
Stanley S., s. Peletiah S. and Caroline R., Oct. 18, 1837, a. 8 m. G.R.2. [Stanly Batts, s. Smith, P.R.1.]

BATTE (see Bates, Batts), Deborah, wid., Oct. 19, 1779. P.R.1.

BATTS (see Bates, Batte), Asenath, July 25 [1819], a. 26. P.R.2.
Lecta, w. Otes, Apr. 22 [1841], a. 58. P.R.1.
Olive, wid., Feb. 5 [1834]. P.R.1.
Sarah, d. Elijah, Oct. 18 [1828]. P.R.1.
Suba, w. Frances [*sic*], Nov. 22 [1847]. P.R.1.
———, ch. Lab, Jan. 5, 1788. P.R.1.
———, w. Elijah, Jan. 28, 1808. P.R.1.
———, w. Ezekel Jr., June 27 [1808]. P.R.1.
———, ch. Elij[a]h, Apr. 23, 1821. P.R.1.
———, ch. Elijah, Nov. 10 [1822]. P.R.1.
———, w. Sulliven, July 8 [1831]. P.R.1.
———, w. Madison, small pox, June 11 [1836]. P.R.1.
———, twin ch. Madison, Nov. 12, 1838. P.R.1.
———, twin ch. Madison, Nov. 12, 1838. P.R.1.
———, ch. Maddison, Oct. 12 [1843]. P.R.1.
———, ch. Madison, Oct. 11, 1844. P.R.1.
———, ch. Madison, Feb. 1 [1846]. P.R.1.
———, twin ch. Madason, Nov. 18 [1847]. P.R.1.

BAXTER, Delevarance, wid., July 12, 1775, a. 72. P.R.1.
Meron, July 12, 1775, a. 72. G.R.1.
Thomas, Mar. 16, 1759, a. 21. G.R.1. [Baxtar Jr., a. 21 y. 6 w. P.R.1.]
Thomas, Mar. 20, 1773, a. 72. G.R.1. [Baxtar, a. 71, P.R.1.]

BEASLEY (see Bezlee).

BEMBO (see Bimbo), Cloe [negro], wid. Jack, May 23, 1790. [Clo Bimbo, P.R.1.]
Cyrus [negro], s. Jack and Cloe, June —, 1787. [June 17, P.R.1.]
Jack [negro], May 13, 1790. [Bimbo, P.R.1.]

BEMIS, Charles, ch. T. and P., Apr. 12, 1847, a. 8 d. G.R.1.
Elnah, ch. T. and P., Mar. 6, 1841, a. 8 m. G.R.1. [Beemus, ch. Theodoer, Mar. 7, P.R.1.]

BENEDICT, Eliza, inf. ———, Dec. 17, 1845. G.R.1.
Henry, Aug. 22, 1843, a. 4 m. G.R.1.

BENEDICT, John Ganow, s. David H. and Olive A., Sept. 1,
1842. [a. 16 m., G.R.1.]
Olive, Aug. 10, 1846, a. 10 m. G.R.1.
Ruth, w. Thomas, Oct. 25, 1847, a. 34. G.R.1.

BENNET, Diana, ——, 1826. C.R.

BEZLEE, Shurlot, Oct. 27 [1821]. P.R.1.

BILLENSSON (see Billings, Billins), ——, ch. William, June
11 [1792]. P.R.1.

BILLINGS (see Billensson, Billins), Easther, w. Willimes, Oct.
28 [1795]. P.R.1.

BILLINS (see Billensson, Billings), ——, ch. Willim, Oct. 3
[1798]. P.R.1.

BIMBO (see Bembo), Pagge, Mar. 13 [1825], a. 4[torn]. P.R.1.

BISHOP, Mary, d. William S. and Jerusha, Aug. 22, 1838, a.
16 m. G.R.1.

BLACKINGTON, Mary, w. Levi Whipple, Oct. 24, 1814, a. 19.
G.R.2.

BLACKMAN, Phillip, s. Eleazer and Mary, Apr. 6, 1769.

BLAK (see Blake), Hannah, w. Asa of Wrentham, May 21, 1790.
P.R.1.

BLAKE (see Blak), Mary, w. Asa, Apr. 21, 1768. [Apr. 21,
1798, G.R.1.]
Sarah L., June 10, 1837, a. 9 m. 19 d. G.R.2.
Silance, May 28, 1829. P.R.1.
Silas, [twin] s. Abraham and Silence, Mar. 10, 1765.

BLOOD, David, s. Abigail, wid., Nov. 3, 1749.
Ichobod, s. Joseph and Abigail, Apr. 10, 1748.
Joanna, d. Abigail, wid., Oct. 25, 1749.
Joseph, Apr. 20, 1748.
Lusee, d. Abigail, wid., Oct. 20, 1749.

BLUE, ——, w. Ammariah, May 25, 1776. P.R.1.

BOLDEN, Joseph, Oct. 24, 1798. P.R.1.

BOOSWORTH (see Bosworth, Bozworth), Lois, d. Stasa, Oct.
7 [1830]. P.R.1.

BOSWORTH (see Boosworth, Bozworth), Ichabod, Nov. 18, 1820, a. 71. G.R.3. [Ichaburd Boosworth, Nov. 16, a. 80, P.R.1.]
Otis, s. Stacy and Abigail, Feb. 24, 1828, a. 1 y. 5 m. 24 d. G.R.2. [Boosworth, ch. Stasa, Feb. 25, P.R.1.]

BOZWORTH (see Boosworth, Bosworth), Phila, May 29 [1830]. P.R.1.

BRICK, Joseph, "a Dwarf," May 28 [1801], a. 35. P.R.1.

BROWN, Esther, w. Joseph Esq., June 6, 1776, in 52d y. G.R.3.
Lucinda Amanda, d. James O. and Nancy G., Nov. 4, 1829, a. 1 y. 5 m. G.R.2.
Mary Ellen, d. James O. and Nancy G., Feb. 10, 1838, a. 1 y. 5 m. 15 d. G.R.2.
———, wid., Aug. 24 [1828]. P.R.1.

BRYANT, Sarah Vose Sumner, w. Philip C., Jan. 25, 1838, a. 37. G.R.1. [Briant, w. Phillip, P.R.1.]

BUCKLEY, John, s. John and Elizabath, drowned, Sept. 1, 1817, a. 5. G.R.1.
Mary Ann, d. Peter and Lucretia, May 9, 1817, a. 1 y. 5 m. G.R.1.

BULARD (see Bullard, Bullerd), ———, ch. Elisher, Oct. 15, 1788. P.R.1.

BULLARD (see Bulard, Bullerd), Albert, [twin] ch. Ellis and Olive, Oct. 8, 1834, a. 14 d. G.R.2. [twin ch. Eles, Oct. 6, P.R.1.]
Amelia, [twin] ch. Ellis and Olive, Oct. 15, 1834, a. 21 d. G.R.2. [twin ch. Eles, Oct. 14, P.R.1.]
Amos Turner, s. Z. and Mary, June 21, 1845, a. 29. G.R.1.
Bethshaba, w. Elisha, June 10, 1774.
Daniel, July 30 [1824]. P.R.1.
Deborah, w. Daniel, Nov. 16, 1775.
Deborah, d. Daniel and Mary, cancer, Aug. 25, 1846, a. 69 y. 4 m. 25 d.
Elisha of Frankling, Mar. 15, 1834. P.R.1.
Elisher, Feb. 26, 1790. P.R.1.
John, s. Whillok, June 22 [1841], in Hartford. P.R.1.
Luis, s. Josh, Apr. 22, 1791. P.R.1.
Maria Louisa, d. Z. and Mary, Aug. 15, 1830. G.R.1.
Mary, w. Daniel, Nov. 5, 1807. [third w. Daniel, P.R.1.]
Olive, w. Ellis, May 21, 1835, a. 27. G.R.2. [Nov. 21, a. 28, P.R.1.]

BULLARD, Seth, s. Elisher, Feb. 26, 1781. P.R.I.
William, s. Ellis and Olive, Sept. 21, 1836, a. 1 y. 5 d. G.R.2.
———, ch. Daniel and Deborah, Nov. 8, 1775.
———, ch. Daniel and ——— (third w.), June 2, 1782. P.R.I.
———, ch. Whiliock, Apr. 12, 1806. P.R.I.
———, ch. Whellock, Feb. 23 [1811]. P.R.I.
BULLERD (See Bulard, Bullard), Mary, second w. Danel, June 17, 1780. P.R.1.
BUR (see Burr), Sabra, d. Asa, Nov. 19 [1830]. P.R.I.
———, ch. Sinneca, July 26 [1828]. P.R.I.
———, twin ch. Nathan, Aug. 30 [1844]. P.R.I.
———, twin ch. Nathan, Sept. 28 [1844]. P.R.I.
BURDICK, Paulina, w. Isaac, Apr. 27, 1837. [Polina, a. 27, G.R.2.]
BURLA, ———, ch. ———, Mar. 24 [1817]. P.R.I.
BURR (see Bur), Abigail, w. Leaben, Oct. 7 [1816]. P.R.I.
Asa, Mar. 28, 1816, a. 77. G.R.2. [Mar. 29, a. 76, P.R.I.]
Charlotte E., d. Seneca A. and Eliza, Sept. 15, 1835, a. 2 y. 4 m. G.R.2. [Bur, d. Senaca, scolt, P.R.I.]
Electe, w. Elisha, Dec. 17, 1834. [Electa, a. 52, G.R.2.] [Lecty Bur, P.R.I.]
Eli, s. Elisha and Electa, Feb. 22, 1811. [Feb. 22, 1841, a. 1 m. 9 d., G.R.2.] [Bur, Feb. 23, 1811, a. 5 w., P.R.I.]
Elisha, May 15, 1804, a. 65. G.R.2.
Elisha, s. Elisha and Electa, Jan. 14, 1813. [Jan. 14, 1818, a. 1 m. 1 d., G.R.2.] [Jan. 18, 1813, P.R.I.]
Elisha, Jan. 12, 1837. [[h. Electa] a. 57, G.R.2.]
Eliza, w. Seneca A., May 15, 1835, a. 33. G.R.2. [Bur, w. Senaca, P.R.I.]
Harriet, d. Elisha and Electa, Mar. 28, 1837. [Harriett, a. 15, G.R.2.] [Hariet, Mar. 29, P.R.I.]
Lucretia, wid. Elisha, Dec. 4, 1828, a. 83. G.R.2. [Lucrete Bur, Dec. 1, P.R.I.]
Nabby, twin d. Laban and Nabby, Jan. 10, 1816, a. 18 d. G.R.2.
Nabby, w. Laban, Oct. 7, 1816, a. 26 y. 27 d. G.R.2.
Olive, d. Elisha and Electa, Nov. 21, 1835.
Polly, d. Asa and Polly, Apr. 22, 1810, a. 6 y. 8 m. G.R.2. [Apr. 21, P.R.I.]
Polly, w. Asa, Jan. 16, 1830. [a. 19, G.R.2.] [Pollay, P.R.I.]

BURR, Rebeckah, d. Elisha and Lucretia, July 6, 1781. [Rebekah, June 6, a. 14 y. 8 m. 2 d., G.R.2.] [Rebekah Bur, d. Elisher, July 6, P.R.1.]
Rhoda, w. Asa, Dec. 4, 1803, in 62d y. G.R.2. [Roda, P.R.1.]
Sally, twin d. Laban and Nabby, Jan. 6, 1816, a. 14 d. G.R.2.
Seneca, Nov. 6, 1842, a. 37. [Seneca A., 1841, G.R.2.] [Nov. 7 [1841], P.R.1.]
———, twin ch. Laben, June 9 [1816]. P.R.1.
———, twin ch. Laben, June 9 [1816]. P.R.1.
———, ch. Laben, Sept. 19 [1821]. P.R.1.
———, twin ch. Asa, Sept. 17 [1833]. P.R.1.
———, ch. Laban, Mar. 26 [1845]. P.R.1.

BUTTERWORTH, Elisabeth, w. Nathanel, May 19, 1778. P.R.1.
Nathaniel, July 13, 1796.
Niles, Nov. 29 [1808]. P.R.1.
Sarah, Apr. 25 [1826]. P.R.1.

CARPENDER (see Carpenter), Amos, s. Reuben, June 21, 1782. P.R.1.
James (Ca[r]pender), s. Danel, Dec. 3, 1776. P.R.1.
Reuben, s. Reuben, June 17, 1782. P.R.1.
———, May 5 [1838], "at the factory." P.R.1.

CARPENTER (see Carpender), Reuben, s. Reuben and Sarah, Oct. 13, 1777.

CASS, Joanna, June 27, 1844, a. 84.

CHAPEN (see Chapin), Elias, Apr. 8 [1826]. P.R.1.

CHAPIN (see Chapen), Daniel, Apr. 7, 1843, a. 81. [Chapen, P.R.1.]
Fanny, Mrs., Feb. —, 1843, [in] Mendon. C.R.
Mary, Jan. 24, 1758, a. 84. G.R.1.

CHASE (see Chease), Amy, w. Cogshall, Feb. 25, 1818, a. 72. G.R.4.
Cogshall, Jan. 26, 1834, a. 96. G.R.4.
Elihu, June 25 [1834], a. 104. P.R.1.
Elisha, Nov. 8, 1834, a. 58. G.R.4.
Lyda, w. Alin, Sept. 13 [1832]. P.R.1.
Narcissa, w. Elisha, Nov. 1, 1839, a. 58. G.R.4.

CHEASE (see Chase), Trifosea, d. Allen, Apr. 9 [1816], a. 18. P.R.1.

CHENE (see Cheny), Anna, wid., of Weard, Apr. 9, 1790. P.R.1.

CHENY (see Chene), Simon of Medfield, "belonging to Captain John Jonis Compiny," "kiled in that fite," Sept. 8, ———. P.R.1.

CHILLSON (see Chilson), Dorcas, d. Walsinham and Susanna, Nov. 18, 1743.
Jedidiah, s. Joseph and Lydia, Oct. 26, 1759.
John, s. Walsinham and Susanna, Oct. 7, 1741.
Marcy, w. Joseph, Aug. 8, 1747, a. 31 y. 6 m. "wanting 10 hours."
Mary, d. Walsinham and Susann, July 14, 1736.
Mettiah, ———, 1825. C.R. [Milletiah Chilson, Nov. 12, in 47th y., G.R.3.] [Miltiah Chilson, Nov. 12, a. 45, P.R.1.]
Sarah, d. Walsinham and Susanna, July 19, 1747.
Walsinham, Jan. 15, 1760, in 79th y.

CHILSON (see Chillson), Abigail, w. John, June 29, 1834, in 78th y. G.R.3. [Abigill, wid., P.R.1.]
Anna, d. Ichabud, Sept. 23 [1832], a. 18. P.R.1.
Hannah, w. Joseph, Mar. 10, 1828, in 72d y. G.R.3.
John, s. John and Abigil, Feb. 12, 1789.
John, Dec. 5, 1830, in 77th y. G.R.3. [John 1st, P.R.1.]
John, Mar. 14, 1841, in 51st y. G.R.4. P.R.1.
Joseph, Feb. 9, 1778. P.R.1.
Joseph, Apr. 5 [1841], a. 86. P.R.1.
Joshua, Jan. 3, 1835. [a. 78, G.R.3.] [a. 77, P.R.1.]
Levina, d. Ichabod and Deborah, Nov. 7, 1847, a. 19 y. 11 m. G.R.4. [Lovina Chillson, d. Ickabud, P.R.1.]
Lyda, wid., Mar. 29, 1789. P.R.1.
Margaret, w. Joshua, Dec. 29, 1837, a. 72. G.R.3. [Margit Chillson, wid., a. 74, P.R.1.]
Martin, s. Ichabod and Deborah, Jan. 11, 1848, a. 23 y. 2 m. 26 d. G.R.4. [s. Icabud (Chillson), Jan. 12, P.R.1.]
Nathen, s. Joshua and Margret, June 20, 1788.
Polly, d. Joshua and Margaret, May 26, 1788.
Polly, d. Joshua and Margaret, Oct. 15, 1791. [ch. Joshaway, Oct. 16, P.R.1.]
———, wid., Dec. 17, 1774, a. 95. P.R.1.
———, ch. Joseph, July 3 [1800]. P.R.1.
———, ch. Icabourd, July 10 [1815]. P.R.1.
———, third ch. Icaburd, Oct. 29 [1815]. P.R.1.
———, fourth ch. Ichaburd, Nov. 9 [1816]. P.R.1.
———, w. Levi, May 31 [1833]. P.R.1.
——— of Mendon, ch. Willard, June 2 [1837]. P.R.1.

BELLINGHAM DEATHS. 175

CHROOKS (see Croks, Crooks), John of Franklin, Aug. 3, 1785. p.r.1.

CLARK, Benj[amin] F., s. Benj[amin] and Lucy, Oct. 18, 1833, a. 28. g.r.2.
Eddy, May 21, 1792, in 27th y. g.r.3.
Elizabeth J., June 15, 1846. g.r.4.
Frankling, Oct. 18 [1833]. p.r.1.
Joel J., Sept. 14, 1849, a. 34. g.r.1.
Laura Catherine, d. Joel J. and Almira, Oct. 10, 1845, a. 4 m. 1 d.
Molly, wid., Feb. 21, 1843. [wid. Eddy, d. Jonathan Draper and Abigail, Feb. 20, in 76th y., g.r.3.] [Feb. 20, a. 80 "or more," p.r.1.]

COB (see Cobb), Amus, s. Capt. Samuel, July 16, 1788, "as he was A coming hom from the Savenna he died at badfurd." p.r.1.

COBB (see Cob), Roda, w. Capt. Samuel, July 30 [1795]. p.r.1.
Samuel, Capt., Dec. 20, 1822, a. 85. g.r.1.
———, second w. Capt. Samuel, Apr. 30, 1801. p.r.1.

COBURN (see Colburn), Amma, Mar. — [1848]. p.r.1.

COLBURN (see Coburn), ———, ch. ———, Nov. 16 [1837]. p.r.1.

COMBS (see Coombs, Coomes, Cooms), John Jr., Jan. 28, 1804. [Coombs, a. 46, g.r.1.] [Cooms, p.r.1.]
Polly, Nov. 16, 1795, a. 25. g.r.1.

COMING, ———, ch. ———, Jan. 14 [1848]. p.r.1.

COOK (see Cooke, Cooks), Aaron, Sept. 28, 1844, a. 25. [Sept. 2, g.r.4.]
Abigail, [twin] d. Caleb and Provided, still born, June 19, 1754.
Abigail, w. Benjamin, Dec. 9, 1813, in 60th y. g.r.3.
Abner, Sept. 3, 1832, a. 53. g.r.2. [Abnah, 1831, p.r.1.]
Adonijah, s. Benjamin and Abigail, Sept. 11, 1787, a. 1 m. g.r.3.
Albinus, Oct. 24, 1847, in 62d y. g.r.4.
Alpheus, s. Benjamin and Abigail, Oct. 25, 1809, in 21st y. g.r.3. p.r.1.
Alpheus, Dec. 19 [1840]. p.r.1.
Alse, wid., Feb. 21 [1842], a. 84. p.r.1.
Alvan, s. Thad, Oct. 24 [1847]. p.r.1.
Amy, Apr. 16, 1834, in 25th y. g.r.3.

Cook, Anson, May 15, 1826. G.R.4.
Been, cancer, May "ye four part" [1831]. P.R.1.
Benjamin, June 18, 1831, in 77th y. G.R.3.
Charles F., s. Seth and Susan, May 9, 1840.
Charlott, w. Daniel, May 5, 1838, a. 74. G.R.2. [Charlotta, wid., P.R.1.]
Daniel, Oct. 12, 1825, a. 69. [Lt. Danil, a. 70, G.R.2.]
David, Oct. 29, 1790, "an old man." P.R.1.
David, Feb. 18, 1836, a. 85. G.R.2. [Dea. David, Feb. 19, a. 84, P.R.1.]
Dennel, Aug. 5, 1784. P.R.1.
Eddy C., ——, 1817. G.R.4.
Elce, w. John, Feb. 21, 1842, a. 84. [Ela, a. 83, G.R.2.]
Eleonia, d. Abner and Wata, Oct. 6, 1808. [Elonera, a. 2 y. 3 m. 29 d., G.R.2.]
Elisabeth, wid., Nov. 28 [1815], a. 86 y. 7 m. P.R.1.
Ellen Eliza, d. Amory B. and Mary, Sept. 25, 1842. [ch. Emary, a. 2, P.R.1.]
Ellis, s. Abner and Wata, Dec. 15, 1812. [Dec. 14, a. 3 y. 4 m. 10 d., G.R.2.]
Elone, second w. David, Dec. 10 [1814], a. 65. P.R.1.
Esther, w. Reuben, Dec. 29, 1838, a. 58. G.R.2. [wid., Oct. 29, P.R.1.]
Eunice, d. Esekel, Sept. 24 [1798]. P.R.1.
Ezekiel Jr., Mar. 6 [1818]. P.R.1.
Freelove, d. Caleb and Provided, Feb. 19, 1758.
Hannah, w. Avery, Mar. 27, 1818, in 27th y. G.R.4.
Hansi, w. Duty, Apr. 25, 1825, in 27th y. G.R.3.
Hansi Angeline, d. Capt. Duty and Abigail, Mar. 21, 1831, a. 2 y. 1 m. 26 d. G.R.3.
Hansi M., d. Capt. Duty and Abigail, Feb. 12, 1838, a. 3 y. 2 m. 25 d. G.R.3.
Harriett Jane, d. Charles and Zilpha, Mar. 24, 1848, a. 5 y. 2 m. 20 d. G.R.2. [adopted d. Charles, P.R.1.]
Horatio, s. Capt. Duty and Abigail, Feb. 9, 1827, a. 22 d. G.R.3.
Horris of Wrentham, May 3 [1845], a. 63. P.R.1.
Jarusha, wid., Jan. 15, 1834. P.R.1.
Jemima, d. Daniel and Elisabeth, Sept. 23, 1748.
Joanna, d. Dea. Nicholas and Elizabeth, Mar. —, 1750, in 10th y. G.R.3.
Joanna, w. Ziba, Oct. 27, 1836, a. 65. G.R.3. P.R.1.
John 2d, s. Elias and Mary, Dec. 5, 1837, a. 43. G.R.2. [a. 42, P.R.1.]
John, Nov. 21, 1840, a. 91. G.R.2. P.R.1.

COOK, John Mayo, s. John 2d and Nancy, consumption, Nov. 29, 1849, a. 18 y. 5 m. 28 d. [Nov. 28, a. 18, G.R.2.]
Joseph, s. Daniel and Elisabeth, May 26, 1769.
Lealan, Aug. 24, 1836. P.R.1.
Lealon, Sept. 23, 1836, a. 48. G.R.2.
Luciete, twin ch. Noah and Olive, Apr. [1], 1764, a. 16 d. G.R.3.
Luther, twin ch. Noah and Olive, Mar. 31, 1764, a. 15 d. G.R.3.
Lyda, Mar. 12 [1844]. P.R.1.
Margera, w. Walter of Mendam, Feb. 24 [1793]. P.R.1.
Mary, d. Benjamin and Abigail, May 1, 1804, in 19th y. G.R.3.
Mayo, s. Elias and Mary, Dec. 9, 1832, a. 35. G.R.2. [a. 34, in Roxboro, P.R.1.]
Moly [dup. W. Molly], w. David [dup. lung fever], Dec. 31, 1848, a. 77 [dup. a. 76]. G.R.2. [Mollay, wid. Dea. David, Dec. 30, P.R.1.]
Naham, s. Ens. Ezekel, Oct. 14 [1798]. P.R.1.
Nancy, wid. John, consumption, Aug. 20, 1849, a. 53 y. 25 d. [d. Dea. Eliab Wight, a. 53, G.R.2.]
Nelson F., s. Capt. Duty and Abigail, Aug. 4, 1831, a. 2 y. 1 m. 12 d. G.R.3.
Nicholas, Dea., Apr. 26, 1779, in 92d y. G.R.3. [Niculus, a. 92, P.R.1.]
Nicklolus Sr., Dec. 1, 1730. [Nicholas, in 71st y., G.R.2.]
Noah, Apr. 29, 1771, in 61st y. G.R.3.
Noah, June 20, 1811, a. 71. G.R.2.
Noah, June 20, 1841, a. 74.
Patience, w. Noah, Jan. 4, 1843, a. 74. [wid., P.R.1.]
Phebe, Mrs., Mar. 7, 1838, a. 75. G.R.2. [Pheba, a. 74 y. 10 m., P.R.1.]
Polly, d. Ben, May 1 [1804]. P.R.1.
Rachel, second w. Benjamin, June 30, 1848, in 80th y. G.R.3.
Reuben, Mar. 29, 1829, a. 48. G.R.2. [Ruban, Mar. 27, P.R.1.]
Rhoda, w. Thaddeus, Oct. 26, 1840, a. 72. G.R.4. P.R.1.
Roxanna, June 7, 1842, a. 60. [Roxana, w. Abijah, a. 59, G.R.1. P.R.1.]
Sally, d. Daniel and Charlotte, Aug. 8, 1788. [a. 2, G.R.2.]
Saly, d. Lt. Daniel and Charlotte, Aug. 18, 1823, a. 34. G.R.2.
Samuel S. Jr., Oct. 27 [1798]. P.R.1.
Sarah, Aug. 8 [1823]. P.R.1.
Seth, s. Daniel and Elisabeth, July 27, 1769.
Seth, s. David Jr. [and] Susannah, June 27, 1783. [ch. Davied, June 28, P.R.1.]
Sofarla, w. Lealend, Sept. 13, 1822. [Soffarly, w. Lealon, Sept. 12, a. 26, G.R.2.] [Sofila, w. Lealand, Sept. 12, P.R.1.]

178   BELLINGHAM DEATHS.

COOK, Susan A., d. William and Eliza, Jan. 29, 1848, a. 11 m.
G.R.2.⁊ [Jan. 28, P.R.1.]
Susanah, w. David, Sept. 21 [1797]. P.R.1.
Susanna, d. Nicholas and Elizabeth, Sept. —, 1748, in 11th y.
G.R.3.
Vernon, s. Daniel and Charlotte, Nov. 14, 1804. [a. 2 y. 11 m.
1 d., G.R.2.] [Varnon, s. Lt. Danil, P.R.1.]
Walter, "old mʳ," of Mendam, Jan. 2, 1794. P.R.1.
William, s. Nicholas and Phillis, Sept. 13, 1775, in 3d y. G.R.3.
[ch. Niculus, P.R.1.]
Ziba, July 15, 1840, a. 76. G.R.3. [July 17, P.R.1.]
———, ch. Ezekel, Sept. —, 1775. P.R.1.
———, w. Daved, Jan. —, 1783. P.R.1.
———, ch. Stephen, July 9, 1787. P.R.1.
———, ch. Arthur, June 4, 1788. P.R.1.
———, ch. Stephen, May 15, 1789. P.R.1.
———, ch. Noah, Dec. 19 [1791]. P.R.1.
———, ch. Esekel Jr., Mar. 30 [1795]. P.R.1.
———, w. Lt. Ruben, May 28, 1828. P.R.1.
———, grand ch. Ziba, Nov. — [1833]. P.R.1.
———, d. Ziba, Apr. 6 [1834]. P.R.1.
———, ch. Emmory, Sept. 9 [1837]. P.R.1.
———, ch. Emmory, Sept. 10 [1837]. P.R.1.
———, inf. s. Charles and Zilpha, July 1, 1846. G.R.2.
———, d. Stephan, Apr. 14 [1849]. P.R.1.

COOKE (see Cook, Cooks), Ezekel, June 15 [1821], a. 80. P.R.1.
Sylvia A., w. Jervis, Sept. 13, 1834, a. 24. G.R.1.

COOKS (see Cook, Cooke), Elisabath, wid., Mar. 3, 1788, a.
89 y. 9 m. P.R.1.

COOMBS (see Combs, Coomes, Cooms), Amos, Mar. 7, 1840, a.
31. G.R.1.
Caroline T., d. Amos, Dec. 14, 1839, a. 3. G.R.1. [Cooms, Dec.
13, P.R.1.]
David, May 27, 1839, a. 27. G.R.1. [Coomes, s. Jessa, P.R.1.]
Eicanors, ch. Valentine R. and Clarissa, Aug. 11, 1839. G.R.1.
George V., ch. Valentine R. and Clarissa, Oct. 2, 1832. G.R.1.
[Gorge Vic Cooms, s. Vallintine (Comes), P.R.1.]
Jesse, m., May 14, 1845, a. 72. [Jessa, G.R.1.] [Jesa Coomes,
P.R.1.]
John N., ch. Valentine R. and Clarissa, Aug. 13, 1829. G.R.1.
[John V. Cooms, s. Vollintine, a. 16 m., P.R.1.]
Mary, Nov. 16 [1795]. P.R.1.

COOMBS, Mary, wid. John, Mar. 28, 1831, a. 93. G.R.1.
Mary Olivia, d. Stephen A. and Charlotte B., dysentary, July 3, 1849, a. 3 y. 11 m. 8 d. [July 11, a. 3, G.R.1.]
Odid, Jan. 14, 1842. [Obed, a. 28, G.R.1.] [Odid Coomes, s. Jessa, a. 28, P.R.1.]

COOMES (see Combs, Coombs, Cooms), Abijah, s. John (Comes), Nov. 23 [1798]. P.R.1.

COOMS (see Combs, Coombs, Coomes), Sarah, wid., Mar. 28 [1831], a. 93 y. 3 m. 7 d. P.R.1.
———, w. Stephen, Mar. 30 [1827]. P.R.1.

COORBET (see Corbet, Corbett, Corbit), Icaburd of Milford, Feb. 20 [1829]. P.R.1.

CORBET (see Coorbet, Corbett, Corbit), Hopestill, w. Dr. John, Jan. 5, 1768, a. 65. G.R.1. [Hopstel Corbett, in 63d y., P.R.1.]
John Jr., Jan. 18, 1758. P.R.1.
Olive, wid., of Milford, Oct. 17 [1837], a. 79. P.R.1.
Priscilla, d. Daniel and Sary, Jan. 20, 1739-40.

CORBETT (see Coorbet, Corbet, Corbit), Elijah, s. John and Hopestill, Mar. 9, 1756.
John, Dr., ———, 1706, a. 48. G.R.1.
John, Dec. 5, 1726, a. 43. [Dr. John, in 43d y., G.R.1.]
John, Dr. [dup. Jr.], Mar. 1, 1794, a. 89. G.R.1. [Corbet, P.R.1.]
Joseph of Milford, Nov. 26 [1797], a. 85. P.R.1.
Josiah, ———, 1705, in 6th m. G.R.1.
Josiah, s. John and Hopstill, Apr. 30, 1753.
Mehetabel, Jan. 7, 1747-8.
Mehetabell, d. John and Hopstill, Dec. 23, 1749.
Priscilla, d. John, Dec. 1, 1728.
Rachel, d. John and Hopestill, July 16, 1754.
Seth, Aug. 1, 1772, a. 29 "Last march." P.R.1.

CORBIT (see Coorbet, Corbet, Corbett), ———, "old mis," wid. Joseph, Oct. 12, 1805. P.R.1.

CORTES (see Curtes, Curtis), Wright, s. Marcurs, Oct. 2 [1824]. P.R.1.

COSHMAN (see Coshmen, Coushman, Coushmon, Cushman), Cyrena, Apr. 25 [1816]. P.R.1.

COSHMEN (see Coshman, Coushman, Coushmon, Cushman),
——, w. Marten, Sept. 30 [1825]. P.R.I.

COUSHMAN (see Coshman, Coshmen, Coushmon, Cushman),
——, ch. Lydia, wid., Nov. 5 [1825]. P.R.I.

COUSHMON (see Coshman, Coshmen, Coushman, Cushman),
Asa, Jan. 26, 1807, a. 27. P.R.I.

CRAIG, Catharine Amelia, June 6, 1842. [Crage, d. Edward C. and Cynthia A., a. 4 y. 11 m. 21 d., G.R.2.] [Crage, a. 5, P.R.I.]
James Otis, June 26, 1842. [Crage, s. Edward C. and Cyntha A., a. 3 y. 3 m., G.R.2.] [Crage, P.R.I.]

CROKS (see Chrooks, Crooks), Brier, Dec. 11 [1819]. P.R.I.

CROOKS (see Chrooks, Croks), Charles Francis, s. Joel and Esther, Feb. 9, 1842. [Charly, a. 7 m. 26 d., G.R.2.] [a. 8 m., P.R.I.]
Mary, d. Jeremiah, Sept. 22, 1843 [dup. a. 24 y. 10 m. 9 d.]. [Mary J., d. Jeremiah and Ann, in 25th y., G.R.4.] [d. Jeremeiah, P.R.I.]

CROSSBY, Sarah Lavina [d. Pardon and Alsada], July 31, 1842.

CUMMINGS (see Coming).

CURTES (see Cortes, Curtis), ——, ch. Wright, Aug. 8 [1826]. P.R.I.

CURTIS (see Cortes, Curtes), Marcus, s. Write, May 18 [1830]. P.R.I.
Philana B., d. Capt. Wright and Aurrilla, Nov. 8, 1820, a. 1 y. 8 m. 17 d. G.R.3.

CUSHMAN (see Coshman, Coshmen, Coushman, Coushmon), Amaziah, June 1, 1800, a. 48. G.R.2. [Lt. Ammaziah (Coshmun), P.R.I.]
Amaziah, Oct. 24, 1825, a. 37 y. 6 m. 10 d. G.R.2. [Ammaziah Coushman, P.R.I.]
Asa, s. Apollas, July 30, 1821, a. 4 y. 3 m. 21 d. G.R.2. [Coushman, ch. Pollus, July 31, a. 4, P.R.I.]
Cyntha, wid., July 24 [1846]. P.R.I.
Fredrieck (Coshmun), s. Amsi, Oct. 6 [1799]. P.R.I.
Lues, s. Lt. Ammasiah (Coshmon), Dec. 17, 1791. P.R.I.
Martin, Aug. — [1832]. P.R.I.
Sabrina, d. Amaziah and Lydia, Jan. 6, 1823, a. 3 y. 6 m. G.R.2.

CUSHMAN, Sabrina, d. Amaziah and Lydia, Nov. 12, 1823, a. 7 m. 22 d. G.R.2.
Sarah, d. Amaziah and Marthe, Oct. 18, 1776.
———, wid., Sept. 17 [1822]. P.R.I.
———, ch. Amasiah, Jan. 5, 1825. P.R.I.

CUTLAR (see Cutler), Ruth, wid., of Holliston, Oct. 19 [1835]. P.R.I.

CUTLER (see Cutlar), Timothy, s. Deborah Kilbon, Feb. 17, 1797, a. 3 y. 1 d. G.R.2.

DAMAN, Benoni, s. Ebenezer and Es[t]her, June 18, 1756.
Ebenezer, s. Ebenezer and Esther, Oct. 15, 1759.
Ebenezer, Feb. 15, 1761, "A Remarkable Instant." [Damman, P.R.I.]

DANIELS (see Danniels), Japhat, Capt., of Holeston, Mar. 3 [1805]. P.R.I.
Samuel of Holliston, May 7, 1788, a. 96. P.R.I.
———, second w. Moses, Sept. 4 [1833]. P.R.I.

DANNIELS (see Daniels), Jessa, July 24 [1830]. P.R.I.

DARLING, Abigail, w. George, d. Dea. Martin Rockwood, May 27, 1838, a. 22. G.R.2. [Abigail L. Rockwood Darlinge, P.R.I.]
Abnar, Nov. 22, 1840, "at the poor house." P.R.I.
Ahimaaz, Oct. 30, 1836, in 72d y. G.R.4.
Allanson, s. Samuel and Sarah, Oct. 2, 1796, a. 1 y. 22 d. G.R.2.
Amasa, Nov. 19 [1825], a. 65. P.R.I.
Anna, d. John and Anna, Oct. 26, 1798, in 28th y. G.R.3. [Oct. 25, P.R.I.]
Asa, July 16 [1819], a. 35. P.R.I.
Caraloine, d. Samuel Jr. and Sarah, Sept. 27, 1801.
Caroline, d. Samuel and Sarah, Sept. 27, 1806, a. 2 d. G.R.2. [Sept. 26, a. 9 d., P.R.I.]
Chalote, Nov. 16, 1792. P.R.I.
Charles, s. Sam[ue]l and Margret, Jan. 31, 1835, a. 19 m. 6 d. G.R.2. [Charls, P.R.I.]
Collins Esq., Dec. 27, 1843, a. 58. G.R.2. [s. Samuel, P.R.I.]
Cornelius, Feb. 17, 1783, in 84th or 85th y. P.R.I.
Cornelius, Mar. 22, 1816. [in 84th y., G.R.3.] [Cornelous, a. 84, P.R.I.]
Danes, Oct. 19, 1775. P.R.I.
David, June 2, 1750.
David, s. Moses, May 29, 1776. P.R.I.

DARLING, Edwin R., Oct. 21, 1828, a. 2 y. 3 m. G.R.2.
Enock, Nov. 10 [1792]. P.R.1.
Esther, wid. Dea. Samuel, Feb. 18, 1816, in 80th y. G.R.3.
  [Easther, Feb. 26, a. 80, P.R.1.]
George Cook, s. George and Susan B., Apr. 26, 1848. G.R.2.
Gorge Stapels, ch. Chalote, Aug. 5 [1792]. P.R.1.
Hannah, w. Cornelus, Mar. 4, 1781, in 89th y. P.R.1.
Hephzibah, w. Cornelous, Mar. 15 [1816], a. 74. P.R.1.
Himas, Nov. 2 [? 24] [1836]. P.R.1.
Huldah, d. Cornelius and Hannah, Mar. 27, 1763. [a. 36 y. 5 m.
  6 d., G.R.3.]
Huldah, d. Job and Margery, Nov. 26, 1765.
Huldah, d. Moss dec'd, Mar. 21, 1790. P.R.1.
Jacob, old age, Feb. 16, 1849, a. 86.
Joab, May —, 1791. P.R.1.
John, Capt., May 29, 1753, in 90th y.
John, Feb. 2 [1800]. P.R.1.
Joshua, May 21, 1815, in 79th y. G.R.3. [a. 80, P.R.1.]
Lanson, s. Samuel Jr. and Sarah, Oct. 2, 1796.
Loiace, wid., May 28 [1816], a. 85. P.R.1.
Margeret, wid., Nov. 17 [1842], a. 84. P.R.1.
Margret, w. Samuel Jr., dropsey, Sept. —, 1847. [Margaret,
  Sept. 4, a. 50, G.R.2.] [Marget, Sept. 4, a. 47, P.R.1.]
Mary, w. Samuel, June 7, 1740.
Mary, w. Ahimaaz, July 17, 1849, a. 75 y. 3 m. 13 d. G.R.4.
Mary H., w. Dr. Elihu, Feb. 12, 1848, a. 52. G.R.2.
Mehitabel, Mar. 15, 1816. [Mehitable, w. Cornelius, in 74th y.,
  G.R.3.]
Michael, July 26, 1795, in 23d y. G.R.3. [Mikel, P.R.1.]
Mikel, Feb. 25, 1803, in Burlintun, N.Y. P.R.1.
Moses, Jan. 26, 1786. P.R.1.
Moses Jr., Dec. —, "bured the 26. day," 1788. P.R.1.
Nancy (Darli[n]g), w. Bengamin, Nov. 17 [1792]. P.R.1.
Nancy, d. Samuel, Oct. 3 [1823]. P.R.1.
Penelope, w. Samuel, July 10, 1759.
Peter Esq., May 16 [1818], a. 93. P.R.1.
Phebe, d. Cornelius and Hannah, May 5, 1761. [May 2, a. 23 y.
  6 m. 1 d., G.R.3.] [May 5, P.R.1.]
Prudence, d. John and Anne, Sept. 11, 1756.
Rachel, d. Moss dec'd, Mar. 1, 1790. P.R.1.
Rachel, wid., Sept. — [1820]. P.R.1.
Rebuen, s. Dea. Samuel, Jan. 6, 1780. P.R.1.
Rhoda, d. Samuel Jr. and Sarah, Oct. 17, 1788. [a. 1 y. 13 d.,
  G.R.2.]

DARLING, Ruth, d. Simon and Peggy, Aug. 8, 1800. G.R.1.
P.R.1.
Samuel, Capt., Feb. 17, 1744, a. 70 y. 11 m. G.R.3. P.R.1.
Samuel, Dea., June 12, 1814, in 95th y. G.R.3. [in 96th y., P.R.1.]
Sarah, w. Samuel, Jan. 31, 1826, a. 62. G.R.2. [Feb. 1, P.R.1.]
Simon, s. Simon and Peggy, Mar. 10, 1801, a. 2. G.R.1. [Mar. 16, P.R.1.]
Stephen, s. John and Anna, June 28, 1773.
Timothy, May 29, 1792. P.R.1.
Timothy Jr., Mar. 28 [1794]. P.R.1.
Uriah, Aug. 27 [1805]. P.R.1.
William, s. Joshua and Martha, Jan. 17, 1810, in 33d y. G.R.3. [Willims, P.R.1.]
———, ch. John, Apr. 25, 1776. P.R.1.
———, ch. Dea. Samuel, Sept. 2, 1777. P.R.1.
———, ch. Benjamen, scalt, Nov. 20, 1790. P.R.1.
———, grand ch. Simon, Aug. 23 [1828]. P.R.1.
———, ch. Jafason, Oct. 21 [1828], a. 2. P.R.1.
———, ch. George, May 12 [1838]. P.R.1.
———, wid., Feb. 11, 1848, a. 91. P.R.1.

DAWLEY, Alvira, Mrs., June 26, 1847. C.R. [Elvira, w. Perry, a. 53, G.R.1.] [Alvira Spear Dorly, w. Pary, P.R.1.]
Benjamin F., Sept. 17, 1840, a. 1. G.R.1. [Dorly, ch. Pary, P.R.1.]
Elvira, d. Perry and Alvira, consumption, Oct. —, 1847, a. 19. [Alvira S., Oct. 27, C.R.] [Elvira S., Oct. 27, G.R.1.] [Dorly, d. Para, Oct. 27, P.R.1.]

DEAN, ———, Mrs. [? Mr.], "killed with a Waggon up hear he came from norton," June 10 [1829]. P.R.1.

DENENS, Marget, wid., of Holliston, Mar. 19, 1791. P.R.1.

DEWEN (see Dewings), ———, ch. Elijah, Feb. 27 [1804]. P.R.1.

DEWINGS (see Dewen), Eligah, Sept. 10 [1844]. P.R.1.
———, w. Eligah, Sept. 10 [1844]. P.R.1.

DRAKE, Betsey, w. John, consumpsion, June 1, 1847, a. 40. [May 31, G.R.1.]
Ichabod J., ch. J. and B., Aug. 16, 1843, a. 2 m. G.R.1. P.R.1.
Mary E., d. Ozius and Elizebath, Aug. 3, 1843, a. 19. G.R.1. P.R.1.

DRAPER, Abigail, w. Jonathan, June 23, 1826, in 96th y. G.R.3. [wid., a. 97, P.R.I.]
Jonathan, May 18, 1803, in 73d y. G.R.3.
Jonathan, Aug. 18 [1803]. P.R.I.
Rachel, d. Jonathan and Abigail, Nov. —, 1814. G.R.3.
Rachel, Dec. 22 [1814], a. 50. P.R.I.
Sarah, Sept. 17 [1815]. P.R.I.

EDDY, Rebecca B., Aug. 6, 1842. G.R.3.

EDWARDS, Silence H., d. Philip and Parnel of Holden, July 29, 1839, a. 20. G.R.5. [July 27, "at the factory," P.R.I.]

ELLARS (see Elles, Ellies, Ellis), Zuba, June 4, 1819. P.R.I.

ELLES (see Ellars, Ellies, Ellis), Vaspheasha, Sept. 4 [1798], at Phellidelffa. P.R.I.

ELLIES (see Ellars, Elles, Ellis), Amos, Capt., May 30 [1817]. P.R.I.

ELLIS (see Ellars, Elles, Ellies), Hannah, d. Amos and Hannah, Nov. 27, 1779.
Hannah, wid., July 3, 1829. [Ellas, a. 80, P.R.I.]
Vispasion, Sept. 3, 1799.
———, ch. Capt. Amous, Nov. 27, 1779. P.R.I.

ESTEN (see Estes), Lucia E., w. Samuel, Apr. 12, 1849. G.R.4.

ESTES (see Esten), Adelbert, inf. s. Samuel and Mary Ann, Aug. 15, 1843. G.R.4.
Clarinda, d. Samuel and Lovina, Nov. 10, 1843. G.R.4.
Harriet A., w. Samuel, Aug. 10, 1840, a. 21 y. 11 m. G.R.4.
Lucina, w. Samuel, Jan. 19, 1819, in 41st y. G.R.4.
Mary Ann, w. Samuel, Aug. 15, 1843, a. 20 y. 4 m. 15 d. G.R.4.
Samuel [h. Lucina], Mar. 22, 1837, in 65th y. G.R.4.

FAIRBANKS (see Farbanks), Asa, Capt., of Franklin, Oct. 29 [1809]. P.R.I.
Calvin, Aug. 11 [1825]. P.R.I.
Emory, Apr. 24 [1814], a. 22. P.R.I.
Hopestil, "Hanged him self," Nov. 30, 1779. P.R.I.
Joseph, Jan. 5, 1835. [a. 74, P.R.I.]
Lucy, w. Joseph of Medway, Mar. 21, 1786. P.R.I.
Mary, w. Joseph, Oct. 4, 1825.
———, wid., of Frankling, June 18, 1788. P.R.I.

FARBANKS (see Fairbanks), Rufus, Mar. 26 [1838]. P.R.I.

FARRAH, ———, Maj., of Uptun, Mar. 9 [1807]. P.R.I.

FARRINGTON, Aaron Jr., Feb. 7, 1841. [a. 51, G.R.2.] [Furrington, a. 51, P.R.I.]
Aaron, Feb. 26, 1841. [Furrington, Feb. 27, a. 86, P.R.I.]
David, Feb. 7, 1833, a. 48 y. 8 m. 23 d. G.R.2.

FISH, Esther, wid., of Shutesbury, Oct. 27 [1826], a. 82. P.R.I.
Seth of Shutesbury, July 1, 1797. P.R.I.

FISHER, Horris, Jan. — [1836], a. 18, in Pautaxit. P.R.I.
John, "fell and brook his neck," July 25 [1836]. P.R.I.
Marget of Wrentham, Oct. 18, 1761. P.R.I.
Oliver, m., Oct. 4, 1845, a. 69. [Oct. 3, a. 79, P.R.I.]
Sarah, d. Abial, Oct. 12, 1828, a. 8 m. P.R.I.
———, w. Abial, Apr. 23 [1832], a. 45, in Sturbridge. P.R.I.
———, twin ch. ———, Sept. 11 [1833]. P.R.I.
———, twin ch. ———, Oct. 23 [1833]. P.R.I.

FLETCHER, ———, w. William, Oct. 24, 1827. P.R.I.

FORASTALL (see Forestall, Foristall, Foristill), Almira, Oct. 4, 1798, a. 3. G.R.I.
Bethiah, wid. Ezra, Sept. 21, 1821, a. 77. G.R.I.
Ezra, Apr. 30, 1811, a. 74. G.R.I. [Forstuel, a. 75, P.R.I.]
Juna, Oct. 4, 1798, a. 1. G.R.I.

FORESTALL (see Forastall, Foristall, Foristill), Caroline N., Sept. 1, 1845. G.R.I.
Edmund H., Nov. 6, 1845. G.R.I.

FORESTER (see Forristar, Forrister), Mary, d. Ezra, Feb. 18, 1775. P.R.I.

FORISTALL (see Forastall, Forestall, Foristill), Amasa, Apr. 22, 1849, a. 75. G.R.I. [Amase Foristar, P.R.I.]
Mary, d. Ezra and Bethiah, Feb. 18, 1775.
Olney D., s. Amasa and Sarah, Oct. 21, 1843, a. 20. G.R.I.
Sally, w. Amasa, Jan. 29, 1835, a. 52. G.R.I.
Sarah, d. Ezra and Bethiah, Sept. 26, 1785. [Forestall, P.R.I.]
Sarah, w. Amasa, June 26, 1821, a. 53. G.R.I.

FORISTILL (see Forastall, Forestall, Foristall), Sarah, second w. Ammasa, Jan. 29 [1835]. P.R.I.

FORRISTAR (see Forester, Forrister), Olny Danil, s. Amasa, Oct. 21 [1843], a. 21. P.R.I.

FORRISTER (see Forester, Forristar), Haven of Holliston, Nov. 12 [1835]. P.R.1.
———, ch. Amma, Oct. 5 [1798]. P.R.1.
———, ch. Amma, Oct. 5 [1798]. P.R.1.

FORSTER (see Forsterster, Forsther, Foster), Bethiah, wid., Sept. 22 [1821], a. 77. P.R.1.

FORSTERSTER (see Forster, Forsther, Foster), ———, twin ch. Amasa, Feb. 6 [1794]. P.R.1.
———, twin ch. Amasa, Feb. 7 [1794]. P.R.1.

FORSTHER (see Forster, Forsterster, Foster), ———, w. Ammesa, June 26 [1821], a. 52. P.R.1.

FORTEN, ——— "old," Feb. 18 [1796]. P.R.1.

FOSTER (see Forster, Forsterster, Forsther), Abigail M., d. Silas and Lucina, Mar. 10, 1819, a. 2 y. 10 m. 25 d. G.R.2. [Forster, ch. Silurs, P.R.1.]

FRANCH (see French), Samuel of Milfurd, Sept. 1, 1790. P.R.1.

FREEMAN (see Freman), Edward, Jan. 21, 1827, a. 46. G.R.2. [Freman, Jan. 27, P.R.1.]
Nancy L., w. James M., Sept. 19, 1843, a. 26 y. 2 m. 23 d.
Nathan, Oct. 2 [1825]. P.R.1.
Philaty Thayer, d. Edward and Sarah, Apr. 2, 1807, a. 2 y. 9 m. 20 d. G.R.2.
Sarah, Sept. —, 1824. C.R. [Sabra, w. Edward, Sept. 10, a. 42, G.R.2.] [Sara Freman, w. Edward, Sept. 10, P.R.1.]
———, w. Nathan, Nov. 11 [1822], a. 82. P.R.1.

FREMAN (see Freeman), Hariet, w. Monroo, Sept. 19 [1843]. P.R.1.

FRENCH (see Franch), Abijah, Dea., of Milford, Jan. 18, 1786. P.R.1.

FROAST, Amariah, "Old mr," of Milford, Mar. 14, 1792. P.R.1.

FULLER, Miltiah, Feb. 7, 1796. P.R.1.

GANZEY, Mary, wid., of Midway, Oct. 11 [1795]. P.R.1.
Samuel of Medway, "Bured" Mar. 27, 1788, in 85th or 86th y. P.R.1.

GILBERT, Lucretia, w. John G., Dec. 20, 1838, a. 21. G.R.2. [Lucreta Gilbut, w. John Gardnar, Dec. 21, P.R.1.]

GILSON, Asa, Aug. 4 [1846]. P.R.I.

GODMAN (see Goodman), Anna, wid., May 31, 1775. P.R.I.
——, wid. John, Nov. 20 [1819]. P.R.I.

GOFF, ——, ch. ——, July 6 [1837], "at the factory." P.R.I.

GOINERS [?], Mary, wid., "ales" Molley Cook, May 8, 1820, a. 80. P.R.I.

GOODMAN (see Godman), Anna, wid., Oct. 11 [1821], a. 69. P.R.I.
Sarah, Oct. 23 [1821]. P.R.I.

GORE, Joseph, July 24, 1786, a. 57. G.R.I.

GOULD, Elizabeth, d. Samuel and Mary, May 18, 1818, a. 8. G.R.2.
Isaiah, Sept. 2, 1849, a. 75. G.R.I.

GOULDSBURY, John, s. John and Abigail, Aug. 5, 1766.

GRANT, Hannah Amanda, w. A. C., Mar. 23, 1849, a. 35. G.R.I.

GREEN, John, s. James and Cyntha, Nov. 13, 1820, a. 20 d. G.R.2.

GUERNSEY (see Ganzey).

HADLY, Mary Kilburn, Oct. 27 [1832]. P.R.I.

HALL, Abigail, w. Seth, Mar. 23, 1753.
Asa Sr., Jan. 3, 1841. P.R.I.
Benjamin [h. Sarah], Feb. 21, 1824. G.R.3. [Bengamen Esq., P.R.I.]
Bridget, Sept. 27, 1821. C.R.
Bridget, w. John, Sept. 26, 1824, in 60th y. G.R.2. [wid., a. 70, P.R.I.]
Jane, w. Zurial, "formerly" wid. Peletiah Smith, Nov. 8, 1746, in 77th y.
Martha, Nov. 1, 1828. G.R.3.
Marvellous, Sept. 3, 1775, in 23d y. G.R.3. [Marvellus, s. Seth, Sept. 2, P.R.I.]
Rebeckah, wid., Jan. 3, 1772. P.R.I.
Sarah, w. Benjamin, Nov. 29, 1821. G.R.3. [w. Benjamen, P.R.I.]
Seth, s. Seth and Abigail, Jan. 28, 1755.
Seth, Lt., Apr. 27, 1780, in 74th y. G.R.3. P.R.I.

HALL, Seth Capen, May 6, 1836. G.R.3.
Susanna, w. Zuriel, June 3, 1742, a. 66.
Zurial, s. Seth and Abigail, May 23, 1738.
Zurial, s. Seth and Abagaial, Dec. 26, 1746, a. 5 y. 5 m. 8 d.
Zuriel [h. Susanna], Apr. 3, 1765, in 88th y.
———, ch. Seth, Sept. —, 1775. P.R.1.
———, oldest s. Lt. Seth and ——— (second w.), Dec. 27, 1779. P.R.1.
———, ch. Asa, Oct. 14 [1798]. P.R.1.
———, ch. Asa, Nov. 3 [1798]. P.R.1.
———, w. Asa, Mar. 25 [1830]. P.R.1.

HARKEL (see Haskel), Salla, wid., colard, June 26 [1829]. P.R.1.

HASKEL (see Harkel), ———, ch. Samuel, Oct. 16 [1818], a. 15 d. P.R.1.

HAVEN, ———, Esq., Mar. 29, 1786. P.R.1.

HAWARD (see Hayward), Ebenezer of Hollastown, June 21, 1782. P.R.1.
Elezer, Jan. 18, 1782. P.R.1.
Hezikiah of Mendam, Mar. 20 [1802]. P.R.1.
Isabel, wid., Mar. 12 [1838], "at the poor house." P.R.1.
John of Milford, June 18 [1794]. P.R.1.
Ruth, Oct. 24, 1762. P.R.1.
Seath, Oct. 11 [1837]. P.R.1.
———, wid., of Mendon, Jan. 12, 1837. P.R.1.

HAWES (see Haws), Levi of Franklin, May 9 [1839]. P.R.1.
Mela, wid., of Franklin, Sept. 4 [1839]. P.R.1.

HAWKINS (see Hokins).

HAWS (see Hawes), Mary of Franklin, Aug. 8, 1785. P.R.1.
Samuel, m., plewrasey fever, ——— [rec. between Jan. 6 and May 19, 1845]. [Hawes, Apr. 6, 1845, a. 70, G.R.1.] [Hawes, Apr. 5 [1845], P.R.1.]

HAYDEN, Handel, s. Lot and Lucinda, Dec. 7, 1837, a. 3 y. 9 m. G.R.2. [Haden, Dec. 8, P.R.1.]
Lucinda H., d. Lot and Lucinda, Dec. 12, 1837, a. 4 y. 11 m. 6 d. G.R.2. [Headen, P.R.1.]

HAYWARD (see Haward), Alce, wid., of Milford, Mar. 8, 1785. P.R.1.
Caleb, s. Samuel and Hannah, "by a very sad accadent," Dec. 1, 1741.

HAYWARD, Eliezer, s. Eliezer and Mary, June 28, 1753.
Eliezer, Jan. 4, 1782, a. 72. [Eleazer, a. 78, G.R.I.]
Elisabath, d. Ebnezer and Hannah, Feb. 17, 1740.
Elisabeth, wid., June 8, 1777. P.R.I.
Grace, w. Jonathan, Aug. 28, 1720.
Mary, wid. Eleazer, Mar. 15, 1814, in 102d y. G.R.I. [Haward, P.R.I.]
Persila, Aug. 10, 1727.
Samuel, Feb. 24, 1755.
Sam[ue]ll, Apr. 9, 1721.
William, s. Eliezer and Mary, May 9, 1753, in 15th y.

HICCOCK (see Hitchcock), ———, wid. Darling, Feb. 12 [1848], a. 52. P.R.I.

HICKSON (see Hixon, Hixson), Mary A., Oct. 20, 1830, in 20th y. G.R.I. [Mary Hixson, d. Ruben, Oct. 19, P.R.I.]

HIDE, Danil, Lt., of Midway, May 30, 1813, a. 80. P.R.I.

HILL, Aaron, Mar. 23, 1799, a. 14. G.R.I. P.R.I.
Aaron, s. M. and P., Oct. 21, 1832, a. 1. G.R.I. [ch. Moses, Oct. 22, P.R.I.]
Abigail, twin ch. Moses and Persis, Oct. 16, 1822, a. 1 y. 7 m. G.R.I. [Oct. 17, P.R.I.]
Amos, Capt., Sept. 6, 1818, a. 25. G.R.I.
David, Nov. 4, 1813, a. 51. G.R.I. [kild, Nov. 5, in Deadham, P.R.I.]
Gilbert, m., s. Moses, apoplexy, Dec. 5, 1848, a. 34.
Jese, Sept. 15 [1832]. P.R.I.
Jonathan, Nov. 22, 1807, a. 90. P.R.I.
Mary, w. Enoch, Jan. 4, 1760.
Mary, wid. Moses, June 6, 1782. P.R.I.
Mary, w. Moses, Sept. 22, 1805, a. 25. G.R.I. P.R.I.
Mary, Nov. 3, 1822. P.R.I.
Mebenezer, Dec. 5, 1734, a. 77. G.R.I.
Mercy, wid. David, July 28, 1841, a. 73. G.R.I.
Paulina, d. David and Mercy, Mar. 17, 1806. [Pauline, a. 4, G.R.I. P.R.I.]
Pauline, Jan. 3, 1817, a. 13 m. G.R.I. [ch. Salvester, Jan. 2, P.R.I.]
Phebe, d. David and Mercy, Oct. 29, 1799. [Oct. 30, P.R.I.]
Polly, Nov. 1, 1822, a. 30. G.R.I.
Roda, wid. Jese, Sept. 15, 1840, a. 84. P.R.I.

HILL, Sarah, d. Jonathan and Rebackah, Sept. 3, 1775. [Sariah, P.R.I.]
Sarah, twin ch. Moses and Persis, Oct. 22, 1822, a. 1 y. 7 m. G.R.I. P.R.I.
Sarah, w. Aaron, Sept. 18, 1836, a. 76. G.R.I.
Solon, s. David and Mercy, Feb. 23, 1799. [1729, a. 6, G.R.I.] [1799, P.R.I.]
Solon, Sept. 1 [1833], in New Orleans. P.R.I.
Sylvester, June 13, 1820. [June 14, a. 35, G.R.I.] [June 14, P.R.I.]
Thoder, s. Jonathan and Rebackah, Sept. 25, 1775.
———, ch. Jesse, Nov. 27 [1790]. P.R.I.
———, d. Jesse, Aug. 26 [1796]. P.R.I.
——— (Heill), w. Joel, Dec. 24 [1796]. P.R.I.
———, w. Jonathen, Nov. 3 [1801]. P.R.I.
———, ch. Moses, June 4 [1804]. P.R.I.
———, second ch. Moses, Sept. 18 [1805]. P.R.I.
———, w. Amos, Sept. 6 [1818]. P.R.I.
———, ch. Ama, July 4 [1835], a. 1, "at the poor house." P.R.I.

HILTON, Abigail, w. W[illia]m, d. Warren Lazele and Betsy, Oct. 3, 1841, a. 20 y. 5 m. 13 d. G.R.2. [Abigill Lazel, a. 19, P.R.I.]

HITCHCOCK (see Hiccock), Thomas, June 8, 1842, a. 83. G.R.2. [Hichcok, P.R.I.]

HIXON (see Hickson, Hixson), Reuben [h. Ruth], July 9, 1837, a. 72. G.R.I. [Ruben Hixson, "found dead in the road," July 10, P.R.I.]
Ruth, w. Reuben, July 8, 1831, a. 55. G.R.I. [Hixson, w. Ruben, P.R.I.]
Ruth, d. Reuben and Ruth, Nov. 20, 1831, a. 32. G.R.I. [Hixson, P.R.I.]

HIXSON (see Hickson, Hixon), ———, ch. Ellara, Nov. 23 [1839], a. 5, "at the poore house." P.R.I.
———, ch. Elary, Oct. 14 [1843]. P.R.I.

HOKINS, Robard, hanging himself, Aug. 3 [1813]. P.R.I.

HOLBROOK, Aaron, Lt., Apr. 15, 1818, a. 87. G.R.I. [Apr. 4, P.R.I.]
Aaron, Apr. 29, 1835. [a. 42, G.R.I.] [s. Amzi, a. 41, P.R.I.]
Abigail, d. Ebenezer, Feb. 15, 1777. P.R.I.

HOLBROOK, Abigail, w. Capt. Jesse, June —, 1805, in 76th y.
  [June 10, a. 76, P.R.1.]
Abigail, w. Eliphelet, Sept. 3, 1808. [Abagail, wid., a. 73 y.
  5 m., P.R.1.]
Abigell, d. Peter and Hannah, May 7, 1722.
Abigil, d. Amariah and Moley, June 24, 1780. [a. abt. 6 w.,
  P.R.1.]
Abijah, Oct. 21 [1812]. P.R.1.
Adaline, Mrs., Oct. 4, 1847. C.R. [Adeline, w. Valentine W.,
  Oct. 3, a. 43, G.R.1.] [Addaline, w. Volentine, Oct. 3, a.
  44, P.R.1.]
Amasa, ——, 1811, a. 46. G.R.1.
Amasa, May 28, 1815.
Ameriah, Sept. 7, 1797, in 42d y. [a. 42, G.R.1.] [Ammariah,
  P.R.1.]
Amos Wales, s. Whitman and Nancy, Apr. 4, 1836. [Apr. 3,
  P.R.1.]
Amsi, Jan. 13, 1848, a. 84. G.R.1. [Amzi, Jan. 14, a. 84 y.
  10 m., P.R.1.]
Anna, w. Asahel, Dec. 22, 1777. [Annar, w. Assel, P.R.1.]
Anna, d. Asa and Meletiah, June 15, 1792. [d. Asa dec'd, P.R.1.]
Anna, wid. Meletiah, June 15, 1792.
Arba, s. Nathan and Sarah, Aug. 29, 1798, a. 3 y. 3 m. 1 d. G.R.2.
  [Arbe, Aug. 24, P.R.1.]
Asa, Mar. 27, 1792.
Assel, Mar. 1 [1810], a. 91. P.R.1.
Benajah, s. Aaron and Hannah, Jan. 30, 1772. [Bena, Jan. 30,
  a. 10 m., G.R.1.] [Bennjah, s. Aron, Jan. 29, P.R.1.]
Benjamin, s. Calvin, Apr. 28 [1820]. P.R.1.
Bettsey, "Mrs.", May 4, 1835, a. 98 [?]. G.R.1. [Betsey, d.
  Amzi, a. 38, P.R.1.]
Caleb, s. El[i]phelet, May 10, 1757.
Calvin, Aug. 8, 1825, a. 63. G.R.1. [a. 60, P.R.1.]
Cazier, Oct. 30, 1756, a. 34. P.R.1.
Cephas Jr., Sept. 1 [1831], a. 5 m. P.R.1.
David, May 29, 1773, in 53d y.
Derius of Brokfield, Apr. 4 [1834]. P.R.1.
Diana, d. Nathan, Aug. 25 [1810]. P.R.1.
Dianna, d. Nathan and Sarah, Aug. 26, 1798. G.R.2. [Diana,
  P.R.1.]
Dinah, Jan. 7, 1827. C.R. [w. Seth, Jan. 8, a. 70, P.R.1.]
Ebenezer of Milfurd, May 31 [1805], a. 88. P.R.1.
Eliab, s. Eliphelet and Abigial, Oct. 16, 1775. [s. Eliphelet Jr.,
  Oct. 15, P.R.1.]

HOLBROOK, Elijah, s. Eliphelet and Joanah, May 2, 1740.
Eliphelet, s. Eliphelet and Abigial, Oct. 15, 1775. [Eliphlet, s. Eliphelet Jr., P.R.I.]
Eliphelet, Oct. 19, 1775, in 84th y. [Eliphler, in 83d y., P.R.I.]
Eliphelet, Apr. 28, 1776, in 51st y. [Eliphalet, a. 52, G.R.I.] [Eliphlet Jr., in 51st y., P.R.I.]
Elisabeth, wid., Sept. 16 [1823], a. 85. P.R.I.
Elizabath, w. Ens. Henery, May 2, 1809. [Elizabeth, w. Ens. Henry, a. 51, G.R.2.] [Elisabeth, in 51st y., P.R.I.]
Elizabeth, w. Lt. Arom, Aug. 4, 1803, in 63d y. [a. 63, G.R.I.] [w. Lt. Aaron, P.R.I.]
Elizabeth, d. Eliab and Betsey, Nov. 25, 1834, a. 23. G.R.2. [Elisabath, P.R.I.]
Elizebeth, d. Peter and Hannah, Mar. 26, 1720.
Elmyra, d. Aaron and Polly, Aug. 16, 1833. [Elmira, P.R.I.]
Elnathan, Mar. 2, 1829, a. 5 w. G.R.I.
Esther, d. Asahael and Anna, Nov. 19, 1764.
Eunice, w. Ens. Henery, Mar. 10, 1818. [Eunis, C.R.] [w. Ens. Henry, a. 49, G.R.2.] [second w. Henry, P.R.I.]
Freelove, w. Abijah, Oct. 1, 1776. P.R.I.
Grace, wid., May 13, 1791, in 76th y. [w. Dea. Joseph, a. 76, G.R.I.]
Hannah, wid. John, Apr. 12, 1770, in 86th y. [wid. Cornet John, a. 86, G.R.I.]
Hannah, d. Jesse and Abigial, Mar. 9, 1776.
Hannah, w. Aaron, Mar. 31, 1782, in 49th y. [1780, a. 49, G.R.I.] [1782, P.R.I.]
Hannah, Mrs., Jan. 9, 1841. C.R. [w. Eliab, d. Ellery Thayer and Abigail, a. 26, G.R.2.] [w. Eliab Jr., P.R.I.]
Hannah Elisabeth, d. Eliab and Julia M., inflammation on the brain, May 16, 1848, a. 4 y. 8 m. 24 d.
Henry, Oct. 1, 1833, a. 77. [Ens. Henry, G.R.2.]
Huldah, d. Jesse and Abigial, Sept. 2, 1775.
James A., s. H. and S., Oct. 23, 1843, a. 6 m. G.R.I. [ch. Horris, Oct. 22, P.R.I.]
Jamime, w. Aaron, Feb. 25, 1810, a. 75. G.R.I. [third w. Lt. Aaron, a. 74, P.R.I.]
Jesse, Capt., Apr. 18, 1815, a. 85 y. 9 m. [a. 85 y. 8 m., P.R.I.]
Joanna, wid., Apr. 6, 1777. P.R.I.
Job of Mendon, Jan. 16, 1786. P.R.I.
John, Cornet, May 11, 1765, in 86th y. [a. 86, G.R.I.]
Joseph, Apr. 25, 1750, in 67th y.
Joseph, Dea., July 14, 1785, in 71st y.
Joseph, Capt., Apr. 18 [1817]. P.R.I.

HOLBROOK, Julia, Oct. 2, 1785, a. 1. G.R.1.
Julia, d. Joseph Jr. and Meletiah, Oct. 9, 1785. [Jule, P.R.1.]
Julian, Mar. 23, 1837, a. 15. G.R.1.
Kezia, d. Derus [Darius] and Olive, Dec. 28, 1792. [Keziah, d. Derious, P.R.1.]
Keziah of Mendon, d. Ebenezer, Dec. 31, 1776. P.R.1.
Lewis, s. Amasa and Sabra, Sept. 29, 1797, a. 10 m. 14 d.
Lois, w. Simon, Aug. 16, 1799, a. 27. G.R.1. [w. Simeoun, P.R.1.]
Lucretia, d. Jesse and Abigail, Jan. 29, 1790. [d. Jasse, P.R.1.]
Lucretia, d. Nathan and Sarah, Oct. 12, 1793, a. 2 d. G.R.2.
Luke, Nov. 3, 1775, in 52d y.
Lurania, Sept. 1, 1845. C.R.
Lyde of Glocester, July 27 [1802], a. 90. P.R.1.
Marcy, w. Asa, July 31, 1834, a. 44. G.R.1.
Martha, d. Joseph and Mary, Jan. 29, 1731.
Martha, d. Joseph and Mary, Jan. 7, 1739-40.
Mary, d. Ziba, Nov. 5 [1819]. P.R.1.
Meranda, d. Seth and Dinah, Oct. 24, 1795. [Merande, d. Lt. Seth, drounde, P.R.1.]
Mercy, wid. Luke, Dec. 3, 1813, a. 83. G.R.1. [Marcy, a. 82, P.R.1.]
Molly, wid., old age, Aug. 24, 1845, a. 86. [w. Amariah, a. 86, G.R.1.] [Molley, wid., a. 88, P.R.1.]
Moses, s. Asahael and Anna, Mar. 14, 1766.
Nancy Polina, d. Whitman and Nancy W., Apr. 23, 1843. [a. 5 y. 6 m., Apr. 23, G.R.1.] [Apr. 22, P.R.1.]
Nathan, ch. Nahan, Oct. 12 [1793]. P.R.1.
Nathan, Capt., Sept. 8 [1819], a. 77. P.R.1.
Nathan, Dec. 29, 1845, a. 77. G.R.2. [a. 77 y. 4 m., P.R.1.]
Naum of Harford, Sept. 7 [1844]. P.R.1.
Olive, d. Calven, Nov. 17 [1817]. P.R.1.
Olive, w. Capt. Seth, Mar. 1, 1826, a. 29. G.R.1.
Pearces, d. Lt. Seth, Sept. 17 [1803]. P.R.1.
Peter, Dec. 24, 1728.
Peter, Ens., of Upton, July 13 [1792]. P.R.1.
Phebe, Dec. 29 [1819], a. 51. P.R.1.
Polly, d. Aaron and Polly, July 18, 1829. [July 19, P.R.1.]
Polly, w. Cephas, May 23, 1831. P.R.1.
Rachel, d. Luke and Mercy, Nov. 7, 1775. [Rachal, d. Luke dec'd, P.R.1.]
Rachel, w. Stephen, Mar. 5, 1810, a. 70. G.R.1. [Mar. 15, a. 80, P.R.1.]
Rhoda, d. Aaron and Hannah, Oct. 26, 1778. [Roda, P.R.1.]

HOLBROOK, Sabin, Feb. 15, 1836, a. 49, G.R.1. [Saban, P.R.1.]
Sabra, wid., Aug. 31 [1839], a. 69, in Worcester. P.R.1.
Sally, w. A., Aug. 11, 1830, a. 76. G.R.1.
Sarah, d. Peter and Sarah, May 23, 1753.
Sarah, w. Peter of Uptown, Aug. 13, 1785. P.R.1.
Sarah, Aug. 12, 1836, a. 34. G.R.1. [d. Amzi, P.R.1.]
Sarah, w. Amzi, May 11 [1839], a. 76. P.R.1.
Sarah, wid. Amasa, Aug. 30, 1839, a. 69. G.R.1.
Seth (Ho[l]brook), s. Eliphelet and Joannah, Sept. 26, 1747.
Seth of Swonzay, Dec. 11, 1833, a. 68 y. 5 m. P.R.1.
Seth, Nov. 13, 1839. [a. 88, G.R.1.] [Lt. Seeth, a. 87, P.R.1.]
Simeon, Oct. 3 [1825], a. 52. P.R.1.
Stephen, June 11, 1812, a. 76. G.R.1.
Susanna Rockwood, w. Naum, July 2 [1840], a. 64, in Harford.
P.R.1.
Ziba of Milford, July 7 [1829]. P.R.1.
———, ch. Abijah, Oct. 2, 1776. P.R.1.
———, ch. Assa, Apr. 28, 1782. P.R.1.
———, second w. Ebenesur of Milfurd, July 16, 1799. P.R.1.
———, ch. Simon and Lois, Aug. 16, 1799. G.R.1. [ch. Simeoun, P.R.1.]
———, ch. Calven, May 5 [1809]. P.R.1.
———, ch. Amos, Sept. 25 [1809]. P.R.1.

HOLLES, Sary, w. Nathan, May 6, 1773. P.R.1.

HOOKER, Abigail, wid., Jan. 14, 1843.
Abigail, Mrs., Jan. 21, 1843, a. 84.

HORTON, Vesta, w. Manly P., only d. Bethuel Slocome and Mary, Dec. 28, 1838, a. 27. G.R.2.

HOUNT (see Hunt), Edward, Dec. 22 [1810], a. 84. P.R.1.

HOWARD, Daniel of Milfurd, May 28 [1798]. P.R.1.
Elisabeth, w. Elisha, Feb. 1, 1815. P.R.1.
Elisha, Jan. — [1819]. P.R.1.
Levina, w. Nathan, Feb. 21, 1810, a. 22. G.R.2.
Marcy, June 21 [1813]. P.R.1.
Martha, wid., of Milfurd, July 3 [1807]. P.R.1.
Parkar, June 27 [1835], "at the poor hous." P.R.1.
———, ch. Rosanna, Dec. 4 [1807]. P.R.1.

HUNT (see Hount), Elisebath, d. Edward and Abagail, May 15, 1739.
Mary E., w. Edward, Aug. 2, 1771, in 39th y. G.R.3.

BELLINGHAM DEATHS.

HUNTER, Martha, wid., of Brantry, Jan. 14, 1827. P.R.1.

HYDE (see Hide).

JENCKS (see Jinks), Hannah E., w. Charles B., Feb. 26, 1818. [Jinks, d. Elias Thayer, P.R.1.]

JINKS (see Jencks), ———, ch. Hannah, Feb. 28 [1818]. P.R.1.

JOHNSON, Abigail, wid., Jan. 17, 1789. P.R.1.
Diana S., w. Benjamin F., Oct. 15, 1842. [in 28th y., G.R.2.] [w. Franklin, P.R.1.]
Eleazer, m., b. Milford, s. Joseph and Hannah, apoplexy, Jan. 31, 1847, a. 63. [Elazer, P.R.1.]
Georg of Framingham, Dec. 26 [1829]. P.R.1.
Julia, d. Benjamin F. and Dianna, consumption, Dec. 30, 1848, a. 14. [Jula, d. Franklin (Jonson), Dec. 29, P.R.1.]
Julia E., d. Benj[amin] F. and Diana S., Dec. 29, 1818, a. 12. G.R.2.

JONES, Briget, d. John and Abigail, June 2, 1756.
Daniel, Dec. 13, 1822. G.R.2. [Joanes, a. 66, P.R.1.]
David, Jan. 26, 1824, a. 95. G.R.2. [June 26, a. 94, P.R.1.]
Elizabeth, w. John Jr., May 30, 1750.
Hannah, w. David, May 5, 1769. [w. Davide, May 4, P.R.1.]
Hannah, Oct. 24, 1831, in 69th y. G.R.2. P.R.1.
Mercy, wid., July 28, 1841, a. 73. [Mrs. Mercy, C.R.] [Marcy, wid., P.R.1.]

JOYCE, Hellen, ch. P. and S., Mar. 15, 1834, a. 3. G.R.1. ["an ediot," P.R.1.]
Henry C., ch. P. and S., Oct. 9, 1834. G.R.1. [a. 7 m., P.R.1.]

KEECH, Warren R., ———, 1848. G.R.2.

KELLE (see Kille, Killey, Killy), Elisha, Jan. 18 [1813]. P.R.1.

KENDALL, Betsey, w. Warren, Feb. 1, 1827, a. 31. G.R.1. [Betssy Kindel, "at the factory," P.R.1.]

KENNEY (see Kinna), William P. of Troy, s. Cyrus, Aug. 19 [1846], a. 21. P.R.1.

KILBURN, Deborah of Milford, June 19 [1833]. P.R.1.
Henry, Sept. 23 [1803]. P.R.1.
Josiah, Mar. 23 [1804]. P.R.1.

BELLINGHAM DEATHS.

KILBURN, Lois, d. Simeon and Luca, Jan. 28, 1794. [Kilbon, s. [*sic*] Simeon and Lucy, Jan. 20, a. 2 y. 4 m., G.R.2.] [Loyes Kilborn, Jan. 29, P.R.I.]
Marcy of Milford, Oct. — [1835]. P.R.I.
Marther, wid., May 29 [1826], a. 92. P.R.I.
Patty, May 26 [1824]. P.R.I.
Simeoun, May 11, 1817, a. 51. P.R.I.
———, ch. Deborah, Feb. 17, 1797. P.R.I.

KILLE (see Kelle, Killey, Killy), ———, ch. Nathan, Jan. 19 [1805]. P.R.I.

KILLEY (see Kelle, Kille, Killy), Zeno, "kiled he had a fall from a hi waggon and the wheel run over his head," Nov. 16 [1835]. P.R.I.

KILLY (see Kelle, Kille, Killey), Elisha, Nov. 26 [1831]. P.R.I.

KINGMON, ———, d. ———, May — [1847]. P.R.I.

KINNA (see Kenney), Roda, w. Rev. Silas of Vt., Nov. 24 [1836], a. 36. P.R.I.

KNAP, Moses, Maj., of Frankling, Nov. 7 [1809]. P.R.I.

LAESL (see Lasel, Lasell, Lazall, Lazele, Lazell, Leasal, Leazal, Leazil), Deborah of Mandem, Nov. 27, 1791. P.R.I.

LAGG (see Leeg, Leg, Legg), ———, wid., July 17 [1792]. P.R.I.

LALON (see Lealand, Lealon), Joanna, w. Aaron of Chaster, N.J., July 28, 1787. P.R.I.

LASEL (see Laesl, Lasell, Lazall, Lazele, Lazell, Leasal, Leazal, Leazil), ———, ch. Joshua of Mendon, Sept. 24, 1788. P.R.I.

LASELL (see Laesl, Lasel, Lazall, Lazele, Lazell, Leasal, Leazal, Leazil), ——— (Laesll), Mr., of Mendom, Jan. 29, 1783, in 82d y. P.R.I.

LATHBRIDGE, Hepzibah, w. Samuel of Franklin, Jan. 24, 1785. P.R.I.

LAURANCE, Maria, d. Jarus [Jarvis] B. and Maria B., Apr. 23, 1843. [Abby M. Lawrence, Apr. 23, a. 2, G.R.2.] [Larrane, Apr. 22, P.R.I.]

LAZALL (see Laesl, Lasel, Lasell, Lazele, Lazell, Leasal, Leazal, Leazil), Abigail, Nov. —, 1814. C.R.
———, ch. Nathan, Oct. 4 [1846]. P.R.I.

LAZELE (see Laesl, Lasel, Lasell, Lazall, Lazell, Leasal, Leazal, Leazil), Abigail, w. Warren, Nov. 7, 1818, a. 36. G.R.2. [Leasuel, P.R.I.]
Ellis, s. Warren and Abigail, May 1, 1806. G.R.2. [Lazel, P.R.I.]
Rebecca, d. Warren and Abigail, Sept. 1, 1821, a. 12. G.R.2. [Rebekah Lazel, d. Warren (Leazel), P.R.I.]
Warren, Nov. 3, 1840, a. 62. G.R.2. [Warrin Lazill, a. 60, P.R.I.]

LAZELL (see Laesl, Lasel, Lasell, Lazall, Lazele, Leasal, Leazal, Leazil), Lorinda, ——, 1826. C.R.
Lovina, wid., Mar. 29 [1845], a. 83. P.R.I.
——, ch. Nathan, Nov. 7 [1847]. P.R.I.

LEALAND (see Lalon, Lealon), Aaron, Rev., of Chester, Aug. 25 [1832]. P.R.I.

LEALON (see Lalon, Lealand), Ruth, d. Aaron of Mendon, Oct. 14, 1785. P.R.I.

LEARNED, Ebenezer, Sept. 19, 1775, a. 19. G.R.I. [Larnard, Sept. 9, a. abt. 19, P.R.I.]

LEASAL (see Laesl, Lasel, Lasell, Lazall, Lazele, Lazell, Leazal, Leazil), Joshua of Mendom, Dec. 3 [1832]. P.R.I.
——, ch. Warrein, Oct. 11 [1826]. P.R.I.

LEAZAL (see Laesl, Lasel, Lasell, Lazall, Lazele, Lazell, Leasal, Leazil), Betsy, w. Daniel of Mendon, Sept. 13 [1838]. P.R.I.

LEAZIL (see Laesl, Lasel, Lasell, Lazall, Lazele, Lazell, Leasal, Leazal), Soliven, Aug. 3 [1828], a. 21. P.R.I.

LEEG (see Lagg, Leg, Legg), ——, ch. Joshua, Oct. 20, 1788. P.R.I.

LEG (see Lagg, Leeg, Legg), Rachel, w. Joshua, Oct. 28, 1776. P.R.I.

LEGG (see Lagg, Leeg, Leg), ——, ch. Joshua, Oct. 21, 1776. P.R.I.

LELAND (see Lalon, Lealand, Lealon).

LEONARD (see Learned).

LEWETT, Phebe, w. Stephen, Dec. 4, 1831, a. 40. [Luet, w. Steven, P.R.I.]

LEWETT, Stephen Vial, s. Stephen and Phebe, Oct. 1, 1840, a. 19. [Stephen W., s. Stephen Esq., a. 20, G.R.2.] [Stephen V. Luet Jr., P.R.1.]
Susanna, wid., mother of Stephen, Dec. 20, 1831, a. 74.

LEWIS, John, "Englesman," June 10 [1807]. P.R.1.

LILLIE, Sybil, w. Henry, Nov. 13, 1833. [Lillee, w. Henri (Lille), P.R.1.]

LOMBARD (see Lumbert).

LOVEL (see Lovell), Edward, s. Rev. Lovel, June 8 [1842]. P.R.1.
———, ch. Rev. Lovel, Sept. 18 [1840], a. 20 m. P.R.1.

LOVELL (see Lovel), Caroline Brooks, June 3, 1842, a. 5. [Lovel, d. Rev. Nehemiah, P.R.1.]
Edward Buffum, June 14, 1842, a. 10 m.
Shubael, Elder, June 8, 1846. C.R.

LUMBERT, James, Dec. 8, 1827, a. 27. G.R.1.

LUTHER, ———, ch. Tom, Oct. 8 [1822]. P.R.1.

MADCALF (see Metcalf), Croner, wid., Jan. 20 [1804], a. 96. P.R.1.
Hipsaba, wid., Aug. 18 [1807]. P.R.1.
Olive, w. Steven Sr., Jan. 30 [1836]. P.R.1.
Presson, Jan. "ye latter part," 1840. P.R.1.
Steven, Judge, July 26 [1800]. P.R.1.
———, ch. Steven, Sept. 13 [1800]. P.R.1.
———, Cornet, of Frankling, Aug. 3 [1803]. P.R.1.
———, ch. Pressin, May 10 [1832]. P.R.1.
———, second ch. Pressin, May 19 [1832]. P.R.1.
———, s. Holes, Mar. 26 [1848]. P.R.1.

MAN (see Mann), Daniel, s. Richard and Susanna, Jan. 2, 1773, in 17th y. G.R.3.
Richard, Feb. 15, 1774, in 44th y. G.R.3.
Richard, "Hung him self," July 9 [1830]. P.R.1. •
[torn]mos, Feb. 24, 1772. P.R.1.
———, wid., Jan. 18, 1805. P.R.1.

MANN (see Man), Abigail, wid., "formerly" w. Rev. Elnathan Wight, Feb. 26, 1802, in 85th y. [Abergial Man, wid., a. 85, P.R.1.]

MANN, Chloe, Miss, Jan. 16, 1840, [in] Franklin. c.r. [Cloe Man of Frankling, Jan. 26, a. 65, p.r.1.]
Livina, d. Benjamin and Chloe, May 28, 181 [*sic*]. g.r.3. [Lovina Man, 1816, p.r.1.]
Lucy, d. Benjamin and Chloe, Apr. 21, 1824, a. 25. g.r.3. [Man, "a Dwaf," Apr. 22, p.r.1.]

MARKEL, James, colard, Mar. 13 [1829]. p.r.1.

MARSH, John, Sept. 8, 1727.

MASSEY, George H., ch. Joseph T. and Catharine P., Oct. —, 1847, in Charlestown. g.r.2.

MATTISON, Marilla A., Miss, Oct. —, 1845. c.r.

MAYO, John, Sept. 8 [1813]. p.r.1.

McKENA, Hannah, Feb. 2, 1788, in 80th y. p.r.1.

MESSENGER, Abigail, d. John and Melariah, May 11, 1761, a. 6 m. g.r.1.
Czarina, Mrs., Oct. 27, 1840. c.r. [Massanger, w. William, a. 41, p.r.1.]
Meltiah, w. John, Mar. 27, 1761, a. 29. g.r.1. [Milatier Messanger, p.r.1.]

METCALF (see Madcalf), Almira A., w. Francis, Apr. 11, 1849, a. 29. g.r.1. [Medcalf, w. Frances [*sic*], Apr. 12, p.r.1.]
Hephzibah, d. Stephen and Hephzibah, Aug. 16, 1775. [Hepsebe Medcalf, p.r.1.]
Hephzibah, d. Stephen Esq. and Hephzibah, Mar. 8, 1796. [Hephziba Madcalf, d. Steven, a. 2, p.r.1.]
Hiram Francis, s. Francis and Almira, dropsey, Feb. 23, 1848, a. 1 y. 9 m. 5 d. [Mar. 23, a. 1, g.r.1.]
John, Feb. 22, 1791. [Madcalf, in 87th y., p.r.1.]
Jonathan of Medway, Jan. 10, 1775. p.r.1.
Mary, w. John, July 28, 1754.
Olive, d. Stephen (Mitcalf) and Olive, Nov. 5, 1809. [Madcalf, p.r.1.]
Olive, d. Hollis and Abigail, Dec. 17 [dup. Dec. 28], 1841. [Dec. 17, a. 16, g.r.1.] [Madcalf, Dec. 18, p.r.1.]
Resign, d. Stephen and Hephzibah, Sept. 2, 1771.
Steven Esq., m., s. Steven, Nov. 11, 1844, a. 71 y. 4 m. 27 d. [Stephen Madcalf Sr., a. 71, p.r.1.]
————, s. John Jr. and Hannah, still born, Dec. 27, 1786.

MILENS, ——, ch. ——, Aug. 27 [1839]. P.R.I.

MILLS, ——, s. Jonathan and Jemimah, July 7, 1730.

MOORE, Dexter, Oct. 8, 1776, a. 6 m. G.R.I.

MORAN, Julius, only s. William F. and Eliza M., Sept. 18, 1834, a. 12 w. G.R.I.

MOREY (see Mowry).

MORGAN (see Morgin), Julius, s. William F. and Eliza, Sept. 18, 1834.

MORGIN (see Morgan), William, Aug. 10 [1839], "at the factory," P.R.I.
——, ch. ——, Sept. 15 [1834]. P.R.I.
——, ch. Wid. Morgin, Aug. 13 [? 18] [1839], "at the factory." P.R.I.

MOWRY, Lewis P., s. Harris J. and Fannie C., June 30, 1848. G.R.3.

NASON, Maron, w. Luther W., July 12, 1848, a. 28. G.R.I. [Maraon Thomson, July 8, P.R.I.]

NEW, Anna, w. James, Feb. 19, 1849, a. 88 y. 6 m. G.R.2.
James, Aug. 28, 1835, a. 84. G.R.2.

NEWTON (see Nuten).

NICHOLS, Samuel W., Feb. 21, 1829, a. 20. G.R.I.

NOCROSS (see Norckros, Norcroos, Norcross), —— (Notros), ch. Silurs, Sept. 10 [1821]. P.R.I.

NORCKROS (see Nocross, Norcroos, Norcross), Selve, wid., Dec. 30 [1824]. P.R.I.

NORCROOS (see Nocross, Norckros, Norcross), Sarah, May 15 [1834]. P.R.I.

NORCROSS (see Norcoss, Norckros, Norcroos), Asa, May 31, 1823. C.R. [May 31, a. 53, G.R.I.] [Norckros, May 30, P.R.I.]
Sally, w. Silas T., Oct. 9, 1830, a. 28. G.R.I. [Sarah Norcros, wid., P.R.I.]
Silas T., Jan. 20, 1829, a. 29. G.R.I. [Silus, P.R.I.]
Silva, Dec. 11 [1836]. P.R.I.
Sylvia, Mrs., Dec. 30, 1824, a. 53. G.R.I.
Sylvia, d. Asa and Sylvia, Apr. 23, 1825, a. 16. G.R.I.

NUTEN, Kier [?], Mar. 30 [1795]. P.R.1.

OCANTON, ———, "old mr," of Franklin, Oct. 1 [1793]. P.R.1.

ONIN (see Onion), ———, ch. Leanord, Feb. 18 [1825]. P.R.1.

ONION (see Onin), Mary, Sept. 1, 1822, a. 7 w. G.R.1.

ORMBY (see Armby).

PAIN (see Paine, Payn), Dan, "beured" May 6 [1804]. P.R.1.
Phebe, Oct. 30, 1825, in 68th y. G.R.3. [w. Thomas, P.R.1.]
Sarah, w. Lt. Gideon, Feb. —, 1824, in 88th y. G.R.3. [wid. Giden, Mar. 28, P.R.1.]
Susanna, d. Thomos, Mar. 29 [1818]. P.R.1.
Thommos, Sept. —, 1837, a. 80. P.R.1.
———, wid., mother of Bishup Paine, June 1, 1776. P.R.1.

PAINE (see Pain, Payn), Gideon, Lt., Apr. 23, 1821, in 88th y. G.R.3. [Pain, a. 88, P.R.1.]
Phebe, d. Capt. William and Ruth, Jan. 31, 1819, in 6th y. G.R.3. [Pain, P.R.1.]
Phila, w. Lt. Alvah, Feb. 5, 1818, in 28th y. G.R.3.
Ruth, w. William, Mar. 15, 1815, in 26th y. G.R.3. [Pain, P.R.1.]
Thomas, July 22, 1837, in 82d y. G.R.3.

PARAY (see Parry, Pary, Perra, Perry), Eb[e]nezer, s. Ebnezer (Parray) and Abagial, Mar. 15, 1745.

PARKIS (see Parkus), Samuel, Aug. —, 1846. C.R.

PARKUS (see Parkis), Milla, w. Jotham, Dec. 1 [1845]. P.R.1.

PARRY (see Paray, Pary, Perra, Perry), Sarah, d. Ebnezer (Perrey) and Abagail, Oct. 30, 1741.
Steven, June —, 1778, "as he was a going to the armi at York." P.R.1.
———, wid., of Milford, Dec. — [1831]. P.R.1.

PARTRADGE (see Partraidge, Partridage, Partridge, Partrige, Parttridge, Patradge, Patridge, Pattridge), Abigail, wid. John, May 26, 1764. G.R.1.
Abigail, w. John, Mar. 11, 1774, a. 50. G.R.1.
Ann, w. John, Mar. 6, 1736, a. 67. G.R.1.
Asa, Dec. 10, 1746, a. 8. G.R.1.
Catherine, w. Joseph, July 13, 1828, a. 75. G.R.1. [Catharine Partridge, wid. Joseph, P.R.1.]

PARTRADGE, Derosah, wid. Job, Nov. 14, 1827, a. 80. G.R.I. [Partridge, P.R.I.]
Elizabath, May 29, 1822, a. 39. G.R.I. [Elisebath Partridge, May 31, P.R.I.]
Ichabod, Apr. 11, 1764. G.R.I.
Job, Sept. 10, 1823, a. 81. G.R.I. [Partridge, a. 84, P.R.I.]
John, Sept. 6, 1750, a. 73. G.R.I.
John, May 14, 1764, a. 26. G.R.I.
John, Dec. 21, 1791, a. 76. G.R.I. [Partridge, of Frankling, P.R.I.]
Joseph, May 24, 1810, a. 63. G.R.I. [Partridge, May 23, P.R.I.]

PARTRAIDGE (see Partradge, Partridage, Partridge, Partrige, Parttridge, Patradge, Patridge, Pattridge), Eleazer, Nov. 8, 1736, in 72d y.

PARTRIDAGE (see Partradge, Partraidge, Partridge, Partrige, Parttridge, Patradge, Patridge, Pattridge), Elisabeth, Feb. 4, 1772. P.R.I.

PARTRIDGE (see Partradge, Partraidge, Partridage, Partrige, Parttridge, Patradge, Patridge, Pattridge), Aaron, s. Benjamin and Sarah, Oct. 18, 1761.
Banjaman Jr., Sept. 16, 1776. P.R.I.
Benjamin, Feb. 10, 1805. [Partradge, Feb. 10, a. 92, G.R.I.] [Bengemen, Feb. 2, a. 93 "ore more," P.R.I.]
Betty, Feb. 4, 1772, in 41st y. [1770, a. 41, G.R.I.]
Caty, d. Joseph and Catherine, Oct. 9, 1797. [Partradge, a. 2, G.R.I.]
Dana, s. Joseph and Catherine, Sept. 30, 1797. [Sept. 29, P.R.I.]
Ebenescer of Frankling, Mar. 15 [1794], "an old man." P.R.I.
Ede, Oct. 12, 1832, a. 53. G.R.I. [Eda, Oct. 11, P.R.I.]
Elezebeth, w. Eleazer (Partraidge), Oct. 26, 1733.
Elizabeth, [twin] d. Job and Deborah, July 18, 1770.
Eunice, w. Joseph, Nov. 3, 1785, in 80th y. [wid., a. 78 or 79, P.R.I.]
Hannah, [twin] d. Job and Deborah, Aug. 5, 1770.
Joseph, June 22, 1770, in 65th y. [a. 65, G.R.I.]
Joseph Jr., Aug. 24, 1814. [Partradge, a. 29, G.R.I.] [Parttridge, P.R.I.]
Lois, d. Benjamin and Sarah, July 8, 1738.
Loyes, Oct. 12 [1795]. P.R.I.
Lucy, wid. Joseph Jr., Dec. 3, 1829, a. 45. [Partradge, a. 46, G.R.I.]
Moses, Sept. 26 [1824]. P.R.I.

PARTRIDGE, Peter, s. Joseph and Eunice, Oct. 8, 1746.
Rhoda, d. Joseph and Eunice, Feb. 20, 1751.
Samuel of Wrentham, Dec. 25, 1774. P.R.I.
Sarah, w. Benja[min], Sept. 4, 1801. [Partradge, Sept. 4, a. 85, G.R.I.] [w. "old mr" Bengamen, Sept. 9, P.R.I.]
Semion, s. Benjamin and Sarah, Oct. 5, 1761.
Simeon, s. Joseph and Catherine, Oct. 9, 1797. [Partradge, a. 7, P.R.I.]
Stephen B., ch. Joseph and Lydiaette, Jan. 12, 1848, a. 6 m. G.R.2.
Timothy of Meedway, Sept. 8, 1787. P.R.I.
———, ch. Joseph, Oct. 13 [1797]. P.R.I.

PARTRIGE (see Partradge, Partraidge, Partridage, Partridge, Parttridge, Patradge, Patridge, Pattridge), Betty, Jan. 13, 1731.

PARTTRIDGE (see Partradge, Partraidge, Partridage, Partridge, Partrige, Patradge, Patridge, Pattridge), ———, ch. Job, May 6, 1790. P.R.I.

PARY (see Paray, Parry, Perra, Perry), Ebenezer, "belonging to Captain John Jonis Compiny," "kiled in that fite," Sept. 8, ———. P.R.I.
James of Milford, Apr. 12 [1823], a. 66. P.R.I.

PATRADGE (see Partradge, Partraidge, Partridage, Partridge, Partrige, Parttridge, Patridge, Pattridge), Bathsheba, Feb. 23, 1824, a. 39. G.R.I. [Beashaba Partridge, Feb. 22, P.R.I.]

PATRIDGE (see Partradge, Partraidge, Partridage, Partridge, Partrige, Parttridge, Patradge, Pattridge), Daniel Cook, s. Joseph and Lydiatte, Dec. 21, 1840. [Partridge, ch. Joseph and Lydiaette, a. 7 m. 23 d., G.R.2.] [Patridge, a. 8 m., P.R.I.]
Joseph, s. Joseph and Eunice, Oct. 7, 1746.

PATTRIDGE (see Partradge, Partraidge, Partridage, Partridge, Patrige, Parttridge, Patradge, Patridge), Lucy, wid., Sept. 4 [1829]. P.R.I.
———, ch. Joseph, croup, May 27 [1845]. P.R.I.

PAYN (see Pain, Paine), Susan Rockwood, w. Nuton, Aug. 22 [1843]. P.R.I.

PENEMAN (see Peniman, Pennaman, Penneman, Penniman), Daniel, s. Daniel and Deborah, Mar. 18, 1757.

PENIMAN (see Peneman, Pennaman, Penneman, Penniman),
——, second w. Daniel, July 1 [1799]. P.R.I.

PENNAMAN (see Peneman, Peniman, Penneman, Penniman),
Josiah Jr. of Mendam, Oct. 19 [1800]. P.R.I.
Samuel, Oct. 1 [1807], a. 90. P.R.I.

PENNEMAN (see Peneman, Peniman, Pennaman, Penniman),
Elisabuth, wid., Nov. 13 [1822], a. 82. P.R.I.
Hannah, w. Samuel Jr. of Milford, Apr. 12, 1802. P.R.I.

PENNIMAN (see Peneman, Peniman, Pennaman, Penneman),
Daniel, Dec. 7 [1805]. P.R.I.
Deborah, w. Daniel, Mar. 13, 1776, a. 52. G.R.I. [Panniman, Mar. 12, P.R.I.]
Elijad of Mendon, June 22, 1789. P.R.I.
Hannah, second w. Nathan, Mar. 7, 1817, a. 43. G.R.I.
Hannah, d. Nathan and Roxanna, Nov. 17, 1838, a. 9. G.R.I.
Mary, w. Nathan, Oct. 6, 1795. [first w. Nathan, Oct. 16, a. 24, G.R.I.] [Pennaman, Oct. 16, P.R.I.]
Nathan, Nov. 30, 1839, a. 77. G.R.I. [Penemon, of Frankling, P.R.I.]
Rhene, d. Silas, Nov. 13, 1775.
Samuel, Maj., of Milford, Dec. 22 [1817]. P.R.I.
Silas, May 12, 1777. [small pox, a. 26, G.R.I.] [Silus Pannaman, smool pox, P.R.I.]
Simeon Partridge, s. Nathan, Oct. 6, 1795. [Simeon I., a. 18 m., G.R.I.] [Pennaman, P.R.I.]

PERRA (see Paray, Parry, Pary, Perry), Oliver, May 9, 1772. P.R.I.

PERRY (see Paray, Parry, Pary, Perra), Elisabeth, w. Oliver, Oct. 6, 1751.
Elisabeth, w. Thomas, Mar. 27, 1755.
Lot, May 31 [1820]. P.R.I.
Nathaniel, s. Ebenezer and Abagail, Oct. 27, 1741.
Susanna (Parry), d. Ebenezer and Abagail, Oct. 18, 1741.
Thomas, Mar. 12, 1763, in 87th y.
——, ch. Lot, Sept. —, 1775. P.R.I.
——, wid., June 19 [1822], a. 80. P.R.I.

PHILIPS (see Phillips, Phlips, Phyleps), ——, ch. Joshua, canker, June 1, 1788. P.R.I.
——, ch. Joshua, canker, June 4, 1788. P.R.I.

PHILLIPS (see Philips, Phlips, Phyleps), Caleb, Dec. 24, 1761. [in 80th y., G.R.3.]
Caleb Jr., Mar. 27, 1776. [Philips, P.R.1.]
Caleb, Oct. 11, 1792, in 88th y. G.R.3. ["old mʳ" Calup Phillups, Oct. 12 [1793], P.R.1.]
Elisabeth, d. Caleb and Susanna, Oct. 5, 1745.
Hannah, Jan. 12, 1762. [w. Caleb, in 91st y., G.R.3.]
Hannah, wid., Nov. —, 1794. P.R.1.
Joshua, Lt., Oct. 25, 1809, in 75th y. G.R.3. P.R.1.
Mary, w. Lt. Joshua, June 25, 1803, in 69th y. G.R.3. [w. Joshuary, P.R.1.]
Sarah, d. Lt. Joshua and Mary, Nov. 8, 1809, in 27th y. G.R.3. [Philliups, P.R.1.]
Susannah, wid. Caleb, Nov. —, 1794, in 87th y. G.R.3.

PHLIPS (see Philips, Phillips, Phyleps), ———, ch. Joshua, July 17, 1776. P.R.1.

PHYLEPS (see Philips, Phillips, Phlips), Nathaniel, s. Caleb Jr. and Susanna, Oct. 31, 1748.

PICERING (see Pickeren, Pickering, Pickern, Pickren), Mary, w. Ben, Dec. 25 [1832], a. 71. P.R.1.
———, wid., "Sume time in the winter" [1832]. P.R.1.

PICKEREN (see Picering, Pickering, Pickern, Pickren), Eunice, d. Samuel, Nov. 6 [1798]. P.R.1.

PICKERING (see Picering, Pickeren, Pickern, Pickren), Elizabeth Jane, d. Simon and Elizabeth, July 30, 1834, a. 10 m. 9 d. G.R.3.
Mary, d. Samuel and Sarah, Dec. 4, 1767. [Dec. 8, in 4th m., G.R.3.]
Newton M., Aug. 23, 1849. G.R.4.

PICKERN (see Picering, Pickeren, Pickering, Pickren), Samuel, May 31 [1807]. P.R.1.
Simon, "fall from his hors," Jan. 11, 1810. P.R.1.

PICKREN (see Picering, Pickeren, Pickering, Pickern), ———, ch. Simon, Nov. 3, 1803. P.R.1.

PLUM, Samuel, Mar. 30 [1822]. P.R.1.

POND (see Poond, Pound), Benjamin, Dec. 3, 1844, a. 71. G.R.1.
Eli, Lt., of Franklin, May 20 [1802]. P.R.1.
Eliab of Frankling, May 11 [1802]. P.R.1.

POND, Ezra of Franklen, Feb. 18, 1788, a. "upward of" 90. P.R.I.
Ichabud, "hang him Self," Aug. 20 [1826]. P.R.I.
Meraanda (Poond), d. Eli of Frankling, Oct. 3 [1795]. P.R.I.
Oliver C., s. Eli and Mari, Oct. —, 1836. G.R.2.
Sara, w. E[?], Aug. 11 [1826]. P.R.I.
———, ch. Eligah, Dec. 1, 1778. P.R.I.

POOND (see Pond, Pound), Hulde, wid., June 18 [1818]. P.R.I.
———, w. Benjaman of Franklen, May 15, 1789. P.R.I.

POUND (see Pond, Poond), ———, w. Eli, July 7 [1813]. P.R.I.

PRAT (see Pratt), Abigail, d. Joseph, Mar. 21, 1765.
Joseph, June 14, 1780. P.R.I.

PRATT (see Prat), Benjamin, ——— 16, 1793, in 63d y. G.R.3. [Bengamen, May 16, P.R.I.]
Elizabeth, w. Joseph, June 9, 1838, a. 77. G.R.2. [Elisabeth Prat, wid., June 8, P.R.I.]
Joseph, Oct. 12, 1836, a. 73. G.R.2. [Oct. 13, a. 74, P.R.I.]
Lydia, w. Joseph, Feb. 7, 1772. [Prat, P.R.I.]
———, ch. Joseph, June 29, 1788. P.R.I.
———, second d. Joseph, Nov. 7 [1812]. P.R.I.

PROCTOR, Clara M., d. James A. and Sarah M., Sept. —, 1849. G.R.I.

PUFFER, Anna, wid. Richard of Wrentham, Oct. 11, 1777.

RATHBUN, Valentine W., May 12, 1813, a. 51 y. 364 d. C.R. [Rev. Valentine W. Rathburn, a. 52, G.R.2.] [Rathburn, P.R.I.]

RAY, Lucius, s. Joseph and Lydia, Feb. 13, 1819, a. 5 d. G.R.3.
Marion, d. Col. Joseph and Lydia, Nov. 14, 1828, a. 7 w. G.R.3.
Mary, d. Joseph and Lydia, Sept. 23, 1819, a. 3 y. 2 m. 14 d. G.R.3.

RAZA (see Razee, Razy, Reaza), Alary, Dec. 9 [1848]. P.R.I.

RAZEE (see Raza, Razy, Reaza), Cyrena, w. Ellery, Nov. 15, 1837, a. 40 y. 7 m. 10 d. G.R.2.
Cyrena, ch. Ellry and Cyrena, Oct. —, 1841. G.R.2.
Ellery, Dec. 10, 1848, a. 28 y. 5 m. 23 d. G.R.2.
Lydia, ch. Ellry and Cyrena, Mar. —, 1843. G.R.2.

RAZY (see Raza, Razee, Reaza), Only, June 10, 1842.

REAZA (see Raza, Razee, Razy), Oliver, Aug. 12 [1825]. P.R.I.

RICHARDSON (see Richarson), Elizabeth, w. Benjamin, Apr. 18, 1783, a. 68. G.R.1.

RICHARSON (see Richardson), Melita of Frankling, Sept. 14 [1844]. P.R.I.

ROCKWOOD, Abigail, Mrs., Oct. —, 1848. C.R.
Abigail B., w. Dea. Martin, Oct. 11, 1848, a. 61 y. 1 m. 8 d. G.R.2. [Abigal B., a. 61, P.R.I.]
Alce, wid. Joseph, May 20, 1819, a. 92. G.R.2. [a. 91 y. 5 m. 18 d., P.R.I.]
Cephas, s. Alce, wid., Dec. 10, 1786, in 21st y. [a. 21, G.R.2.] ["being cast a way a coming hom from The Estward on louvels eilon," P.R.I.]
Deborah, wid. Levi, May 10, 1807, a. 59. G.R.2. P.R.I.
Deborah Batty, d. Alce, wid., Oct. 19, 1779, in 26th y.
Francis Albert, s. Martin and Julia M., Aug. 23, 1844, a. 10 m. 2 d. G.R.2. [s. Martin Jr., P.R.I.]
Hannah, d. Levi, Nov. 18, 1778, in 7th m. [Hanah, P.R.I.]
John, s. Alce, wid., Dec. 9, 1786, in 31st y. [a. 31, G.R.2.] ["being cast a way a coming hom from The Estward on louvels eilon," P.R.I.]
Joseph Jr., s. Joseph, Oct. 6, 1778, in 19th y. [in Danbar, P.R.I.]
Joseph, Nov. 10, 1778, in 51st y.
Julia Maria, w. Martin Jr., Apr. 24, 1844. [Apr. 23, a. 25, G.R.2. P.R.I.]
Levi, June 15, 1806, a. 54. [a. 54 y. 5 m., P.R.I.]
Levi 2d, June 16 [1837], in York. P.R.I.
Sena E., d. Martin [and] Abigail, Oct. 2, 1822. [ch. Marten, Oct. 1, P.R.I.]

SAILLS (see Sayles), Daniel, cancer, Jan. 19 [1844]. P.R.I.

SANFORD, Seth of the Contry goar, "belonging to Captain John Jonis Compiny," "kiled in that fite," Sept. 8, ——. P.R.I.

SAYLES (see Saills), Judith, w. Lyman, Jan. 3, 1848, a. 32. G.R.2.
Louisa Ann, d. Lyman and Judith Ann, July 15, 1841, a. 2 m. 21 d. G.R.2.
Martha D., w. John, d. Ahimaaz Darling and Mary, Mar. 4, 1818, a. 16. G.R.4.

SCAMEL (see Scamell, Scammeal, Scammel, Scammell), Hopstel, d. Dr. John (Scammiel), Oct. 14 [1808]. P.R.I.

SCAMELL (see Scamel, Scammeal, Scammel, Scammell),Hannah, w. Dr. John, Sept. 9, 1823, a. 62. G.R.5. [Scammel, a. 61, P.R.I.]

SCAMMEAL (see Scamel, Scamell, Scammel, Scammell), Bethiah, d. Dr. John, Mar. 8, 1816. P.R.I.

SCAMMEL (see Scamel, Scamell, Scammeal, Scammell), Jane, "Old Mrs.," of Milford, Jan. 25, 1794. P.R.I.

SCAMMELL (see Scamel, Scamell, Scammeal, Scammel), Alexander, "Adj't, Gen, of the American Armies and Col, of the first Regt, of N.H. while he commanded a chosen corps of light infantry at the successful siege of York-Town Virginia, in the gallant performance of his duty as field officer of the day was unfortunately captured and afterward insidiously wounded of which wounds he expired at Williamsburg," Oct. —, 1781, a. 37. G.R.5.
Bethiah, w. Dr. Samuel Lisle, Nov. 27, 1805, a. 66. G.R.I. [Scamel, Nov. 29, a. 64 [?], P.R.I.]
Hannah, w. John, Sept. 9, 1825, a. 62. G.R.I.
John, Dr., widr., b. Mendon, Mar. 9, 1845, a. 83. [Scamell [h. Hannah], May 18, G.R.5.] [Scammel, Mar. 8, P.R.I.]
John C., Jan. 2, 1848, a. 54. G.R.5. [Maj. John Scamel, P.R.I.]
Samuel, Dr. [dup. Dr. Samuel Leslie Jr.], Dec. 5, 1805, a. 67 [dup. a. 66]. G.R.I. [Dr. Samuel L. Scammel, Dec. 8, a. 66, P.R.I.]
Samuel Leslie, Dr., ———, 1753, a. 45, in Milford. G.R.5.

SCOOT (see Scoott, Scot, Scott), Ickabud of Frankling, Nov. 1 [1843]. P.R.I.
Mary, wid., Apr. 16 [1800]. P.R.I.
Samuel, Dea., Nov. 27 [1793]. P.R.I.
Sylvenurs, May 6 [1818]. P.R.I.
———, wid., "fal down Stares broak her neak," June 11 [1847], "at poor house." P.R.I.

SCOOTT (see Scoot, Scot, Scott), David, Apr. 28 [1846]. P.R.I.
———, w. Samuel, Mar. 22 [1823]. P.R.I.

SCOT (see Scoot, Scoott, Scott), Charls, s. Salvenus and Mary, Jan. 18, 1759.
David, Feb. 1, 1782. P.R.I.

Scot, John, second s. Lues, "dronded at frankling bever pond," June 25 [1791], "this is otes Scot" [added]. P.R.I.

SCOTT (see Scoot, Scoott, Scot), Abigail, d. Saul and Selah, Apr. 19, 1809, a. 18 y. 1 m. 1 d. G.R.3. [Apr. 18, P.R.I.]
Almena, d. Emory and Watie, Mar. 16, 1835, a. 2 y. 17 d. G.R.3.
Almira, d. Emory and Watie, Dec. 29, 1842, a. 1 y. 10 m. 25 d. G.R.3.
Anna (Scoot), w. Jonathen, Aug. 15 [1795]. P.R.I.
Anna, d. William and Selah, June 10, 1834, a. 22. G.R.3. [Scoot, June 15, P.R.I.]
Bathsheba, Mar. —, 1823. C.R.
Clarissa, Nov. 25, 1846. C.R. [d. William and Selah, Nov. 25, a. 42, G.R.3.] [Claracee Scoot, Nov. 24, a. 43, P.R.I.]
Elisha, June 7, 1843, a. 63 y. 6 m. 7 d. [a. 64, G.R.3.] [Scoot, P.R.I.]
Hannah, wid. Samuel, Mar. 25, 1844. [Mar. 26, a. 73, P.R.I.]
Joanna, w. Silvanus, Apr. 26, 1777, in 68th y. G.R.3. [w. Silvens, smol pox, P.R.I.]
Leah, w. Joseph, June 24, 1752.
Leonard, s. Samuel and Bathsheba, Sept. 25, 1798. [Sept. 25, a. 3 y. 4 m. 7 d., G.R.3.] [Sept. 26, P.R.I.]
Mary, Aug. 19, 1844, a. 7. [d. Emory and Watie, Aug. 17, G.R.3.]
Nancy, d. Samuel and Bathsheba, Sept. 26, 1798. [Sept. 26, a. 5 y. 5 m. 16 d., G.R.3.] [Sept. 25, P.R.I.]
Nathaniel, s. Samuel and Mary, Aug. 28, 1748.
Olney, Sept. 12, 1838, a. 56. G.R.3. [Ony, Sept. 13, P.R.I.]
Paulina, Apr. —, 1822. C.R. [Pollina, d. Samuel and Bathsheba, Apr. 16, a. 20 y. 1 d., G.R.3.] [Pelina, Apr. 6, P.R.I.]
Samuel, s. Samuel and Bathsheba, Oct. 28, 1798. [Oct. 27, in 28th y., G.R.3.]
Samuel, Sept. 12, 1829, in 79th y. G.R.3. [Scoott, Sept. 13, P.R.I.]
Sarah Ann, d. Elisha and Nancy, Aug. 27, 1832, in 17th y. G.R.3. [Scoot, P.R.I.]
Saul, Apr. 22, 1834, in 70th y. G.R.3. [Scoot, Apr. 21, P.R.I.]
Selah, w. William, Jan. 8, 1813, a. 33. G.R.3. [Jan. 28, P.R.I.]
Silvanus, Apr. 27, 1777, in 76th y. G.R.3. [Silvens, smol pox, Apr. 26, P.R.I.]
Thankfull, d. Samuel and Mary, Sept. 4, 1748.
William, Apr. 11, 1846, a. 71. G.R.3. [Apr. 12, P.R.I.]
———, ch. Jonathan, Sept. —, 1775. P.R.I.
———, ch. Jonathan, Sept. —, 1775. P.R.I.

SCOTT, ———, ch. Jonathan, Sept. —, 1775. P.R.1.
———, last ch. Jonthan, Oct. 9, 1775. P.R.1.
———, ch. Jonathan, May 6, 1777. P.R.1.
———, twin ch. William, Jan. 28 [1813]. P.R.1.
———, twin ch. William, Jan. 28 [1813]. P.R.1.
———, w. Welcom, Mar. 7 [1826]. P.R.1.

SEBLEY (see Sibly), ———, ch. Phebe, Aug. 19 [1821]. P.R.1.

SHAMAN (see Shamean, Shamon, Sharemon, Sheamon, Sherman), ———, ch. Elisha, Mar. 26 [1817]. P.R.1.

SHAMEAN (see Shaman, Shamon, Sharemon, Sheamon, Sherman), Seth, Jan. 1, 1804. P.R.1.

SHAMON (see Shaman, Shamean, Sharemon, Sheamon, Sherman), Leuse, Dec. 4 [1821]. P.R.1.

SHAREMON (see Shaman, Shamean, Shamon, Sheamon, Sherman), ———, wid., Mar. 13 [1807]. P.R.1.

SHEAMON (see Shaman, Shamean, Shamon, Sharemon, Sherman), ———, w. Elisha, Apr. 13 [1810]. P.R.1.

SHEPARD, Deborah, w. Daniel, Mar. 5, 1771. [Shapord, P.R.1.]
Elisabeth, d. Isaac and Sarah, Sept. 19, 1760.

SHERBORN, Lewis, s. Geo[rge] and Abigail, May 17, 1839, a. 2. G.R.2. [Luis Sharbarn, s. Jorge, P.R.1.]

SHERMAN (see Shaman, Shamean, Shamon, Sharemon, Sheamon), Almina P., d. Elisha and Rhoda, June 21, 1842, a. 1 y. 1 m. 24 d. G.R.4.
Mary, d. Reuben and Patience, Dec. 23, 1821, in 15th y. G.R.4.
Patience, w. Reuben, Feb. 21, 1840, a. 67. G.R.4.
Reuben, Aug. 12, 1819, in 45th y. G.R.4. [Sheamen, Aug. 10, a. 45, P.R.1.]
———, inf. s. Elisha and Rhoda, June —, 1848. G.R.4.

SHUMWAY, Jabez of Midway, June 30 [1821], a. 74. P.R.1.

SIBLY (see Sebley), ———, Mr., Apr. 22 [1843], "at the South part." P.R.1.

SLOCOM (see Slocome, Slocoom, Slocum), Asa, July 31, 1811, a. 31. G.R.1. P.R.1.
Clarassa H., July 24, 1819, a. 3. G.R.1.

SLOCOM, Esther, May —, 1826. C.R. [Slocome, w. Simon, May 30, a. 66, G.R.2.] [Easther, wid., May 29, a. 70, P.R.1.]
Horace, s. Simon and Esther, Oct. 25, 1798. [Slocome, a. 1 y. 7 m., G.R.2.]
Polly, d. Simon and Esther, June 20, 1787. [Slokcom, P.R.1.]
Vasty Hawton, d. Bethuel, Oct. 28 [1838]. P.R.1.
Vesta, [twin] d. Simon and Esther, Jan. 11, 1801. [Slocome, Aug. [?] 11, a. 8 m. 12 d., G.R.2.] [Scloscum, Jan. 11, P.R.1.]
———, ch. Simon, Oct. 30 [1798]. P.R.1.
———, ch. Bethuel Jr., Sept. 1 [1845]. P.R.1.

SLOCOME (see Slocom, Slocoom, Slocum), Asa G., s. Bethuel and Mary, Nov. 21, 1831, a. 13. G.R.2. [Slocom, s. Thuel, a. 12, P.R.1.]
Charles E., Aug. 28, 1847, a. 31. G.R.2. [Slocoome, Aug. 27, "at the falls," P.R.1.]
Simon, June 11, 1818, a. 70. G.R.2. [Slocom, P.R.1.]

SLOCOOM (see Slocom, Slocome, Slocum), ———, ch. Clarasa, July 24 [1819], a. 7. P.R.1.

SLOCUM (see Slocom, Slocome, Slocoom), Esther, d. Simon and Esther, Feb. 7, 1789. [Slocome, Feb. 1, a. 5, G.R.2.] [Slokcom, Feb. 7, P.R.1.]

SMEETH (see Smith), ———, ch. Tamer, Feb. 21, 1779. P.R.1.

SMITH (see Smeeth), Abigail, w. Samuel, Sept. 2, 1780, in 59th y. G.R.3.
Augustus, ch. Peletiah and Julia B., Aug. 9, 1840. G.R.1. [Augustus M., s. Peltiah, a. 7 m., P.R.1.]
Catherine Massey, d. Peletiah Jr., Dec. 5, 1843. [ch. Peletiah and Julia B., Dec. 7, G.R.1.]
Celia Ann, d. John and Celia Ann, Sept. 18, 1843. [Sila Ann, Sept. 18, a. 11 d., G.R.2.] [Sept. 16, P.R.1.]
David, Jan. 3, 1822. P.R.1.
Deborah, d. Wid. Smith, Oct. 31, 1776. P.R.1.
Edward, Jan. 22, 1800. P.R.1.
Elemuel, s. Samuel and Anna, Oct. 14, 1811, a. 5 hrs. G.R.2.
Emily Olivey, d. John and Celia Ann, Sept. 19, 1837. [a. 5 m. 24 d., G.R.2.]
Eunice, wid. Peletiah, Feb. 19, 1757.
George H., s. John and Celia Ann, Sept. 15, 1841, a. 5 m. 5 d. G.R.2.
Joanah, d. James and Sarah, Sept. 17, 1738.
John Atwood, s. John and Celia Ann, Sept. 11, 1840. [1839, a. 9 m. 13 d., G.R.2.]

SMITH, Lemuel, s. Samuel and Anna, Oct. 14, 1811.
Margret, w. Capt. Robert, Nov. 4, 1791, a. 81. G.R.I. [Margit, wid. Capt. Robeard, P.R.I.]
Mathew, Oct. 20, 1776. P.R.I.
Pellitiah, Sept. 10, 1727. [Peltiah, Sept. 18, G.R.I.]
Rebecca, w. Samuel, Nov. 19, 1804, in 47th y. G.R.3.
Robard Jr., Jan. 3, 1794. P.R.I.
Robert, Capt., ——— 4, 1787, a. 83. G.R.I. [Capt. Robbord, Mar. 24, in 81st y., P.R.I.]
Robert, June 2, 1794, a. 42. G.R.I.
Samuel, Oct. 4, 1809, in 51st y. G.R.3. [Sam, P.R.I.]
Sarah, w. James, July 10, 1749.
Simon, s. Robert Jr. and Levina, Aug. 3, 1790. [ch. Robeard, Aug. 23, P.R.I.]
Warren A., ch. Peletiah and Julia B., Aug. 1, 1848. G.R.I.
———, ch. Matthew, Oct. 10, 1776. P.R.I.
———, d. Mathew, Oct. 18, 1776. P.R.I.
———, ch. Levi, Dec. 16 [1828]. P.R.I.
———, ch. John, June 6 [1831]. P.R.I.
———, ch. John, Sept. 11 [1839]. P.R.I.
———, ch. John, Sept. 25 [1841]. P.R.I.
———, h. Ruth of Potucet, Oct. 17 [1847]. P.R.I.

SNOW, Ruth, Mrs., Oct. 5, 1848. C.R.

SPEAR (see Speer), Benja[min] Jr., s. Benjamin and Elizabeth, June 24, 1792. [a. 3, G.R.I.] [Bengamen (Spears), s. Bengamen, P.R.I.]
Benjamin, Capt., Nov. 27, 1820, a. 60. G.R.I. [Capt. Bengemen Speare, a. 59, P.R.I.]
Benjamin F., Feb. 2, 1839, a. 36. G.R.I.
Elizabeth, wid. Benjamin, old age, Nov. 20, 1847, a. 82. [w. Capt. Benjamin, G.R.I.] [Elisebath, P.R.I.]
Horatio, s. Benjamin and Elizabeth, July 17, 1787. [Horaito, a. 32 d., G.R.I.] [Speer, ch. Bengaman, P.R.I.]
Vesta, Nov. 9, 1839, a. 47. G.R.I. [Vasta, P.R.I.]

SPEER (see Spear), Frankling, Feb. 2 [1839]. P.R.I.

STACY, ———, ch. ———, drowned, Feb. — [1848], "at the factory." P.R.I.
———, ch. ———, drowned, Feb. — [1848], "at the factory." P.R.I.

STAPELS, Susan, wid., of Mendam, Aug. 27, 1847. P.R.I.

STONE, ———, ch. Limon, July 27, 1839, "at the factory."
P.R.I.

STOW, Lurana, m., consumption, Sept. 1, 1845, a. 29. [Lurania Stowe, w. Walter D., Sept. 4, a. 29, G.R.2.] [Sept. 1, a. 30, P.R.I.]

STREETER (see Streter), ——— (Street[e]r), wid., Oct. 24, 1778. P.R.I.
———, ch. Elazer (St[r]eeter), May 28, 1788. P.R.I.

STRETER (see Streeter), ———, ch. Berzil, Oct. 19, 1785. P.R.I.

SUMNER, Davis, Dec. —, 1826. C.R. [Dec. 12, a. 65, G.R.I.] [Sumnah, P.R.I.]
Dolly, w. Davis, Dec. 31, 1830, a. 65. G.R.I. [Sumnah, wid. Davis, P.R.I.]
James of Milford, Aug. 29 [1795]. P.R.I.

SUNDERLAND, Ella C., d. Daniel and Frances, Mar. 21, 1845, a. 5 w. G.R.I.

SWIFT, Abram, s. Samuel and Chloe, Feb. 15, 1775, in 12th m. G.R.3.

TAFT, Jorge, Dec. 2 [1831]. P.R.I.
Vernera, d. James and Almira, Oct. 11, 1826, a. 1 y. 8 m. G.R.I. [Oct. 12, P.R.I.]

TENNEY, George N., "A student of Medicine in the New York University," Nov. 23, 1847, a. 24. G.R.2. [Gorge Tinny, in N.Y., P.R.I.]

THAYER, Aaron, Apr. 28, 1785, a. 70. G.R.2. [Lt. Aaron of Mendon, P.R.I.]
Aaron, Capt., Oct. 9, 1829, a. 71.
Aaron, s. Aaron and Mary Ann, Nov. 23, 1829, a. 2 y. 5 m. G.R.2. [third ch. Aaron Jr., Nov. 25, P.R.I.]
Aaron, s. Aaron and Mary Ann, Feb. 3, 1831, a. 3 m. 26 d. G.R.2. P.R.I.
Aaron, Mar. 16 [1831]. P.R.I.
Abba S., d. James P., dropsy, Nov. 22, 1845, a. 28. [Mrs. Abby S., Nov. 21, C.R.] [Abby S., d. Asa Burr, Nov. 22, G.R.I. [Abigill, Nov. 22, P.R.I.]
Abigail, d. Dependance and Hannah, Nov. 7, 1763.
Abraham, s. Isaac and Miriam, Nov. 20, 1729.

THAYER, Adelia, d. Lewis of Worcester, Sept. —, 1842.
Alpheus Jr., Feb. 2, 1823, a. 29. G.R.2. [Alpha Jr., a. 28, P.R.1.]
Alpheus, widr., s. Elias and Hannah, liver complaint, Apr. 27, 1846, a. 81 y. 3 m. 27 d. [Apr. 17, a. 81, C.R.] [Capt. Alpheus, Apr. 17, a. 81, G.R.2.] [Capt. Alphaus, Apr. 17, a. 81, P.R.1.]
Andrue, June 20 [1818]. P.R.1.
Benjamin, June 29, 1826, a. 82 y. 2 m. 2 d. G.R.2. [Bengaman, a. 83, P.R.1.]
Betsey, w. Alpheus, Sept. 29, 1842. [w. Capt. Alpheus, a. 75, G.R.2.]
Caroline Elizabeth, d. Thompson and Charlotte, Feb. 10, 1828, a. 1 y. 4 m. 25 d. G.R.2. [ch. Thomson, P.R.1.]
Catharine, d. Elijah and Catharine, Sept. 22, 1793, a. 4 hrs. G.R.1.
Catharine, w. Elijah, Sept. 29, 1793, a. 26. G.R.2. [Thayar, w. Elijah (Thayer) of Mendon, P.R.1.]
Catherine, w. Alpheus Jr., Nov. 2, 1836, a. 41. G.R.2. [Catharine, wid., Nov. 22, P.R.1.]
Daniel, Apr. 3 [1820]. P.R.1.
Dexter, Nov. 12, 1813, a. 31 y. 9 m. G.R.2.
Ebenezer, May 5, 1771, a. 73. G.R.1. [Capt. Ebenezer, May 3, P.R.1.]
Ebenezer of Killingly, Dec. 19, 1774, a. 44. P.R.1.
Ebenezer, Apr. 30, 1782, in 44th y. G.R.2. P.R.1.
Ebenezer, s. Elias and Hannah, June 9, 1788. [s. Lt. Elias and Hannah, Jan. 9, a. 3, G.R.3.] [s. Elies, June 10, P.R.1.]
Elias, Lt., Sept. —, 1806, a. 66. G.R.2. [Sept. 10, a. 65, P.R.1.]
Elias Jr., s. Elias and Ruth, Nov. 2, 1808. [Nov. 2, a. 2, G.R.2.] [Nov. 12, P.R.1.]
Elias, Capt., June 26, 1833, a. 61. G.R.2. P.R.1.
Elias N., s. Elias and Ruth, Aug. 6, 1835, a. 22. G.R.2.
Elias N., ch. Capt. Lyman W. and Eliza, Sept. 3, 1839, a. 5 m. G.R.2. [ch. Capt. Limon, Sept. 13, P.R.1.]
Elisabath, w. Capt. Alphaus, Sept. 29 [1842], a. 75. P.R.1.
Eliza, w. Lyman W., Nov. 6, 1842, [a.] 40. [w. Capt. Lyman W., a. 41, G.R.2.] [second w. Capt. Limon, a. 40, P.R.1.]
Elizabeth, w. Silas F., Sept. 26, 1848, a. 26. G.R.2. [Elisabath Rockwood, w. Foster, Sept. 6, P.R.1.]
Ezekiel, June 22, 1791. [June 21, P.R.1.]
Ezra, Mr., of War, Feb. 12, 1775. P.R.1.
File, Aug. 25 [1810], a. 37. P.R.1.

THAYER, Hannah, w. Capt. Ebenezer, Feb. 20, 1783, in 76th y. G.R.2. [wid., P.R.1.]
Hannah, w. Lt. Elias, Oct. 23, 1822, a. 78. G.R.2. [wid., Oct. 3, a. 82, P.R.1.]
Hannah E., d. Lyman W. and Rachel, Aug. 19, 1829, a. 9 m. G.R.2. [Hannah Ellas, d. Capt. Limon, Aug. 20, P.R.1.]
Harding, s. Dexter and Esther, Feb. 18, 1809, a. 1 y. 11 m.. G.R.2.
Harding, s. Dexter and Esther, June 12, 1811, a. 4 m. G.R.2.
Helena Abby, d. James P. and Abby S., canker rash, Sept. 16, 1848, a. 4 y. 4 m. 10 d. [Sept. 16, a. 1 y. 4 m. 10 d., G.R.2.] [Sept. 15, P.R.1.]
Irane, Apr. 13 [1825]. P.R.1.
Jacob, s. Isaac and Miriam, [? Sept. 4, 1726].
Jacob, s. Isaac and Miriam, Sept. 13, 1747.
Jacob, s. Isaac and Mary, Aug. 8, 1752.
Jemima, wid. Lt. Aaron, Oct. 16, 1815, a. 99. G.R.2. [of Mandam, a. 98 y. 11 m., P.R.1.]
John, Jan. 14, 1816, a. 27. P.R.1.
Jonathan Jr., June 14, 1746.
Jonathan, Apr. 12, 1747.
Julia, w. Marvel, dropsey, Sept. 16, 1848, a. 64 y. 2 m. 16 d. [Jula, wid., P.R.1.]
Julia Ann, d. Marvel and Julia, Aug. 6, 1823, a. 6. G.R.2. [Jeulean, P.R.1.]
Julia Ann, d. Capt. Elias and Ruth, Feb. 17, 1833, a. 25. G.R.2. [Julean, P.R.1.]
Leovinea, May 18 [1810]. P.R.1.
Luther, Nov. 4, 1804, a. 39. G.R.2. [Theayer, P.R.1.]
Lydda, Oct. —, 1826. C.R. [Lyda, wid., Oct. 18, a. 7[torn], P.R.1.]
Lyman W., Capt., s. Elias and Ruth, hung himself, Apr. —, 1848, a. 49. [Apr. 5, 1849, a. 50, G.R.2.] [Capt. Limon, hanged him self, Apr. 5, 1848, P.R.1.]
M. Bertram, s. John M. and Mary T., Oct. 3, 1848, a. 4. G.R.2.
Martha, d. Elias and Hannah, June 18, 1782. [d. Lt. Elias and Hannah, a. 15, G.R.2.] [d. Elius, P.R.1.]
Martha, wid., Mar. 30 [1807]. P.R.1.
Marvel [h. Julia], June 17, 1824, a. 41. G.R.2. [Marvalus, June 18, P.R.1.]
Marvelous, June —, 1821. C.R.
Mary, wid. Luther, Sept. 26, 1815, a. 49. G.R.2.
Mary Kimball, d. Ellery and Abigail, ——, 1826. [Aug. 6, a. 1 y. 3 m. 25 d., G.R.2.]

THAYER, Mathew [? Martha], d. Alpheus and Elizebath, Aug.
12, 1788. [ch. Alfeas, Aug. 2, P.R.I.]
Meary, "the blind woman," July 1 [1791]. P.R.I.
Moses of Mendon, Sept. 24, 1783. P.R.I.
Moses, June 18 [1847]. P.R.I.
Nathaniel of Frankling, June 4 [1824], a. 71. P.R.I.
Nehemiah, s. Jonathan and Elezebath, Nov. 9, 1740.
Nelson, Aug. 6, 1835, a. 21. P.R.I.
Noah, s. Isaac and Miriam, Sept. 26, 1736.
Polly, wid., Sept. 26 [1815], a. 40. P.R.I.
Rachel, w. Capt. Lyman W., Oct. 28, 1829, a. 29. G.R.2. [w. Capt. Limon, Nov. 2, P.R.I.]
Rhoda B., w. Willard, Mar. 19, 1817, a. 28. G.R.2. [Mar. 9, P.R.I.]
Rosanna, w. Capt. Aaron, Feb. 26, 1821. [Feb. 28, a. 61, G.R.2.] [Feb. 26, a. 63, P.R.I.]
Rufus, s. Calvin and Abigil, Apr. 13, 1789. [ch. Calven, P.R.I.]
Ruth, wid., Dec. 9 [1839], a. 80, in Woster." P.R.I.
Sabra, w. Ebenezer, July 28, 1833, a. 59 y. 3 m. G.R.3.
Sarah, w. Benjamin, July 22, 1792, a. 46. G.R.2. [w. Ben of Mendam, P.R.I.]
Sarah B., w. Alanson, d. Samuel Darling and Sarah, Feb. 8, 1828, a. 28. G.R.2. P.R.I.
Sarah E., ch. Capt. Lyman W. and Eliza, Aug. 13, 1831, a. 3 m. G.R.2.
Silars, Mar. 11 [1816], a. 70. P.R.I.
Susan, d. Elias and Ruth, ——, 1812. [Sept. —, a. 1 y. 1 m., G.R.2.] [ch. Capt. Elias, Sept. 7, a. 15 m., P.R.I.]
Susana, w. Nathanel of Franklen, Jan. 30, 1788. P.R.I.
William C., s. Manning and Abigail, inflanatory feaver, Aug. 2, 1848, a. 15 y. 4 m. 6 d. [a. 16, G.R.2.] [s. Mannan, a. 15, P.R.I.]
Ziba, s. Dependance and Hannah, "Scald from Dish-Kettel," Mar. 16, 1756.
Ziba, s. Dependance and Hannah, June 4, 1760.
——, ch. Willard and Rhoda, Feb. 20, 1817. [s. Willard and Rhoda B., a. 27 d., G.R.2.]
——, ch. Willard, Feb. 25 [1817]. P.R.I.
——, ch. Aaron Jr., June 26 [1826]. P.R.I.
——, ch. Capt. Limon, Aug. 7 [1836]. P.R.I.
——, w. Luis, Oct. 14 [1840]. P.R.I.
——, ch. Capt. Limon, Feb. 9 [1841]. P.R.I.
——, ch. Fostor, Feb. 20 [1847]. P.R.I.
——, ch. Milton, Oct. 4 [1848]. P.R.I.

THOMPSON (see Thomson, Tompson), Abigail, w. Joseph, Jan. 6, 1843, a. 48. [Thomson, a. 58, G.R.1.] [Abigial Thomson, P.R.1.]
David, Jan. 21, 1775, a. 35. G.R.1.
David, Oct. 1 [?] [1819], a. 80. P.R.1.
Ebenezer, Mar. 6, 1760. [Thomson, a. 61, P.R.1.]
Hannah, w. John, Nov. 24, 1759. [Thomson, wid., in 93d y., P.R.1.]
John [h. Hannah], Mar. 6, 1749. [Mar. 5, a. 82, G.R.1.]
Jonathan, June 7, 1782, in 83d y. G.R.2. [Thomson, 1783, P.R.1.]
Joseph, s. Joseph and Mary, Oct. 10, 1730.
Joseph, Jan. 2, 1755.
Martha, wid. Peter, Nov. 14, 1757. [Thomson, Nov. 13, P.R.1.]
Olive, d. Peter and Martha, Sept. 23, 1747.
Peter, Sept. 30, 1755, "In his Joyrney homeward from Lake Gorge." [Thomson, Lt., P.R.1.]
Sarah, d. David and Lucy, June 4, 1765.

THOMSON (see Thompson, Tompson), Abigail, w. John, Aug. 25, 1756. C.R.
Ab[i]gail, Sept. 26, 1756. P.R.1.
Abigail, Mar. 24 [1823], a. 90. P.R.1.
Amos, June 15, 1833. [a. 75, G.R.2.]
Baxter, s. Jonathan Jr. and Jemima, Oct. 8, 1761.
Benjamin of Glocester, July 4, 1786. P.R.1.
Chloe [d. Joseph and Mary], Jan. 6, 1776.
Dan, Aug. 5, 1841, a. 67, in Ohio. P.R.1.
Elisabuth, wid., of Peru, May — [1810]. P.R.1.
Esther, d. Joseph, Oct. 26, 1740.
Eunice, Oct. 29 [1822], a. 96 "wanting 34 day." P.R.1.
Eunice, wid., Dec. 1 [1822], a. 78. P.R.1.
Hannah, May 20, 1761. P.R.1.
Hannah, d. Calib and Lydia, Aug. 9, 1788. [d. Calup, P.R.1.]
Irene, d. Baxter, and Abigail, May 14, 1823, a. 8 m. 14 d. G.R.2.
Joel, Sept. 13 [1835], a. 67, "at the poor house." P.R.1.
John, Feb. 27, 1756, in 67th y. C.R. P.R.1.
Jonathen of Ward, Jan. —, 1793. P.R.1.
Joseph, Jan. 19, 1801, in 68th y. [a. 68, G.R.1.] [a. 67 y. 29 d., P.R.1.]
Lois, w. Joseph, May 5, 1838, a. 91. G.R.1. [wid., a. 94 y. 5 m., P.R.1.]
Lucy, w. David, Jan. 21, 1775. [w. Davied, P.R.1.]
Martha, w. Banjamin of Glocester, Jan. —, 1783. P.R.1.

THOMSON, Mary, wid. Joseph, Mar. 4, 1781, in 79th y.
Mary, w. Amos, Dec. 16, 1833. [a. 72, G.R.2.] [wid., P.R.I.]
Moses of Midway, June 23 [24, written below] [1794]. P.R.I.
Polley, d. David and Eunice, Aug. 21, 1788. [Thompson, Aug. 23, a. 3, G.R.2.] [d. Daved, Aug. 21, P.R.I.]
Ruth, d. Joseph and Mary, June 8, 1749.
Ruth, d. Joseph and Lois, Jan. 29, 1779, in 2d y.
Samuel of Dover Hill, Oct. 11, 1779. P.R.I.
Sarah, wid., of Dadham, Sept. 6, 1786. P.R.I.
Silence, d. Calib and Lydia, June 22, 1771.
———, d. Laban, July 4 [1832]. P.R.I.
———, w. Baxter, Mar. 27, 1833, a. 45. G.R.2. P.R.I.

THURBER, Daniel, Dr., of Mendon, Jan. 21 [1836], a. 69. P.R.I.
———, w. Dr. Thurber, Sept. 14 [1823]. C.R.I.

TILER, John of Mendon, "keled by the fall of a tree," Sept. 27, 1788. P.R.I.
Nathan Esq. of Mendon, Dec. 27, 1782, a. 96 or 97. P.R.I.

TILLINGHAST, Albert T., s. L. B. and Mary, July 14, 1844, a. 7 m. 4 d. G.R.2.
Betsey J., d. L. B. and Mary, Sept. 10, 1844, a. 2 y. 6 m. 9 d. G.R.2.
Rhoda, w. L. B., Feb. 14, 1834, in 25th y. G.R.2.

TINGLEY, George D., s. Charles W. and Margaret, July 12, 1842, a. 2 y. 5 m. 18 d. G.R.3.

TOBE, ———, ch. Selvenes, Feb. 18, 1790. P.R.I.

TOMPSON (see Thompson, Thomson), Benonie, s. Benjamin and w., May 11, [17]27.

TRUMAN, William, May 30 [1824]. P.R.I.

TUCKER, Daved, Aug. —, 1775. P.R.I.

TURNER, Amos, Cornet, of Midway, Dec. 4 [1820], a. 60. P.R.I.
Edward of Medfield, Dec. —, 1774. P.R.I.
Marcy, wid., of Medfeld, Jan. 4, 1783, a. 80 y. 6 w. P.R.I.

TYLER (see Tiler).

UPHAM, John, Sept. 16, 1783. P.R.I.
Patience, wid. John, July 13, 1829, a. 95. G.R.2. [a. 92, P.R.I.]

VERRY, Sarah, wid., of Mendom, Dec. 24 [1816], a. 84. P.R.1.

WAG, Experiance, w. Daniel, Jan. 29, 1774, a. 80 y. 10 m. " & sume od days." P.R.1.

WALDEN, Job, Oct. 24, 1798.

WALES, Abigail, w. George F., dropsey, July 31, 1849, a. 32 y. 8 m. 25 d.
Amos O., s. Amos and Rhoda, Feb. 13, 1841, a. 1 y. 20 d. G.R.1.
Gilbert A., s. Otis Jr. and Jerusha, Sept. 10, 1849, a. 9 m. 10 d. G.R.2.
John, m., b. Franklin, consumpsion, Dec. 13, 1846, a. 76. [Dec. 13, G.R.1.] [Dec. 12, P.R.1.]
Nabby, wid. James, Sept. 17 [1847]. P.R.1.
Ruth, w. John, Mar. 2 [1796]. P.R.1.
Sarah A., b. Franklin, d. Willard and Sarah, consumption, Oct. 31, 1849, a. 19 y. 7 m. 12 d.
———, ch. George F. and Abigail, consumption, Sept. 13, 1849, a. 3 m.

WARD, Elizabeth A., June 23, 1837, a. 5. G.R.1. [Woard, Jan. 23, "at the factory," P.R.1.]
George S., Feb. 17, 1836, a. 9 m. G.R.1. [Woard, "at the factory," P.R.1.]

WARE (see Wares, Weares, Wears), Sarah, wid., of Franklin, July 11 or 12 [1831]. P.R.1.
Tamah, w. Eli of Frankling, Mar. 1 [1821]. P.R.1.

WARES (see Ware, Weares, Wears), Celei [?], Aug. 21 [1821], a. 72. P.R.1.
Eleasar of Frankling, Oct. 28 [1843]. P.R.1.
Eli of Frankling, Nov. 1 [1835], a. 87. P.R.1.

WARFEEL, Elihu Parmer, Dec. 14 [1806]. P.R.1.

WARNER (see Worner).

WEARES (see Ware, Wares, Wears), Hamah, wid., of Franklen, Aug. 25 [1801], a. 90. P.R.1.

WEARS (see Ware, Wear, Wares, Weares), Creta of Frankling, Jan. 19, 1844. P.R.1.
Jerushe of Frankling, Mar. 8 [1844]. P.R.1.

WEDGE, Daniel of Oxford, Oct. 5, 1778. P.R.1.
Experance, w. Daniel, Jan. 29, 1774.

WHEELER, John, Mar. 7, 1816, a. 25. G.R.1.

WHEELOCK (see Whelock, Whillock), Ebenesar of Milford, May 6 [1801]. P.R.1.

WHELOCK (see Wheelock, Whillock), Eunice, Nov. 2 [1818]. P.R.1.
Johannah, wid., Feb. —, 1823, a. 84. P.R.1.
Silas of Mendam, Apr. 22 [1793]. P.R.1.

WHICKACOUR (see Whicker, Whittaker), ———, w. Dr. Whickacour, Apr. 6 [1807]. P.R.1.

WHICKER (see Whickacour, Whittaker), Alpha, d. Dr. Whicker, Dec. 5 [1796]. P.R.1.

WHILLOCK (see Wheelock, Whelock), ———, wid., of Milford, Jan. 28 [1807]. P.R.1.

WHISTON, Joseph, Mar. 13 [1818], a. 75. P.R.1.

WHIT (see White), Seusane, Nov. 7 [1815], a. 80. P.R.1.

WHITE (see Whit), James, "belonging to Captain John Jonis Compiny," "kiled in that fite," Sept. 8, ———. P.R.1.
John (Wh[i]te), June 29, 1776, at Crown Point. P.R.1.
Jonathan, b. Medway, old age, Feb. 11, 1849, a. 74.
Susanna, w. J., "formerly" w. Richard Williams, Feb. 22, 1843, a. 86. G.R.2.
———, ch. Leanard, Feb. 11, 1833. P.R.1.
———, w. Lanard, July 11 [1835]. P.R.1.

WHITING, Susanna, d. Pelletiah and Hannah, Feb. 10, 1767.

WHITNE (see Whitney, Whitny), Elias, July 29 [1810], a. 94. P.R.1.
Leaben, June 20 [1818]. P.R.1.

WHITNEY (see Whitne, Whitny), Harriette, d. Ethan and Betsey M., Mar. 15, 1811, a. 27. G.R.2. [Hariat, 1841, a. 26, P.R.1.]
Lauria Ann, d. Nelson and Ruth M., consumption, Nov. 21, 1849, a. 5 m. 4 d.
———, ch. Nelson, Aug. 6 [1848]. P.R.1.

WHITNY (see Whitne, Whitney), Helen E., d. Dexter and Adeliza, Oct. 17, 1840, a. 1 y. 1 m. 18 d. G.R.2.

WHITTAKER (see Whickacour, Whicker), William, Dea., Aug. 12 [1830]. P.R.1.

WIGHT, Aaron, Dr., Feb. 8 [1813]. P.R.1.
Abigail, w. Rev. Elnathan, Feb. 26, 1802, a. 85. G.R.1.
Abigail, w. Aaron, consumption, July 13, 1849, a. 74.
Austin, s. Eliab and Jemima, June 2, 1798. [s. Capt. Eliab and Jemima, a. 6, G.R.2.] [Orsten, P.R.1.]
Elnathan, Rev., Nov. 6, 1761. [[h. Abigail] a. 46, G.R.1.] [a. 45, P.R.1.]
Isabel, d. Elnathan and Abigail, Oct. 22, 1761. [1762, a. 5 y. 8 m. 21 d., P.R.1.]
Jemima, d. Eliab Esq., Sept. 26 [1823]. P.R.1.
Jemima, w. Dea. Eliab, Apr. 26, 1835, a. 74. G.R.2. [Jamima, w. Eliab Esq., P.R.1.]
Jerusha, w. Nathan, Apr. 8 [1817], a. 57. P.R.1.
Jonathan of Medfield, Feb. 19, 1779, in 97th y. P.R.1.
Joseph, s. Joseph and Martha, Aug. 25, 1749.
Joseph, Oct. 25, 1758. [a. "gast entred" 81st y., P.R.1.]
Joseph, Dea., Apr. 25, 1792, in 89th y. [in 87th y., G.R.2.] [a. 87 y. 3 m., P.R.1.]
Maray, d. Joseph and Mathew [Martha], Dec. 26, 1741.
Marget, w. Samuel, Oct. 26, 1775. P.R.1.
Margret, wid., of Springfield, Oct. 31, 1787, in 102d y. P.R.1.
Martha, w. Joseph, Oct. 14, 1759. [in 82d y., P.R.1.]
Martha, w. Joseph, Dec. 5, 1781, in 76th y. [w. Dea. Joseph, a. 77, G.R.2.] [a. 76 y. 8 m. 3 d., P.R.1.]
Mary, wid. Samuel, Mar. 4, 1817, a. 88. G.R.2.
Nathan, s. Joseph and Martha, Feb. 5, 1743-4.
Nathan, s. Nathan and Jarusha, Feb. 1, 1782. [s. Nathan and Jerusha, a. 1 m., G.R.2.] [a. abt. 4 w., P.R.1.]
Peter, s. Joseph and Martha, Aug. 12, 1749.
Peter, s. Samuel and Mary, Feb. 21, 1758.
Presson, s. Nathan and Jerusha, June 23, 1793, a. 2 m. 2 d. G.R.2.
Rebekah of Attleborough, Jan. 12, 1785, a. 75. P.R.1.
Samuel, May 8, 1790. [a. 60, G.R.2.]
Samuel, Sept. 4 [1831]. P.R.1.
———, [twin] d. Seth, Apr. 22, 1845, a. 8 d.
———, [twin] d. Seth, Apr. 23, 1845, a. 9 d.

WILCOX, Amelia, w. Jeraul O., intermitant fever, Feb. 27, 1849, a. 44. [a. 45 y. 10 m. 8 d., G.R.4.]
Amos, s. Daniel and Nancy, June 17, 1833, a. 8 m. 11 d. G.R.4.
Oliver B., s. Jeraul O. and Amelia, Aug. 30, 1832, in 4th y. G.R.4.

WILCOX, Samuel, "Killed in skirmish at Middleburgh Va. 1st R. I Cav. Vols.," Dec. 28, 1831. G.R.4.
Stephen, eldest s. Stephen and Nancy, May 27, 1849, a. 28. G.R.4.
WILLIAMS (see Willims), Charles, s. Charles and Mary, Sept. 12, 1846, a. 8 m. G.R.1.
Elias R., s. Thomas and Polly, Dec. —, 1820, a. 6 m. G.R.3.
Franklin, s. Parsen, June 27, 1823. P.R.1.
Nancy, w. Parsons, Mar. 20, 1823, a. 35. G.R.2. [w. Parsen, P.R.1.]
William, Rev., of Wrentham, Sept. 22 [1823], a. 86. P.R.1.
———, ch. Parsen, Nov. 8 [1822], a. 1. P.R.1.
WILLIMS (see Williams), John, Aug. 19 [1826], a. 53. P.R.1.
WISWALL, ———, ch. Eliza, Oct. 27 [1836]. P.R.1.
WOOD (see Woods), C. H., July 25, 1725, a. 90. G.R.1.
WOODS (see Wood), ———, ch. ———, Aug. 17 [1839]. P.R.1.
WORNER, Samuel of the Contry goar, "belonging to Captain John Jonis Compiny," "kiled in that fite," Sept. 8, ———. P.R.1.
WRIGHT, Hannah, wid., Dec. 28 [1841]. P.R.1.
Henry Augustus, s. Jonathan and Susan, dysentery, Aug. 4, 1846, a. 2. [s. Jonathan and Susan M., 1840 [?], G.R.2.] [Rite, 1846, P.R.1.]
Seth, Jan. 11, 1830. P.R.1.

UNIDENTIFIED.

Da[torn], Huldah, Mar. 27, 1763. P.R.1.
———, ———, m., d. Ahimus Darling, Mar. 4 [1818]. P.R.1.
———, ———, ch. of d. of Ahimus Darling, Mar. 4 [1818]. P.R.1.
———, ———, "and irishman at C Picering," Jan. 17, 1836. P.R.1.
———, ———, "an iresh woman at madison battses," Sept. 23 [1847]. P.R.1.

NEGROES, ETC.

Hagar, "A woman of coller," Nov. 4 [1805], a. 105. P.R.1.

www.ingramcontent.com/pod-product-compliance
Lightning Source LLC
Chambersburg PA
CBHW071157160426
43196CB00011B/2106